ZB
SPELLING
CONNECTIONS

J. Richard Gentry, Ph.D.

4

Series Author
J. Richard Gentry, Ph.D.

Editorial Development: Cottage Communications

Art and Production: PC&F

Photography: George C. Anderson: cover; pages 1, 4, 6, 7, 254, 255, 256, 257;
The Stock Market: p. 287 © Kennan Ward; Tony Stone Images: p. 276 © Robert Shafer; p. 278
© Ambrose Greenway; p. 282 © Dugald Bremner; p. 286 © Tim Brown

Illustrations: Laurel Aiello: pages 10, 21, 28, 34, 45, 51, 57, 63, 69, 81, 87, 105, 118, 123, 129,
142, 224, 229, 232, 233, 236, 238, 239, 240, 242, 244, 245, 246, 247, 248, 249, 252;
Dave Blanchette: pages 9, 16, 27, 52, 58, 70, 88, 93, 94, 106, 112, 117, 124, 201, 209, 214, 215,
219, 221; Len Ebert: pages 136, 141; Tom Elliot: pages 35, 77, 97, 121, 156, 163; Ruth Flanigan:
pages 11, 17, 23, 29, 47, 53, 59, 65, 71, 83, 89, 95, 101, 107, 119, 125, 131, 137, 143, 155; Rusty
Fletcher: pages 203, 213, 220; Colin Fry: pages 202, 207, 219, 222; Kate Gorman: pages 172,
196; Benton Mahan: pages 38, 39, 40, 42, 74, 75, 76, 77, 110, 111, 114, 147, 148, 150, 182, 183,
184, 186; Bill Ogden: pages 64, 146, 153, 159, 178, 189, 190; Vicki Woodworth: pages 161, 166,
167, 173, 179, 191, 197

Illustration for **Vocabulary Connections** pages by Sam Snyder

The following references were used in the development of the **Word Study** activities included on
the **Vocabulary Connections** pages in each developmental spelling unit:

Ayto, John. *Arcade Dictionary of Word Origins: The Histories of More Than 8,000 English-
Language Words.* New York: Arcade Publishing, Little, Brown, and Company, 1990.
Barnhart, Robert K., ed. *The Barnhart Dictionary of Etymology: The Core Vocabulary of Standard
English.* New York: The H.W. Wilson Company, 1988.
Makkai, Adam, ed. *A Dictionary of American Idioms.* New York: Barron's Educational Series,
Inc., 1987.
Rheingold, Howard. *They Have a Word for It: A Lighthearted Lexicon of Untranslatable Words
and Phrases.* Los Angeles: Jeremy P. Tarcher, Inc., 1988.
Terban, Marvin. *Time to Rhyme: A Rhyming Dictionary.* Honesdale, PA: Wordsong, Boyds Mills
Press, 1994.

ISBN: 0-7367-2062-6

Copyright © 2004 Zaner-Bloser, Inc.

Zaner-Bloser, Inc., P.O. Box 16764, Columbus, Ohio 43216-6764 (1-800-421-3018)
www.zaner-bloser.com
Printed in the United States of America   09 10 330 10 09 08

Contents

Spelling Study Strategy

Look ➡ **Say** ➡ **Cover** ➡ **See** ➡ **Write** ➡ **Check**

1 **Look** at the word.

2 **Say** the letters in the word. Think about how each sound is spelled.

3 **Cover** the word with your hand or close your eyes.

4 **See** the word in your mind. Spell the word to yourself.

5 **Write** the word.

6 **Check** your spelling against the spelling in the book.

short a

1. _____

2. _____

3. _____

4. _____

short e

5. _____

6. _____

7. _____

8. _____

9. _____

10. _____

short i

11. _____

12. _____

13. _____

14. _____

15. _____

16. _____

short o

17. _____

short u

18. _____

19. _____

20. _____

Spelling and Thinking

READ THE SPELLING WORDS

1.	crust	*crust*	Lucas cut the **crust** off his bread.
2.	pass	*pass*	I **pass** that computer store every day.
3.	else	*else*	Who **else** is coming to this party?
4.	skill	*skill*	Writing poetry is a **skill** I admire.
5.	brag	*brag*	It is rude to **brag** about your deeds.
6.	zipper	*zipper*	Maria sewed a **zipper** into her skirt.
7.	began	*began*	He was so happy he **began** to sing.
8.	collar	*collar*	Mom has a lace **collar** on her dress.
9.	drag	*drag*	We **drag** our boats into the water.
10.	smell	*smell*	Did you stop to **smell** the roses?
11.	brick	*brick*	Follow the yellow **brick** road.
12.	felt	*felt*	In the sun the sand **felt** hot.
13.	spill	*spill*	You must not **spill** your milk.
14.	button	*button*	Kwan lost a **button** from his shirt.
15.	held	*held*	I **held** the injured bird in my hand.
16.	trust	*trust*	Can I **trust** you to keep a secret?
17.	kept	*kept*	This show has **kept** me in suspense.
18.	trick	*trick*	The magician tried to **trick** us.
19.	shell	*shell*	The turtle's head was in its **shell**.
20.	begin	*begin*	Let me **begin** to tell you a story.

SORT THE SPELLING WORDS

1.–4. Write the words that have the **short a** sound spelled **a**.

5.–10. Write the words that have the **short e** sound spelled **e**.

11.–16. Write the words that have the **short i** sound spelled **i**.

17. Write the word that has the **short o** sound spelled **o**.

18.–20. Write the words that have the **short u** sound spelled **u**.

REMEMBER THE SPELLING STRATEGY

Remember that many short vowel sounds are spelled with a single letter: **a** in **pass**, **e** in **held**, **i** in **skill**, **o** in **collar**, and **u** in **trust**.

Spelling and Vocabulary

Word Analysis

Write the spelling word that does not belong in each group.

1. start, begin, felt
2. dump, pass, spill
3. collar, shell, sleeve
4. kept, trick, fool
5. boast, held, brag
6. skill, faith, trust

Word Structure

7.–9. Write the two-syllable spelling words that have a short vowel in the first syllable. Draw a line between the syllables.

10.–11. Write the two-syllable spelling words that have a short vowel in the second syllable. Draw a line between the syllables.

Phonics

12.–13. Write the spelling words that rhyme with **nag**.

14.–15. Write the spelling words that rhyme with **sick**.

16.–20. Words in a dictionary are in alphabetical order. Write these words in alphabetical order.

held   else   trust   kept   crust

◆ ■ ◆

Dictionary Check Be sure to check the alphabetical order of the words in your **Spelling Dictionary**.

Word Analysis
1. _____
2. _____
3. _____
4. _____
5. _____
6. _____

Word Structure
7. _____
8. _____
9. _____
10. _____
11. _____

Phonics
12. _____
13. _____
14. _____
15. _____

Using the Dictionary
16. _____
17. _____
18. _____
19. _____
20. _____

crust	pass	else	skill	brag
zipper	began	collar	drag	smell
brick	felt	spill	button	held
trust	kept	trick	shell	begin

Complete the Sentences

Complete the Sentences Write a spelling word to complete each sentence.

1. We will _____ each sentence with a capital letter.
2. If you fill your glass too full, you may _____ your drink.
3. It takes great _____ to play professional sports.
4. The magician taught us a new _____.
5. I hope I can _____ you to keep this secret.
6. I like to _____ about my brother's paintings.
7. Because I was hot, the _____ of my shirt got wrinkled.
8. A _____ in a jacket makes it easy to open and close.
9. Did anyone _____ get the right answer to that question?
10. A turtle goes into its _____ when it is frightened.

Solve the Analogies

Solve the Analogies Write a spelling word to complete each analogy.

11. **Skin** is to **apple** as _____ is to **bread**.
12. **Stroller** is to **push** as **sled** is to _____.
13. **See** is to **eye** as _____ is to **nose**.
14. **Sleep** is to **slept** as **keep** is to _____.
15. **Say** is to **said** as **hold** is to _____.

Solve the Riddles

Solve the Riddles Write a spelling word for each riddle.

16. I am round and have eyes.
17. I rhyme with **glass** and mean "to go by."
18. I am the "yesterday" word of "today's" word **feel**.
19. One of the three little pigs used me to build a house.
20. I am a two-syllable word that means "started."

Complete the Sentences
1.
2.
3.
4.
5.
6.
7.
8.
9.
10.

Solve the Analogies
11.
12.
13.
14.
15.

Solve the Riddles
16.
17.
18.
19.
20.

Spelling and Writing

Proofread a Story

Six words are not spelled correctly in this story. Write the words correctly.

A Gift From the Beach

At the beach, I found a shel I could not pas by. It had a pink edge that looked like a colar. When I helt it in my hand, it felled smooth. I could smell the sea on it. I trusst it will always remind me of that happy day.

Proofreading Marks

☰ Make a capital.

／ Make a small letter.

∧ Add something.

℮ Take out something.

⊙ Add a period.

⌗ New paragraph

ⓢⓟ Spelling error

Write a Story

Narrative Writing

Write a story about an interesting place you have visited. Include all the information the reader will need to know. Be sure to tell the following:

- the name of the place you visited
- names of people, if any, you went with
- what you did there
- how long you stayed
- what interesting sights you saw
- what interesting things you did
- what you liked best about your visit

Use as many spelling words as you can.

Writing Process

Prewriting

Drafting

Revising

Editing

Publishing

Proofread Your Writing During

Proofread your writing for spelling errors as part of the editing stage in the writing process. Be sure to check each word carefully. Use a dictionary to check spelling if you are not sure.

VOCABULARY CONNECTIONS

Strategy Words

Review Words: Short Vowel Sounds

Write a word from the box to complete each sentence. The word you write will rhyme with the underlined word.

| crop | dinner | land | lunch | test |

I. Each day I miss my _____, I get a little <u>thinner</u>.

2. The rabbit ate a <u>bunch</u> of carrots for its _____.

3. Our teacher chose the <u>best</u> questions for the _____.

4. That farmer couldn't <u>stop</u> bringing in his _____.

5. A pilot cannot _____ a seaplane on the <u>sand</u>.

Preview Words: Short Vowel Sounds

Synonyms are words that have the same meanings. **Antonyms** are words with opposite meanings.

| camera | contest | discuss | public | swift |

6. Write the word from the box that is a synonym of **fast**.

7. Write the word from the box that is a synonym of **competition**.

8. Write the word from the box that is an antonym of **private**.

Write the word from the box that could replace the underlined words in each sentence.

9. Our class will <u>talk about</u> the Civil War.

10. Bring your <u>device that takes pictures</u> on a trip.

Content Words

Science: Human Body

Write the word from the box that fits each definition.

digest	pulse	exert	rate	lungs

1. to put forth
2. to absorb food into the body
3. pace or measurement
4. a regular throbbing caused by the beat of a heart
5. organs that remove carbon dioxide and supply oxygen

Social Studies: Islands

Write the word from the box that matches each clue.

canal	inlet	coastal	river	England

6. Land along the shore is called this.
7. It is a stream of water that flows into the ocean.
8. This island is also a country in Europe.
9. This waterway is usually dug out across land.
10. This is another word for **bay** or **cove**.

Apply the Spelling Strategy

Circle the letter that spells the **short u** sound in two of the Content Words you wrote.

Word Study

Clipped Words

A **clipped word** is a short, familiar form of a longer word. For example, **ad** is a clipped word. It is short for **advertisement**. Write the Strategy Word that is the clipped form of **luncheon**.

Science: Human Body

1. _____
2. _____
3. _____
4. _____
5. _____

Social Studies: Islands

6. _____
7. _____
8. _____
9. _____
10. _____

Clipped Words

1. _____

a-consonant-e

1. _____
2. _____
3. _____
4. _____
5. _____

i-consonant-e

6. _____
7. _____
8. _____
9. _____
10. _____
11. _____
12. _____
13. _____
14. _____

o-consonant-e

15. _____
16. _____
17. _____
18. _____

u-consonant-e

19. _____
20. _____

Spelling and Thinking

READ THE SPELLING WORDS

1.	wise	*wise*	Owls are described as **wise** birds.
2.	huge	*huge*	An elephant is a **huge** animal.
3.	case	*case*	We bought a **case** of spring water.
4.	alone	*alone*	Are you **alone** or with friends?
5.	rise	*rise*	Soap bubbles **rise** in the air.
6.	cube	*cube*	A **cube** has six sides.
7.	fame	*fame*	Movie stars earn **fame** and money.
8.	beside	*beside*	Magda sits **beside** me in school.
9.	blame	*blame*	He did not **blame** us for the mistakes.
10.	chose	*chose*	They **chose** sides for the game.
11.	tire	*tire*	My bicycle **tire** is flat.
12.	became	*became*	The hiker **became** lost in the woods.
13.	awhile	*awhile*	Rest **awhile** if you are tired.
14.	spoke	*spoke*	Joy **spoke** her lines well.
15.	wife	*wife*	I met Uncle Theo's new **wife**.
16.	drove	*drove*	Mother **drove** the truck to work.
17.	surprise	*surprise*	Aunt Belle paid us a **surprise** visit.
18.	scale	*scale*	Use the **scale** to check the cat's weight.
19.	alive	*alive*	Grandfather is **alive** and well.
20.	invite	*invite*	I will **invite** you to the party.

SORT THE SPELLING WORDS

Write the spelling words that have a long vowel sound spelled the following ways:

1.–5. **a-consonant-e**   15.–18. **o-consonant-e**

6.–14. **i-consonant-e**   19.–20. **u-consonant-e**

REMEMBER THE SPELLING STRATEGY

Remember that the long vowel sounds you hear in **case, rise, chose,** and **cube** are spelled with the **vowel-consonant-e** pattern.

Spelling ᵃⁿᵈ Vocabulary

Synonyms

Words that have the same or almost the same meaning, such as **simple** and **easy,** are called **synonyms**. Write a spelling word that is a synonym for each of these words.

1. carton   **3.** recognition   **5.** smart

2. gigantic   **4.** accuse

Word Structure

6.–12. Write the spelling words that have two syllables. Draw a line between the syllables.

Phonics

Change one or two letters at the beginning of each of these words to write spelling words.

13. life   **15.** broke   **17.** tube

14. wire   **16.** tale   **18.** those

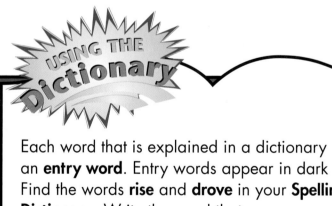

USING THE Dictionary

Each word that is explained in a dictionary is called an **entry word**. Entry words appear in dark print. Find the words **rise** and **drove** in your **Spelling Dictionary**. Write the word that answers each question.

19. Which word is a past tense?

20. Which word can mean to "move upward or ascend"?

Synonyms

1. _____

2. _____

3. _____

4. _____

5. _____

Word Structure

6. _____

7. _____

8. _____

9. _____

10. _____

11. _____

12. _____

Phonics

13. _____

14. _____

15. _____

16. _____

17. _____

18. _____

Using the Dictionary

19. _____

20. _____

wise	huge	case	alone	rise
cube	fame	beside	blame	chose
tire	became	awhile	spoke	wife
drove	surprise	scale	alive	invite

Solve the Analogies

Solve the Analogies Write a spelling word to complete each analogy.

1. **Small** is to **tiny** as ____ is to **big**.
2. **Down** is to **up** as **descend** is to ____.
3. **Skate** is to **foot** as ____ is to **car**.
4. **Ruler** is to **measure** as ____ is to **weigh**.
5. **Ignorance** is to **wisdom** as **ignorant** is to ____.
6. **Came** is to **come** as ____ is to **become**.
7. **Four** is to **six** as **square** is to ____.

1. ____
2. ____
3. ____
4. ____
5. ____
6. ____
7. ____

Substitute a Word

Substitute a Word Sometimes authors save space by using one word that has the same meaning as two or more words. Write one spelling word for each of these phrases.

8. ask to come
9. a box for carrying something
10. went by car
11. for a short time
12. at the side of
13. the quality of being well known

8. ____
9. ____
10. ____
11. ____
12. ____
13. ____

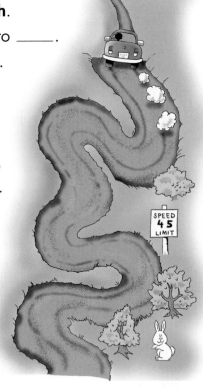

Complete the Paragraph

Complete the Paragraph Write the spelling words from the box that complete the paragraph.

The detective __14.__ to the __15.__ of the missing man. "It will come as no __16.__ to learn that your husband is __17.__ and well. You __18.__ knew where he was hiding, and you __19.__ to keep it a secret. You and he must take the __20.__ for this deceit."

14. ____
15. ____
16. ____
17. ____
18. ____
19. ____
20. ____

surprise
alone
chose
alive
blame
spoke
wife

Spelling and Writing

Proofread a Letter

Write the six words that are not spelled correctly below.

17 Oak Drive
Willowdale, Ohio
September 17, 2001

Dear Joe,

I paid a sirprise visit to Mr. Jackson and his wise wive. They live aloan on a huje farm. Their house was built baside a beautiful lake. They want me to stay with them awile.

Love,

Ricky

Write a Letter

Narrative Writing

Imagine that you have taken a trip. Write a letter to your family or friends. Be sure to include the following information:

- where you are
- why you went there
- what you like about the place
- how long you plan to stay
- what you plan to do after you leave
- when you will visit or call

Use as many spelling words as you can.

Writing Process

Prewriting
⇩
Drafting
⇩
Revising
⇩

Proofread Your Writing During → **Editing**
⇩
Publishing

Proofread your writing for spelling errors as part of the editing stage in the writing process. Be sure to check each word carefully. Use a dictionary to check spelling if you are not sure.

VOCABULARY CONNECTIONS

Strategy Words

Review Words

1. _____
2. _____
3. _____
4. _____
5. _____

Preview Words

6. _____
7. _____
8. _____
9. _____
10. _____

Review Words: Vowel-Consonant-e

Write a word from the box to complete each sentence.

close	face	size	write	wrote

1. Yesterday I _____ a letter to my friend Sheila.
2. I hope that Sheila will _____ to me soon.
3. I need to know what _____ gloves to buy for her.
4. I can hardly wait to see her _____ again.
5. I always _____ my letters to her with my nickname.

Preview Words: Vowel-Consonant-e

Write the word from the box that matches each clue.

complete	froze	include	locate	underline

6. It means "to find."
7. It is another word for "whole" or "having everything."
8. What you do when you draw a line under a word or a phrase.
9. What you do when you add an item to a collection of things.
10. What water did last night when it was very cold.

Content Words

Math: Numbers

Write the word to solve each of these math problems.

fifty	ninety	nineteen	thousand	seventy

1. Five hundred plus five hundred equals one _____.
2. Twenty-five plus twenty-five equals _____.
3. The number between eighty and one hundred if you count by tens is _____.
4. The highest whole number under twenty is _____.
5. Eighty minus ten equals _____.

Health: Nutrition

Write the word from the box that fits each definition.

dessert	sandwich	diet	spinach	dine

6. a green leafy vegetable
7. something made with two slices of bread and a filling
8. something usually eaten after the main meal
9. a word meaning "to eat"
10. the food a person eats

Apply the Spelling Strategy

Circle the three Content Words you wrote in which **long i** is spelled **i-consonant-e**.

Word Study

More Than One Meaning

Many words have more than one meaning. Write the one Strategy Word that can have these meanings:

- the front of a clock
- to turn in a certain direction
- to stand up to
- your eyes, nose, etc.

Math: Numbers
1. _____
2. _____
3. _____
4. _____
5. _____

Health: Nutrition
6. _____
7. _____
8. _____
9. _____
10. _____

More Than One Meaning
1. _____

Spelling and Thinking

READ THE SPELLING WORDS

1.	aim	*aim*	Her **aim** is to become a doctor.
2.	holiday	*holiday*	Which **holiday** falls on January 1?
3.	paper	*paper*	Todd forgot to sign his **paper**.
4.	station	*station*	The radio **station** went off the air.
5.	able	*able*	Humans are **able** to travel in space.
6.	crayon	*crayon*	Blue **crayon** is good for coloring sky.
7.	flavor	*flavor*	I use toothpaste with mint **flavor**.
8.	lazy	*lazy*	Successful people are usually not **lazy**.
9.	brain	*brain*	Our **brain** controls our emotions.
10.	anyway	*anyway*	You may not win, but try **anyway**.
11.	remain	*remain*	Sleep and eat well to **remain** healthy.
12.	favor	*favor*	Do a **favor** for your friends.
13.	rail	*rail*	The **rail** for the train was made of steel.
14.	taste	*taste*	I like the sour **taste** of lemon.
15.	trailer	*trailer*	I got a **trailer** to pull my boat.
16.	lady	*lady*	A **lady** is known for her good manners.
17.	nation	*nation*	Our **nation** is a vast land.
18.	relay	*relay*	I will **relay** the good news to all.
19.	fail	*fail*	Try again if at first you **fail**.
20.	radio	*radio*	Karl is host of a **radio** talk show.

SORT THE SPELLING WORDS

1.–10. Write the words that have the **long a** sound spelled **a**.

11.–16. Write the words that have the **long a** sound spelled **ai**.

17.–20. Write the words that have the **long a** sound spelled **ay**.

REMEMBER THE SPELLING STRATEGY

Remember that the **long a** sound can be spelled **a** as in **lady, ai** as in **aim,** and **ay** as in **relay**.

a

1.

2.

3.

4.

5.

6.

7.

8.

9.

10.

ai

11.

12.

13.

14.

15.

16.

ay

17.

18.

19.

20.

Spelling ᵃⁿᵈ Vocabulary

Word Structure

I.–2. Write the spelling words that have two syllables and have the **long a** sound in the second syllable. Draw a line between the syllables. Refer to your dictionary if you need help.

3.–12. Write the spelling words that have two syllables and have the **long a** sound in the first syllable. Draw a line between the syllables. Refer to your dictionary if you need help.

Word Meanings

Write a spelling word for each clue.

13. You use your mouth to do this to food.

14. Thanksgiving is an example.

15. It is the opposite of **pass**.

16. It is located in your skull.

USING THE Dictionary

Write each pair of words in alphabetical order.

17.–18. anyway, aim   **19.–20.** radio, rail

◆ ◆ ◆

Dictionary Check Be sure to check the alphabetical order of the words in your **Spelling Dictionary**.

Word Structure

I. _____

2. _____

3. _____

4. _____

5. _____

6. _____

7. _____

8. _____

9. _____

10. _____

II. _____

12. _____

Word Meanings

13. _____

14. _____

15. _____

16. _____

Using the Dictionary

17. _____

18. _____

19. _____

20. _____

Spelling and Reading

aim	holiday	paper	station	able
crayon	flavor	lazy	brain	anyway
remain	favor	rail	taste	trailer
lady	nation	relay	fail	radio

Fill in the Blanks

Fill in the Blanks Write the spelling word that completes each sentence.

1. If your _____ is poor, you will not hit the target.
2. I never _____ to enjoy a good book.
3. You must be strong if you are _____ to carry that heavy load.
4. I used pencil and _____ to draw and color that picture.
5. Please _____ in your seat until your name is called.
6. Jimmy and I went to the bus _____ to meet my aunt.
7. Goods are often sent by _____ or by sea.
8. Once you have had a _____ of Mother's cooking you will want more.
9. The car pulled a _____ full of furniture.
10. Dad told Jim not to open the present, but he did _____.
11. We heard a traffic report on our car's _____.
12. Do me the _____ of returning a book to the library.
13. Chocolate is my favorite ice cream _____.
14. The player will _____ the coach's message to the team.
15. Columbus Day is a _____ in some states.

Solve the Analogies

Solve the Analogies Write a spelling word to complete each analogy.

16. **Paint** is to **canvas** as **pencil** is to _____.
17. **Gentleman** is to **man** as _____ is to **woman**.
18. **Heart** is to **chest** as _____ is to **head**.
19. **Country** is to _____ as **car** is to **automobile**.
20. **Slim** is to **thin** as **idle** is to _____.

Fill in the Blanks

1. _____
2. _____
3. _____
4. _____
5. _____
6. _____
7. _____
8. _____
9. _____
10. _____
11. _____
12. _____
13. _____
14. _____
15. _____

Solve the Analogies

16. _____
17. _____
18. _____
19. _____
20. _____

Spelling and Writing

Proofread a Diary Entry

Six words are not spelled correctly in this diary entry.
Write the words correctly.

October 8

Each weekend is a holliday at our house. We
remain at home and listen to music on our
favorite raydio station, read the daily papur,
and are lazey without feeling guilty. I give my
brane a rest from school, and we all relax. I
did have to do some chores, but it was a
great weekend enyway.

Proofreading Marks

≡ Make a capital.

/ Make a small letter.

∧ Add something.

℮ Take out something.

⊙ Add a period.

⌗ New paragraph

(SP) Spelling error

Write a Diary Entry

Narrative Writing

Write a diary entry for a real or an imagined day.
Include all the information that is important. Be sure to
include the following:

- the date you are writing your entry
- the date or dates you are writing about
- what you did during that time period
- what feelings you had about what happened
- what changes in your life, if any, you will make because
  of that experience

Writing Process

Prewriting

Drafting

Revising

Proofread Your Writing During **Editing**

Publishing

Proofread your writing for spelling errors as part of the editing
stage in the writing process. Be sure to check each word
carefully. Use a dictionary to check spelling if you are not sure.

VOCABULARY CONNECTIONS

Strategy Words

Review Words: Long a Spelled a, ai, ay

Write a word from the box for each definition.

away	laid	mail	maybe	paint

1. perhaps; possibly
2. past tense and past participle of **lay**
3. letters, postcards, packages and other print material sent through the postal system
4. absent; a distance from; in another direction
5. to color

Preview Words: Long a Spelled a, ai, ay

Someone mixed up the second syllables of the words in the box. Replace the second syllable in each word. Then write each word correctly.

explain	grayest	midday	prepaid	reclaim

6. grayclaim
7. preday
8. expaid
9. reest
10. midplain

Review Words

1. _____
2. _____
3. _____
4. _____
5. _____

Preview Words

6. _____
7. _____
8. _____
9. _____
10. _____

Content Words

Social Studies: Sailing

Write words from the box to complete this story.

barrier	scrape	reef	surf	sailboat

Since we wanted to go sailing, my friend and I borrowed a __1.__ . We sailed around the __2.__ island into the open sea. Because the wind was strong, the boat was hard to handle. The __3.__ was driving us toward a coral __4.__ . I was afraid we would __5.__ the bottom of the boat if we were driven ashore. Luckily, we got back safely.

Fine Arts: Making Models

Write a word from the box to solve each riddle.

cardboard	poster	clay	wire	modeling

6. I am a material that can be molded. What am I?
7. I am thin but strong. What am I?
8. I am forming an animal from clay. What am I doing?
9. I am large and announce something. What am I?
10. I am a stiff material often used for making boxes. What am I?

Apply the Spelling Strategy

Circle the two Content Words you wrote in which the **long a** sound is spelled **ai** or **ay**.

Word Study

Prefixes

The prefix **mid-** means "near, in, or of the middle." **Midsummer** is near the middle of summer. Write the Strategy Word that means "around noon" or "in the middle of the day."

Social Studies: Sailing

1. _____
2. _____
3. _____
4. _____
5. _____

Fine Arts: Making Models

6. _____
7. _____
8. _____
9. _____
10. _____

Prefixes

1. _____

Spelling and Thinking

READ THE SPELLING WORDS

1.	field	*field*	The cows are grazing in the **field**.
2.	lead	*lead*	If you **lead,** I will follow.
3.	speed	*speed*	Do bikers **speed** on this path?
4.	believe	*believe*	I **believe** you are telling the truth.
5.	deal	*deal*	That **deal** was too good to be true.
6.	piece	*piece*	We lost a **piece** of the puzzle.
7.	reach	*reach*	Ava cannot **reach** the top shelf.
8.	breeze	*breeze*	The **breeze** helped cool us today.
9.	speak	*speak*	We are learning to **speak** Italian.
10.	agree	*agree*	Yes, I **agree** with your plan.
11.	least	*least*	It has rained for at **least** six days.
12.	season	*season*	Summer is the **season** I like best.
13.	between	*between*	This secret is **between** you and me.
14.	chief	*chief*	A **chief** is head of a group.
15.	steam	*steam*	You can **steam** these vegetables.
16.	degree	*degree*	The temperature rose one **degree** today.
17.	reason	*reason*	What is your **reason** for being so early?
18.	brief	*brief*	A **brief** tale is a short story.
19.	repeat	*repeat*	Do not **repeat** everything you hear.
20.	peach	*peach*	The skin of a **peach** is fuzzy.

SORT THE SPELLING WORDS

1.–10. Write the words that have the **long e** sound spelled **ea**.

11.–15. Write the words that have the **long e** sound spelled **ee**.

16.–20. Write the words that have the **long e** sound spelled **ie**.

REMEMBER THE SPELLING STRATEGY

Remember that the **long e** sound can be spelled in different ways:
ea in **deal**, **ee** in **speed**, and **ie** in **field**.

ea
1.
2.
3.
4.
5.
6.
7.
8.
9.
10.

ee
11.
12.
13.
14.
15.

ie
16.
17.
18.
19.
20.

Spelling ᴬⁿᵈ Vocabulary

Word Meanings

Write a spelling word for each definition.

1. a fuzzy, sweet fruit
2. a leader; head of a group
3. to handle in a certain way; cope
4. gas made from water
5. to talk
6. a part
7. smallest in size or amount
8. to extend

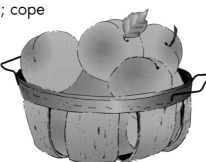

Word Categories

Write a spelling word to complete each category.

9. area, meadow, _____
10. current, wind, _____
11. swiftness, rapidity, _____
12. short, concise, _____

Syllables

13.–19. Write the spelling words that have two syllables. Draw a line between the syllables.

USING THE Dictionary

20. Words that have the same spellings but different origins, meanings, and sometimes pronunciations are called **homographs**. The dictionary usually has a separate entry for each homograph. Write the spelling word that is a homograph.

◆ ◆ ◆

Dictionary Check Be sure to check your answer in your **Spelling Dictionary**.

Word Meanings
1. _____
2. _____
3. _____
4. _____
5. _____
6. _____
7. _____
8. _____

Word Categories
9. _____
10. _____
11. _____
12. _____

Syllables
13. _____
14. _____
15. _____
16. _____
17. _____
18. _____
19. _____

Using the Dictionary
20. _____

field	lead	speed	believe	deal
piece	reach	breeze	speak	agree
least	season	between	chief	steam
degree	reason	brief	repeat	peach

Solve the Analogies
Write a spelling word to complete each analogy.

1. **Carrot** is to **vegetable** as _____ is to **fruit**.
2. **Huge** is to **big** as **gale** is to _____.
3. **Monarch** is to **ruler** as **talk** is to _____.
4. **Happy** is to **sad** as **follow** is to _____.
5. **Country** is to **state** as **whole** is to _____.
6. **Seek** is to **search** as _____ is to **short**.
7. **Heat** is to _____ as **cold** is to **ice**.
8. **Question** is to **ask** as _____ is to **think**.

Complete the Sentences
Write a spelling word to complete each sentence. The spelling word rhymes with the underlined word.

9. The farmer's _____ will surely <u>yield</u> a crop.
10. You must never _____ that dangerous <u>feat</u>.
11. I swim at a <u>beach</u> that is not out of _____.
12. When biking, you <u>need</u> to be aware of your _____.
13. We dined at a <u>feast</u> with five courses at _____.
14. To appoint him a _____ is beyond my <u>belief</u>.
15. A five-dollar <u>meal</u> is a very good _____.

Complete the Paragraph
Write words from the box to complete the paragraph.

My friends and I have different ideas about which 16. _____ is best. I 17. _____ summer is perfect, but Marcie does not 18. _____. She prefers winter while Paul is torn 19. _____ spring and fall. He needs a high 20. _____ of cool, brisk weather.

believe
agree
degree
between
season

Solve the Analogies
1.
2.
3.
4.
5.
6.
7.
8.

Complete the Sentences
9.
10.
11.
12.
13.
14.
15.

Complete the Paragraph
16.
17.
18.
19.
20.

Proofread a Newspaper Rental Ad

Six words are not spelled correctly in this newspaper rental ad. Write those words correctly.

·❧ DAILY NEWS ·❧·

For Rent

Why pay high hotel rates? Rent for the seasun. A peech of a house on a lovely piese of land between a grassy feild and a clear blue lake. Enjoy the summer breeze and catch a load of fish. $175 per week. I will not be able to repeet this offer, so act now!

Proofreading Marks

≡ Make a capital.

/ Make a small letter.

∧ Add something.

℆ Take out something.

⊙ Add a period.

⌗ New paragraph

SP Spelling error

Write a Newspaper Rental Ad — Persuasive Writing

Write a newspaper rental ad. You can rent your house, a house you know, or an imaginary house. Be sure to include the following information:

- the advantages of the house itself
- why the person should rent it
- what period of time the house is to be rented (week? month? season?)
- where the house is located
- the rental price

Proofread Your Writing During

Proofread your writing for spelling errors as part of the editing stage in the writing process. Be sure to check each word carefully. Use a dictionary to check spelling if you are not sure.

Writing Process

Prewriting

⬇

Drafting

⬇

Revising

⬇

Editing

⬇

Publishing

VOCABULARY CONNECTIONS

►Strategy Words◄

Review Words: Long e Spelled ea, ee, ie

Write a word from the box for each clue.

cheese	leave	mean	peace	speech

1. the opposite of **war**
2. to go away
3. an antonym of **kind**
4. a solid food made from milk
5. a public talk

Preview Words: Long e Spelled ea, ee, ie

Substitute a word from the box to replace each underlined word.

beliefs	beneath	decrease	freedom	make-believe

6. The store owner has promised that he will <u>lower</u> his prices.
7. Some children have <u>imaginary</u> friends.
8. Our <u>strong opinions</u> are that we will play and win the game.
9. Be thankful for your <u>independence</u>.
10. The new subway system runs <u>under</u> all the city streets.

Review Words

1. _____
2. _____
3. _____
4. _____
5. _____

Preview Words

6. _____
7. _____
8. _____
9. _____
10. _____

Content Words

Science: Animals

Write a word from the box to fit each description.

beetle	lizard	grasshopper	reptile	insect

1. an animal with long rear legs for jumping
2. a hard-shelled animal with two sets of wings
3. class of animals that includes fly, bee, and mosquito
4. scaly animal with long body, four legs, and tapering tail
5. class of animals that includes snake and turtle

Health: Diseases

Read the following clues and write the word from the box that solves each mystery.

chicken pox	itch	fever	measles	flu

6.–7. We cover your body with red spots.
8. I often follow the handling of poison ivy.
9. I raise your temperature and make you feel hot.
10. I am worse than a cold and may send you to bed.

Apply the Spelling Strategy

Circle the two Content Words you wrote in which the **long e** sound is spelled **ea** or **ee**.

Word History

An Old English word, **bitela,** meant "to bite." Write the Content Word that came from this word and means "a kind of insect."

Science: Animals

1. _____
2. _____
3. _____
4. _____
5. _____

Health: Diseases

6. _____
7. _____
8. _____
9. _____
10. _____

Word History

1. _____

Long i: i, i-C-e, y, igh, ey, uy

i

1. ____
2. ____
3. ____
4. ____
5. ____
6. ____

i-consonant-e

7. ____
8. ____

y

9. ____
10. ____
11. ____

igh

12. ____
13. ____
14. ____
15. ____
16. ____
17. ____
18. ____

ey or uy

19. ____
20. ____

Spelling and Thinking

READ THE SPELLING WORDS

1.	eyes	*eyes*	Sunglasses protect our **eyes**.
2.	icicle	*icicle*	An **icicle** is a hanging stick of ice.
3.	tight	*tight*	My shoes are too **tight** for comfort.
4.	climb	*climb*	Some bears can **climb** trees.
5.	umpire	*umpire*	The **umpire** called the pitch a strike.
6.	highway	*highway*	A **highway** is wider than a street.
7.	idea	*idea*	Whose **idea** was it to hold this meeting?
8.	flight	*flight*	In **flight,** bats scoop up insects.
9.	cycle	*cycle*	The water **cycle** supports life.
10.	fright	*fright*	The haunted house gave us a **fright**.
11.	iron	*iron*	Steel and **iron** are strong materials.
12.	slight	*slight*	A **slight** rip can be sewn easily.
13.	tiny	*tiny*	A dot is a **tiny** mark.
14.	higher	*higher*	Go to **higher** ground during floods.
15.	shy	*shy*	A **shy** person tries to avoid notice.
16.	hire	*hire*	Will the city **hire** more workers?
17.	buy	*buy*	I **buy** my shoes at that store.
18.	might	*might*	She was afraid they **might** be late.
19.	reply	*reply*	I must **reply** to the invitation.
20.	title	*title*	What is the **title** of your story?

SORT THE SPELLING WORDS

Write the words that have the **long i** sound spelled:

1.–6. **i**.

7.–8. **i-consonant-e**.

9.–11. **y**.

12.–18. **igh**.

19.–20. **ey** or **uy**.

REMEMBER THE SPELLING STRATEGY

Remember that the **long i** sound is spelled **i** in **climb**, **i-consonant-e** in **hire**, **y** in **cycle**, **igh** in **might**, **ey** in **eyes**, and **uy** in **buy**.

Spelling and Vocabulary

Word Meanings

Replace each underlined word or group of words with a spelling word.

1. We took a <u>plane ride</u> from Denver to Seattle.
2. Because we were on a <u>close</u> schedule, we had to hurry.
3. After a <u>brief</u> delay, the plane took off.
4. I <u>could</u> have relaxed, but then I realized I had forgotten my suitcase.
5. That gave me quite a <u>scare</u>.

Word Structure

6.–15. Write the spelling words that have more than one syllable. Draw a line between syllables.

Phonics

16. Write the one-syllable word that ends with a consonant that is not sounded.
17. Write the one-syllable word that ends with a **silent e**.
18. Write the one-syllable word that starts like **ship** and ends like **try**.

USING THE Dictionary

Look at these dictionary respellings. Say each word. Write the spelling word for each dictionary respelling.

19. /bī/   20. /īz/

◆ ◆ ◆

Dictionary Check Be sure to check your answer in your **Spelling Dictionary**.

Word Meanings
1. _____
2. _____
3. _____
4. _____
5. _____

Word Structure
6. _____
7. _____
8. _____
9. _____
10. _____
11. _____
12. _____
13. _____
14. _____
15. _____

Phonics
16. _____
17. _____
18. _____

Using the Dictionary
19. _____
20. _____

Spelling and Reading

eyes	icicle	tight	climb	umpire
highway	idea	flight	cycle	fright
iron	slight	tiny	higher	shy
hire	buy	might	reply	title

Complete the Sentences Write a spelling word to complete each sentence.

1. Volunteering to help the needy is a good _____.
2. Even _____ people can learn to speak in public.
3. It is hard to follow the ball with the sun in your _____.
4. Many people have tried to _____ Mount Everest.
5. The plant is going to _____ more workers.
6. The _____ called the player out at third base.
7. What is the _____ of the book you are reading?
8. I thought her _____ to the question was excellent.
9. I want to _____ my mother a birthday present.
10. Jill thinks she _____ have a plan to raise money.

Solve the Riddles Write a spelling word to solve each riddle.

11. I am little; I rhyme with **fight**. Who am I?
12. As a verb, I press; as a metal, I am heavy. Who am I?
13. I am wide and black; cars ride on my back. Who am I?
14. I am best in the cold but drip in the heat. Who am I?

Solve the Analogies Write a spelling word to complete each analogy.

15. **Big** is to **huge** as **small** is to _____.
16. **Up** is to **down** as **loose** is to _____.
17. **Gallop** is to **horse** as _____ is to **bird**.
18. **Canoe** is to **paddle** as **bike** is to _____.
19. **Leave** is to **go** as **scare** is to _____.
20. **Empty** is to **full** as **lower** is to _____.

Complete the Sentences

1. _____
2. _____
3. _____
4. _____
5. _____
6. _____
7. _____
8. _____
9. _____
10. _____

Solve the Riddles

11. _____
12. _____
13. _____
14. _____

Solve the Analogies

15. _____
16. _____
17. _____
18. _____
19. _____
20. _____

Spelling and Writing

Proofread a Poster

Six words are not spelled correctly on this poster. Write those words correctly.

THE MAN IN THE IREN MASK

by that famous theater group
the Season Cicle Players!

Where? Main Street Theater, Hiway 66 When? June 17–20

Your eys will pop out of your head. Your heart will pound.

Chills, joy, and frite. All for the slight price of $2.50.

Don't be shi. Call 555-2633 now to reserve your seats.

SEE YOU THERE!!

Write a Poster

Persuasive Writing

Write a poster urging people to attend something. It may be to go to a show, a fireworks display, a rodeo, or an ice-cream social. Be sure to tell the following:

- name of the event
- location
- reasons for taking part
- price of tickets
- who is giving the event
- date or dates
- where to get tickets

Use as many spelling words as you can.

Proofread Your Writing During

Proofread your poster for spelling errors as part of the editing stage in the writing process. Be sure to check each word carefully. Use a dictionary to check spelling if you are not sure.

Writing Process

Prewriting

Drafting

Revising

Editing

Publishing

35

VOCABULARY CONNECTIONS

◄Strategy Words►

Review Words

1. _____
2. _____
3. _____
4. _____
5. _____

Preview Words

6. _____
7. _____
8. _____
9. _____
10. _____

Review Words:
Long i Spelled i, i-C-e, y, igh, ey, uy

Write a word from the box that fits each clue.

fight	find	price	right	wild

1. This is a bad way to settle an argument.
2. This word is an antonym of **wrong**.
3. This is an antonym of **lose**.
4. This is a synonym of **cost**.
5. This rhymes with **mild**.

Preview Words:
Long i Spelled i, i-C-e, y, igh, ey, uy

Write a word from the box to complete each sentence.

arrive	delight	silent	style	supply

6. The audience remained ____ during the president's speech.
7. The happy baby shook the rattle and squealed with ____.
8. I will cook the dinner if you will be good enough to ____ the food.
9. Our flight will ____ at 4:30 this afternoon at the city's new airport.
10. I like her ____ of singing.

Content Words

Language Arts: Verbs

Write the word that best matches each definition.

carried	grabbed	chased	hurried	climbed

1. ran after
2. went up
3. took, transported
4. went fast
5. seized, grasped

Language Arts: Exact Meaning

Write the word from the box that best fits each sentence.

hiked	wandered	marched	wobbled	strolled

6. The spinning top _____ as it slowed down.
7. The brook _____ through the woods and down the hill.
8. The soldiers _____ to the parade ground.
9. Wearing backpacks, the friends _____ the mountain trail.
10. The musicians _____ from house to house.

Apply the Spelling Strategy

Circle the spelling of the **long i** sound in two of the Content Words you wrote.

Word Study

Silent Letters

The letters **gh** are usually pronounced /**f**/ at the end of syllables or words, as in **laugh**. In the middle of a syllable or word, **gh** is generally silent, as in **right**. Write the Strategy Word that has a silent **gh** and means "great pleasure."

Language Arts: Verbs

1. _____
2. _____
3. _____
4. _____
5. _____

Language Arts: Exact Meaning

6. _____
7. _____
8. _____
9. _____
10. _____

Silent Letters

1. _____

Assessment and Review

Assessment Units 1–5

Each Assessment Word in the box fits one of the spelling strategies you have studied over the past five weeks. Read the spelling strategies. Then write each Assessment Word under the unit number it fits.

Unit 1

1.–4. Many short vowel sounds are spelled with a single letter: **a** in **pass**, **e** in **held**, **i** in **skill**, **o** in **collar**, and **u** in **trust**.

Unit 2

5.–10. The long vowel sounds you hear in **case**, **rise**, **chose**, and **cube** are spelled with the **vowel-consonant-e** pattern.

Unit 3

11.–14. The **long a** sound can be spelled **a** as in **lady**, **ai** as in **aim**, and **ay** as in **relay**.

Unit 4

15.–18. The **long e** sound can be spelled in different ways: **ea** in **deal**, **ee** in **speed**, and **ie** in **field**.

Unit 5

19.–20. The **long i** sound can be spelled in different ways: **i** in **climb**, **i-consonant-e** in **hire**, **y** in **cycle**, **igh** in **might**, **ey** in **eyes**, and **uy** in **buy**.

skull
stroke
betray
series
magic
fired
icy
beast
slope
rainy
crime
raft
claim
gift
male
screen
basin
type
seep
sty

 **Unit 1: Short Vowel Sounds**

begin	kept	trust	zipper	pass
collar	held	button	began	felt

Write the spelling word that rhymes with each of these words.

1. slept   3. melt   5. flipper

2. mass   4. yelled   6. just

Write a spelling word to complete each sentence.

7. The dog wore a red ____.

8. I lost one shiny gold ____ from my new coat.

9. What time does the school day ____?

10. Last year, school ____ one hour earlier.

 **Unit 2: Vowel-Consonant-e**

awhile	became	beside	invite	case
drove	huge	wife	surprise	alone

Write the missing spelling word. Use the underlined word as a clue.

11. They are <u>husband</u> and ____.

12. These horses ran <u>together</u> while one stood ____.

13. One package was <u>big</u>, but the other was ____!

14. There are seats <u>behind</u> and also ____ me.

Find the misspelled word in each sentence. Write the word correctly.

15. My party was a real suprise.

16. Don't wait for me, I will be along in awile.

17. Anna will inveit the whole class to her party.

18. Mary bicame ill from eating too much ice cream.

19. Can the lawyer win this kase?

20. We were lost and drov three blocks out of our way.

Unit 1
1. _____
2. _____
3. _____
4. _____
5. _____
6. _____
7. _____
8. _____
9. _____
10. _____

Unit 2
11. _____
12. _____
13. _____
14. _____
15. _____
16. _____
17. _____
18. _____
19. _____
20. _____

 **Review**   Unit 3: Long a Spelled a, ai, ay

favor	holiday	relay	trailer	able
paper	nation	radio	station	lady

Write the spelling word that goes with each meaning.

1. another word for **woman**
2. something you ask someone to do for you
3. another word for a country under one government
4. a place to stand or an official building
5. a special kind of day
6. a sheet you write on
7. something that might be pulled by a truck or car
8. having skill or talent
9. a kind of race in which a stick might be passed from one runner to another
10. equipment that might have earphones

 **Review**   Unit 4: Long e Spelled ea, ee, ie

agree	believe	field	reason	between
reach	speak	lead	chief	piece

Write the spelling word that completes each sentence.

11. What is your _____ for saying that?
12. You will need a stool to _____ that upper shelf.
13. I _____ that is the right answer.
14. The house stands _____ two huge old trees.
15. Tall corn grew in the farmer's _____.
16. Would you like a _____ of chocolate cake?
17. If we follow Rover, he will _____ us to the right place.
18. The _____ reason I can't go is that I have homework to do.
19. Please _____ a little more softly.
20. Do you _____ that the party was a big success?

buy	climb	might	cycle	flight
eyes	tiny	idea	iron	shy

Write the spelling words for these clues.

1.–2. These words rhyme with **right**.

3. This word has three syllables.

Write the spelling word that completes each sentence.

4. Rain is part of the water ____.

5. It is fun to ____ that big old tree in our yard.

6. I have just enough money to ____ that book.

7. Most animals have two ____.

8. A very small insect is a ____ ant.

9. A tool we use to press clothes is called an ____.

10. Speak up. Don't be ____.

Unit 5

1. _____
2. _____
3. _____
4. _____
5. _____
6. _____
7. _____
8. _____
9. _____
10. _____

 GAME **Spelling Study Strategy**

Spelling Tic-Tac-Toe

Practicing spelling words can be fun if you make it into a game. Here's an idea you can try with a friend.

1. Write your spelling words in a list. Ask your friend to do the same with his spelling words. Trade spelling lists.

2. Draw a tic-tac-toe board on a piece of scrap paper. Decide who will use **X** and who will use **O**.

3. Ask your partner to call the first word on your spelling list to you. Spell it out loud. If you spell it correctly, make an **X** or an **O** (whichever you are using) on the tic-tac-toe board. If you misspell the word, ask your partner to spell it out loud for you. You miss your turn.

4. Now you call a word from your partner's spelling list.

5. Keep playing until one of you makes "tic-tac-toe." Keep starting over until you both have practiced all your spelling words.

Grammar, Usage, and Mechanics

Possessive Nouns

A possessive noun shows ownership.
Some possessive nouns are singular. Only one person or animal is the owner.

> **Jess's** bike is old, but **Jill's** is new.
>
> Do not remove the **dog's** collar.

Other possessive nouns are plural. More than one person or animal are the owners.

> All the **boys'** teams are here but not the **men's** teams.
>
> The **horses'** hooves could be heard in the canyon as they galloped over the hill.

Practice Activity

A. Write the correct possessive form in each sentence.

1. My (mothers'/mother's) birthday is tomorrow.
2. One (teams'/team's) coach is late.
3. A (pigs'/pig's) tail is curly.
4. I knit both of my (uncles'/uncle's) hats.
5. It was (Jakes'/Jake's) turn to feed the rabbits.

B. Change each underlined phrase to make one possessive noun.

6. I will borrow the sweater <u>of Carlos</u>.
7. The shoes <u>of everyone</u> need to be polished.
8. The kennel <u>where the dogs stay</u> is very clean.
9. Kim found the lost key <u>that belongs to your cousins</u>!
10. The books <u>of the student</u> were piled high.

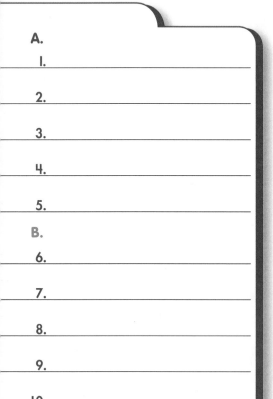

A.
1.
2.
3.
4.
5.
B.
6.
7.
8.
9.
10.

WORKSHOP

Read It Backwards!

Good writers always proofread their writing for spelling errors. Here's a strategy you can use to proofread your papers.

Instead of reading your paper from the first word to the last word, try reading it from the last word to the first word. So you would read the sentence **The computer was brand new** like this: **new brand was computer The**.

Does this sound like a funny thing to do? It is! But reading your paper backwards helps you think about how to spell each word instead of thinking about what the whole sentence means. Try it!

Electronic Spelling

Search Engines

When you use a computer to find information in an on-line encyclopedia or on the Internet, you often use search engines. These are very useful tools. You type in a word or phrase, and the search engine looks for information on that topic. However, you must spell the word correctly or the search engine will report, "No matches found."

Sometimes it makes sense to type in both the singular and plural forms of a noun. Then the search engine will find both or either. Be careful typing plural forms. Make sure you spell them correctly. If you type **tornaedos,** most search engines will say "No matches found for tornaedos."

Look at these plural words. Which are misspelled? Write those words correctly. Write **OK** if a word is correct.

1. radioes
2. holidayes
3. cases
4. eyeses
5. zippers
6. monkeys

Electronic Spelling

1. _____
2. _____
3. _____
4. _____
5. _____
6. _____

Spelling and Thinking

o

1.

2.

3.

4.

5.

6.

7.

8.

9.

10.

11.

12.

13.

oa

14.

15.

16.

ow

17.

18.

19.

20.

READ THE SPELLING WORDS

1. poet	*poet*	Which **poet** wrote those lines?
2. coast	*coast*	Along the **coast** lie sunken ships.
3. pillow	*pillow*	A soft **pillow** cradled her head.
4. hotel	*hotel*	The **hotel** was ten stories high.
5. also	*also*	I can sing and **also** dance.
6. clothes	*clothes*	My **clothes** hang in a closet.
7. pony	*pony*	The **pony** trotted around the ring.
8. bold	*bold*	Catching the snake was a **bold** move.
9. moment	*moment*	In a **moment** the sun will set.
10. obey	*obey*	Dogs can learn to **obey** commands.
11. grown	*grown*	She has **grown** an inch this year.
12. hello	*hello*	I say **hello** to everyone I know.
13. motel	*motel*	A **motel** is a motor hotel.
14. boast	*boast*	Do not **boast** of our success yet.
15. glow	*glow*	I followed the **glow** of the lamp.
16. goal	*goal*	The ball bounced over the **goal** line.
17. poem	*poem*	That **poem** contains rhyming words.
18. shown	*shown*	We were **shown** to our room.
19. hero	*hero*	A **hero** does brave deeds.
20. fold	*fold*	Do not **fold** or wrinkle your paper.

SORT THE SPELLING WORDS

1.–13. Write the words with the **long o** sound spelled **o**.

14.–16. Write the words with the **long o** sound spelled **oa**.

17.–20. Write the words with the **long o** sound spelled **ow**.

REMEMBER THE SPELLING STRATEGY

Remember that the **long o** sound can be spelled in different ways: **o** in **pony**, **oa** in **goal**, and **ow** in **glow**.

Spelling and Vocabulary

Word Meanings

Write a spelling word for each definition.

1. a form of **grow**
2. land along the ocean
3. place offering guests rooms, meals, and other services
4. a form of **show**
5. something usually found on a bed

Syllables

Say a word to yourself and listen to the beats to determine how many syllables it has. You can also tell how many syllables a word has by the number of vowel sounds it contains. Check a dictionary to be sure.

6.–9. Write the four-letter spelling words that have one syllable.

10.–15. Write the four-letter spelling words that have two syllables.

The dictionary lists the part of speech for each entry word after the respelling. Write each word and the abbreviation for its part of speech.

16. motel	19. moment
17. hello	20. boast
18. clothes	

◆ ◆ ◆

Dictionary Check Be sure to check your answer in your **Spelling Dictionary**.

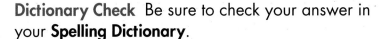

Word Meanings

1. _____
2. _____
3. _____
4. _____
5. _____

Syllables
one-syllable

6. _____
7. _____
8. _____
9. _____

two-syllables

10. _____
11. _____
12. _____
13. _____
14. _____
15. _____

Using the Dictionary

16. _____
17. _____
18. _____
19. _____
20. _____

poet	coast	pillow	hotel	also
clothes	pony	bold	moment	obey
grown	hello	motel	boast	glow
goal	poem	shown	hero	fold

Complete the Sentences

I.
2.
3.
4.
5.
6.
7.
8.
9.
10.

Solve the Riddles

II.
12.
13.
14.
15.

Complete the Paragraph

16.
17.
18.
19.
20.

Complete the Sentences   Write a spelling word to complete each sentence.

1. While driving to Chicago, we stopped for the night at a _____ right on the highway.
2. A _____ was at the head of the bed.
3. Mother has _____ both flowers and vegetables.
4. Many beachgoers swam and picnicked along the sandy _____.
5. Say _____ to your brother for me.
6. We play ball and _____ fly kites in the park.
7. Peter was _____ a map of the city when he was lost.
8. She is a _____, a writer, and a musician.
9. He is a doorman at a fancy _____ in New York City.
10. The _____ of fireflies lights up the night sky.

Solve the Riddles   Write a spelling word to solve each riddle.

11. I am a brief period of time. Who am I?
12. Everyone loves me because I am brave. Who am I?
13. I am something everyone wants to reach. Who am I?
14. Sometimes I rhyme, and sometimes I do not. Who am I?
15. I am something you do with paper and with clothes. Who am I?

Complete the Paragraph   Write words from the box to fill in the blanks in the story.

Children, dressed in their best __16.__, were taking turns riding a __17.__. They were having their pictures taken and felt quite __18.__ when they could make the pony __19.__. I heard one boy __20.__ that he was the best rider and was going to be a cowboy.

pony
bold
obey
boast
clothes

Spelling  Writing

Proofread Directions

Six words are not spelled correctly in these directions. Write those words correctly.

Continue down this street, along the coist. You will come to a grand hotle on your right. A little past that will be a store that sells women's cloaths. Turn left there, as shown on your map, and continue walking. In a momint you can foald up your map, for you will have reached your goil. Harris Street crosses the street you are on.

Proofreading Marks

Make a capital.

Make a small letter.

Add something.

Take out something.

Add a period.

New paragraph

Spelling error

Write Directions

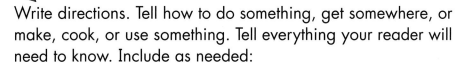

Write directions. Tell how to do something, get somewhere, or make, cook, or use something. Tell everything your reader will need to know. Include as needed:

- simple directions your reader can follow
- each step in order
- materials, if any, your reader will need
- how far it is to your reader's destination
- how long it will take to cook or make the item
- how hard or easy it will be to accomplish the goal

Use as many spelling words as you can.

Proofread Your Writing During

Writing Process

Prewriting
⇩
Drafting
⇩
Revising
⇩
Editing
⇩
Publishing

Proofread your writing for spelling errors as part of the editing stage in the writing process. Be sure to check each word carefully. Use a dictionary to check spelling if you are not sure.

VOCABULARY CONNECTIONS

Strategy Words

Review Words

1. _____
2. _____
3. _____
4. _____
5. _____

Preview Words

6. _____
7. _____
8. _____
9. _____
10. _____

Review Words: Long o Spelled o, oa, ow

Write a word from the box for each definition.

below	nobody	over	rainbow	soap

1. above
2. band of colors, usually in the sky
3. item to wash with
4. under
5. not anyone

Preview Words: Long o Spelled o, oa, ow

Write a word from the box to complete each sentence.

bowl	groceries	growth	loaves	narrow

6. Mother bought a pound of butter and two _____ of bread.
7. For breakfast this morning I had a _____ of cereal and a glass of juice.
8. Joe had to squeeze through a _____ slit in the fence.
9. I must go to the store to buy some _____.
10. We were pleased to discover new _____ on our plant.

Content Words

Social Studies: Farming

Write words from the box to complete the paragraph.

farming	sowing	prairie	visit	reaper

I am going to __1.__ my aunt and uncle, who have a farm on a western __2.__ . I have learned that __3.__ is not easy. It includes __4.__ the seed in the spring and using a large __5.__ to harvest the crops in the fall.

Fine Arts: Stringed Instruments

Write a word from the box for each clue.

cello	viola	harp	violin	strings

6. My name has three vowels, one at the end.
7. I am the "little sister" of the word you just wrote.
8. I am the "big sister" of the words you just wrote; you sit to play me.
9. You probably have seen pictures of angels playing me.
10. Some musical instruments have few or many of these.

Apply the Spelling Strategy

Circle the one-letter spelling of the **long o** sound in three of the Content Words you wrote. Circle the two-letter spelling of the **long o** sound in one of the Content Words you wrote.

Anagrams

Anagrams are words that have all the same letters, but the letters are in a different order in each word. **Blow** and **bowl** are anagrams. Write the Strategy Word that is an anagram of **elbow**.

Social Studies: Farming

1. _____
2. _____
3. _____
4. _____
5. _____

Fine Arts: Stringed Instruments

6. _____
7. _____
8. _____
9. _____
10. _____

Anagrams

1. _____

Spelling and Thinking

READ THE SPELLING WORDS

1.	flute	flute	A **flute** is a musical instrument.
2.	view	view	We had a clear **view** of the sea.
3.	student	student	The **student** studied for her test.
4.	whose	whose	I wonder **whose** shoes these are.
5.	clue	clue	That **clue** helped solve the mystery.
6.	human	human	We all belong to the **human** race.
7.	juice	juice	Orange **juice** is a healthful drink.
8.	few	few	She has **few** faults and many friends.
9.	true	true	Is that story **true** or false?
10.	tube	tube	That thin **tube** is a drinking straw.
11.	truth	truth	The **truth** serves better than a lie.
12.	glue	glue	We can **glue** the pieces together.
13.	dew	dew	The grass sparkled with morning **dew**.
14.	lose	lose	Whether you win or **lose,** be a good sport.
15.	tulip	tulip	The **tulip** is a flower of spring.
16.	used	used	My bike, though **used,** is new to me.
17.	due	due	Yesterday's homework is **due** today.
18.	fruit	fruit	Those **fruit** trees bear sweet pears.
19.	music	music	I listen to **music** to relax.
20.	rule	rule	No school **rule** should be broken.

/o͞o/

1.
2.
3.
4.
5.
6.
7.
8.
9.
10.
11.
12.
13.
14.
15.

/yo͞o/

16.
17.
18.
19.
20.

SORT THE SPELLING WORDS

1.–15. Write the spelling words with the /o͞o/ vowel sound. Circle the letters that spell this vowel sound.

16.–20. Write the spelling words with the /yo͞o/ vowel sound. Circle the letters that spell this vowel sound.

REMEMBER THE SPELLING STRATEGY

Remember that the vowel sound you hear in **true** and the vowel sound you hear in **few** can be spelled in different ways.

Spelling ᵃⁿᵈ Vocabulary

Word Meanings

Write a spelling word for each of the following definitions.

1. a scene; a range or field of sight
2. water droplets that form on cool surfaces
3. expected or scheduled
4. information that helps solve a problem
5. a sticky liquid that holds things together
6. a musical instrument

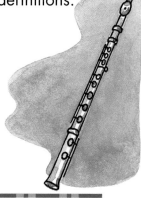

Phonics

Follow the directions to write new words.

7. toy – oy + ube = _____
8. rail – ail + ule = _____
9. useful – ful + d = _____
10. train – ain + ue = _____
11. fool – ool + ew = _____
12. jug – g + ice = _____
13. whole – le + se = _____
14. frost – ost + uit = _____
15. troop – oop + uth = _____
16. low – w + se = _____

USING THE Dictionary

Find each word in your **Spelling Dictionary**. Write the word, and draw a line between the syllables.

17. tulip
18. student
19. music
20. human

◆ ◆ ◆

Dictionary Check Be sure to check your answers in your **Spelling Dictionary**.

Word Meanings

1. _____
2. _____
3. _____
4. _____
5. _____
6. _____

Phonics

7. _____
8. _____
9. _____
10. _____
11. _____
12. _____
13. _____
14. _____
15. _____
16. _____

Using the Dictionary

17. _____
18. _____
19. _____
20. _____

flute	**view**	**student**	**whose**	**clue**
human	**juice**	**few**	**true**	**tube**
truth	**glue**	**dew**	**lose**	**tulip**
used	**due**	**fruit**	**music**	**rule**

Complete the Sentences   Write the spelling word that completes each sentence.

1. From the hill we had a great _____ of the lake.
2. Do you prefer talk shows or _____ programs on the radio?
3. My teacher said our project is _____ tomorrow.
4. In the morning _____ covered the car's windshield.
5. I squeezed the _____ of toothpaste.
6. We asked _____ book was left on the table.
7. That safety _____ will protect you from harm.
8. They used _____ to attach their pictures to paper.

Solve the Analogies   Write a spelling word to solve each analogy.

9. **Strike** is to **drum** as **blow** is to _____.
10. **Animal** is to **deer** as **flower** is to _____.
11. **Huge** is to **tiny** as **false** is to _____.
12. **Puzzle** is to **piece** as **riddle** is to _____.
13. **Joy** is to **win** as **sorrow** is to _____.
14. **Coat** is to **beaver** as **skin** is to _____.
15. **More** is to **many** as **less** is to _____.

Complete the Paragraph   Write the spelling word from the box that fits each blank.

An encyclopedia was __16.__ by the __17.__ to learn the __18.__ about a healthy diet. She wanted to know if we should eat __19.__ and drink __20.__ at every meal or only once a day.

student
juice
truth
used
fruit

Complete the Sentences

1. _____
2. _____
3. _____
4. _____
5. _____
6. _____
7. _____
8. _____

Solve the Analogies

9. _____
10. _____
11. _____
12. _____
13. _____
14. _____
15. _____

Complete the Paragraph

16. _____
17. _____
18. _____
19. _____
20. _____

Spelling and Writing

Proofread a Paragraph

Six words are not spelled correctly in this paragraph. Write those words correctly.

It was a frigid day but as fine as any human could want. As a rool, I would shun the cold, but I am a troo football fan. Therefore, I appeared when I was doo at the stadium. The vue was breathtaking. The band, sparkling with bright colors, was playing spirited musik. Soon the teams, in splendid uniforms, trotted onto the springy turf. Whether my team would win or luze, this would be a day to remember.

Proofreading Marks

≡	Make a capital.
/	Make a small letter.
∧	Add something.
ℓ	Take out something.
⊙	Add a period.
⌗	New paragraph
SP	Spelling error

Write a Paragraph

Descriptive Writing

Write a paragraph describing something you remember fondly. It may be a person, an interesting place, or a pleasant experience. Be sure to include

- the name of the person or place.
- the kind of experience.
- what you liked about the person, place, or experience.
- descriptive words that make the experience come alive for the reader.

Use as many spelling words as you can.

Writing Process

Prewriting

Drafting

Revising

Editing

Publishing

Proofread Your Writing During ➤ **Editing**

Proofread your writing for spelling errors as part of the editing stage of the writing process. Be sure to check each word carefully. Use a dictionary to check spelling if you are not sure.

VOCABULARY CONNECTIONS

Strategy Words

Review Words: Vowel Sounds /yoo/, /oo/

Write a word from the box that has the same meaning as the underlined word or words.

balloon	drew	news	pool	threw

1. Did you read today's underline account of happenings in the paper?
2. Let's blow up a underline rubber bag for the party.
3. How fast the pitcher underline hurled the ball!
4. The artist underline sketched the waterfront scene.
5. We swam in the stream's underline still, deep part.

Preview Words: Vowel Sounds /yoo/, /oo/

Write a word from the box that is a synonym of each word or phrase.

amuse	beauty	continue	movies	suitcase

6. motion pictures
7. entertain
8. keep on
9. luggage
10. a pleasing quality

Review Words
1. _____
2. _____
3. _____
4. _____
5. _____

Preview Words
6. _____
7. _____
8. _____
9. _____
10. _____

Content Words

Social Studies: Rural Life

Write a word from the box for each of these definitions.

blue jeans	railroad	matter	waterfall	mind

1. a path built of tracks for trains
2. the part of a person that thinks
3. denim pants
4. a stream that falls from a high place
5. something that takes up space

Science: Birds

Write a word from the box to complete each sentence.

canary	parrot	chicken	plumage	feather

6. We have taught our ＿＿＿ to say many words.
7. The package felt light as a ＿＿＿.
8. What beautiful ＿＿＿ the peacock has!
9. A hen or a rooster is also called a ＿＿＿.
10. I have a ＿＿＿ that sings a lovely tune.

Apply the Spelling Strategy

Circle the letter or letters that spell the /o͞o/ vowel sound in two of the Content Words you wrote.

Word Study

Word History

In Italy, in the 1400's, a strong cotton cloth was described as **jene**. This was based on the Italian city of Genoa, where the cloth was first made. Write the Content Word that comes from this word.

Social Studies: Rural Life
1. ＿＿＿＿＿＿＿＿
2. ＿＿＿＿＿＿＿＿
3. ＿＿＿＿＿＿＿＿
4. ＿＿＿＿＿＿＿＿
5. ＿＿＿＿＿＿＿＿

Science: Birds
6. ＿＿＿＿＿＿＿＿
7. ＿＿＿＿＿＿＿＿
8. ＿＿＿＿＿＿＿＿
9. ＿＿＿＿＿＿＿＿
10. ＿＿＿＿＿＿＿＿

Word History
1. ＿＿＿＿＿＿＿＿

Spelling AND Thinking

READ THE SPELLING WORDS

1.	flour	*flour*	Bread contains **flour** and yeast.
2.	however	*however*	He is polite **however** he feels.
3.	coil	*coil*	Please **coil** the hose on its reel.
4.	enjoy	*enjoy*	Relax and **enjoy** the sunset.
5.	amount	*amount*	The **amount** of our bill was $25.
6.	powder	*powder*	We dusted the dog with flea **powder**.
7.	moist	*moist*	The ground is **moist** after it rains.
8.	vowel	*vowel*	Ina's name begins and ends with a **vowel**.
9.	spoil	*spoil*	Do not let the rain **spoil** your fun.
10.	flower	*flower*	Plant a seed to grow a **flower**.
11.	joint	*joint*	Your arm bends at the elbow **joint**.
12.	joy	*joy*	The hero was greeted with shouts of **joy**.
13.	power	*power*	Those who rule have **power**.
14.	royal	*royal*	Guards protected the **royal** family.
15.	foil	*foil*	Wrap food in **foil** to keep it fresh.
16.	plow	*plow*	The **plow** turned over the soil.
17.	choice	*choice*	We had a **choice** of peas or beans.
18.	mouth	*mouth*	How many teeth are in your **mouth**?
19.	crowd	*crowd*	Follow your heart, not the **crowd**.
20.	mount	*mount*	Learn to **mount** before riding a horse.

SORT THE SPELLING WORDS

1.–9. Write the spelling words in which the /**oi**/ sound is spelled **oi** or **oy**.

10.–20. Write the spelling words in which the /**ou**/ sound is spelled **ou** or **ow**.

REMEMBER THE SPELLING STRATEGY

Remember that the /**oi**/ sound can be spelled in different ways: **oi** in **coil** or **oy** in **joy**. The /**ou**/ sound can be spelled in different ways: **ou** in **mouth** or **ow** in **plow**.

oi or oy
1.
2.
3.
4.
5.
6.
7.
8.
9.

ou or ow
10.
11.
12.
13.
14.
15.
16.
17.
18.
19.
20.

Spelling ᴬⁿᵈ Vocabulary

Word Meanings

Write a spelling word that has the same meaning as each definition below.

1. nevertheless
2. get on a horse
3. to ruin; damage
4. great strength; force
5. get pleasure from
6. selection
7. powder of ground grain
8. of kings and queens
9. total; sum
10. wind around
11. type of sound or letter

Analogies

Write a spelling word to complete each analogy.

12. **Chicken** is to **flock** as **person** is to _____.
13. **Dry** is to **arid** as _____ is to **wet**.
14. **Sneeze** is to **nose** as **yawn** is to _____.
15. **Tree** is to **leaf** as **bush** is to _____.

USING THE Dictionary

Read each sentence below. Write the spelling word and its part of speech. Use the **Spelling Dictionary** if you need help.

16. The candy was covered with foil.
17. Bath powder has a nice smell.
18. My shoulder joint aches.
19. The farmer will plow his fields.
20. You bring joy to everyone.

Word Meanings

1. _____
2. _____
3. _____
4. _____
5. _____
6. _____
7. _____
8. _____
9. _____
10. _____
11. _____

Analogies

12. _____
13. _____
14. _____
15. _____

Using the Dictionary

16. _____
17. _____
18. _____
19. _____
20. _____

flour	however	coil	enjoy	amount
powder	moist	vowel	spoil	flower
joint	joy	power	royal	foil
plow	choice	mouth	crowd	mount

Complete the Sentences

Complete the Sentences   Write a spelling word to complete each sentence.

1. Mix water and _____ to make a thick paste.
2. The daffodils will _____ in the spring.
3. The tractor has replaced the horse and _____.
4. The reward is a large _____ of money.
5. Every tooth in his _____ sparkled.
6. His lasso was a _____ of rope.
7. The baby can _____ the stairs.
8. A consonant may be followed by a _____.
9. Bake these potatoes in aluminum _____.
10. The dry earth had turned to _____.
11. Throwing a ball can injure your shoulder _____.
12. Some foods _____ if left out of the refrigerator.
13. She was given the _____ to govern the state.
14. Air that is _____ feels warmer than air that is dry.

Complete the Paragraph   Write the spelling word that fits each blank.

I hoped to have fun. Little did I expect to **15.** myself as much as this, **16.**. Following the **17.**, we came to the changing of the queen's **18.** guard. It was a great **19.** to see the beautiful castle and all the guards. If given a **20.** of tourist attractions in England, you might want to choose the changing of the guard.

Complete the Sentences
1. _____
2. _____
3. _____
4. _____
5. _____
6. _____
7. _____
8. _____
9. _____
10. _____
11. _____
12. _____
13. _____
14. _____

Complete the Paragraph
15. _____
16. _____
17. _____
18. _____
19. _____
20. _____

Spelling and Writing

Proofread a Newspaper Ad

Six words are not spelled correctly in this newspaper ad. Write those words correctly.

Giant Yard Sale!

We are selling a large amownt of goods. Take your choyce. There are flouer pots, powre tools, boxes of bath and soap pouder, and more. Come and enjoy yourself—and buy, buy, buy. We expect a big croud so arrive early. Hours are from 9 a.m. until 3 p.m., 28 Darling Street, Sweetlife, Florida.

YARD SALE

YARD SALE TODAY!

Proofreading Marks

≡ Make a capital.

/ Make a small letter.

∧ Add something.

℘ Take out something.

⊙ Add a period.

⌗ New paragraph

SP Spelling error

Write a Newspaper Ad

Write a newspaper ad offering something for sale. You may have a large sale or offer a single item. Be sure to include the following information:

- the kind of sale you are having
- the items you are selling
- a description of the items
- prices (optional)
- hours of sale (optional, depending on kind of sale)
- a telephone number or an address

Use as many spelling words as you can.

Writing Process

Prewriting

⇩

Drafting

⇩

Revising

⇩

Proofread Your Writing During ➤ **Editing**

⇩

Publishing

Proofread your writing for spelling errors as part of the editing stage in the writing process. Be sure to check each word carefully. Use a dictionary to check spelling if you are not sure.

VOCABULARY CONNECTIONS

Review Words

1. _____
2. _____
3. _____
4. _____
5. _____

Preview Words

6. _____
7. _____
8. _____
9. _____
10. _____

Strategy Words

Review Words: Vowel Diphthongs /oi/, /ou/

Write a word from the box that could replace each underlined word or group of words.

about	boil	found	house	join

1. We <u>discovered</u> an injured bird.
2. I am going to <u>become a member of</u> the Boy Scouts as soon as I am old enough.
3. We studied for <u>around</u> an hour.
4. They live in the <u>dwelling</u> by the bay.
5. To make hot chocolate, heat milk in a pan but do not allow it to <u>bubble</u>.

Preview Words: Vowel Diphthongs /oi/, /ou/

Write the word from the box that is suggested by each clue below.

allowance	avoid	couch	employ	tower

6. hire for wages
7. money given on a regular basis
8. a tall, slender part of a building
9. to stay clear of
10. a sofa

Content Words

Language Arts: Parts of Speech

Write a word to complete each sentence.

adjective	pronoun	adverb	verb	noun

1. A word that can show action is a _____.
2. A word such as **you, me,** and **they** is a _____.
3. A word that names a person, place, or thing is a _____.
4. A word that describes a noun is an _____.
5. A word that describes a verb is an _____.

Fine Arts: Singing

Write a word from the box for each clue.

duet	tenor	solo	bass	trio

6. three singers
7. high male voice
8. singing alone
9. deep male voice
10. music sung by two

Apply the Spelling Strategy

Circle the spelling of the /**ou**/ sound in two of the Content Words you wrote.

Word Study

Prefixes

The prefix **tri-** means "three." For example, a **triangle** has three angles. Write the Content Word that also includes this word part and means "a group of three."

Language Arts: Parts of Speech

1. _____
2. _____
3. _____
4. _____
5. _____

Fine Arts: Singing

6. _____
7. _____
8. _____
9. _____
10. _____

Prefixes

1. _____

/ôr/

1. _____
2. _____
3. _____
4. _____
5. _____
6. _____
7. _____
8. _____
9. _____
10. _____

/ô/

11. _____
12. _____
13. _____
14. _____
15. _____
16. _____
17. _____
18. _____
19. _____
20. _____

Spelling and Thinking

READ THE SPELLING WORDS

1. forgot	*forgot*	I almost **forgot** my friend's birthday.
2. bought	*bought*	Wayne **bought** a new pair of shoes.
3. nor	*nor*	Neither rain **nor** snow will bother us.
4. haul	*haul*	A mule can **haul** heavy loads.
5. ought	*ought*	You **ought** to eat a balanced diet.
6. forest	*forest*	Squirrels prefer a **forest** of oak.
7. sport	*sport*	Baseball is my favorite **sport**.
8. thought	*thought*	We **thought** it would rain today.
9. daughter	*daughter*	Her **daughter** is taller than she is.
10. port	*port*	The storm kept the ship in **port**.
11. sort	*sort*	We will **sort** the mail by date.
12. record	*record*	I will **record** the things I did today.
13. taught	*taught*	We **taught** our dog to do tricks.
14. brought	*brought*	My brother **brought** a friend home.
15. forth	*forth*	Go **forth** and do your best.
16. because	*because*	I ran home **because** I was late.
17. fought	*fought*	My grandfather **fought** in a war.
18. report	*report*	Please **report** your findings.
19. forty	*forty*	My aunt lives **forty** miles away.
20. caught	*caught*	I **caught** six fish at the lake.

SORT THE SPELLING WORDS

1.–10. Write the spelling words in which the /ôr/ sound is spelled **or**.

11.–20. Write the spelling words in which the /ô/ sound is spelled **au**, **augh**, or **ough**.

REMEMBER THE SPELLING STRATEGY

The **r**-controlled vowel sound you hear in **sport** (/ôr/) is spelled **or**. The vowel sound you hear in **haul** (/ô/) can be spelled in different ways: **au** in **haul, augh** in **caught,** and **ough** in **ought.**

Spelling ᴬⁿᵈ Vocabulary

Word Meanings
Write the spelling word that goes with each meaning.

1. past tense of **buy**
2. a harbor town where ships dock
3. and not; or not; not either
4. forward; into full sight
5. past tense of **bring**
6. a game, often a competition
7. an account

Synonyms
Write the spelling word that is a synonym for each word.

8. carry
9. should
10. battled
11. arrange
12. idea
13. captured
14. instructed

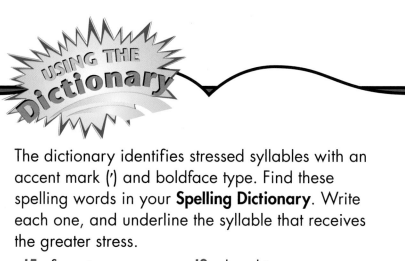

USING THE Dictionary

The dictionary identifies stressed syllables with an accent mark (') and boldface type. Find these spelling words in your **Spelling Dictionary**. Write each one, and underline the syllable that receives the greater stress.

15. forgot
16. because
17. forest
18. daughter
19. report
20. forty

Word Meanings

1. _____
2. _____
3. _____
4. _____
5. _____
6. _____
7. _____

Synonyms

8. _____
9. _____
10. _____
11. _____
12. _____
13. _____
14. _____

Using the Dictionary

15. _____
16. _____
17. _____
18. _____
19. _____
20. _____

forgot	bought	nor	haul	ought
forest	sport	thought	daughter	port
sort	record	taught	brought	forth
because	fought	report	forty	caught

Replace the Words

Replace the Words   For each sentence, write the spelling word that is the past tense of the underlined verb.

1. Show me what you <u>buy</u> at the store.
2. I almost <u>forget</u> that today is your birthday.
3. Carlos <u>brings</u> his stamp collection to school.
4. Maria <u>catches</u> the ball for the third out.
5. Before they became friends, the two boys <u>fight</u> a lot.
6. I <u>think</u> the answer was simple.
7. Mrs. King <u>teaches</u> us how to paint with water colors.

Use the Clues

Use the Clues   Write a spelling word for each clue.

8. a good place for ships
9. a parent's female child
10. put in groups
11. twenty-eight and twelve

Complete the Paragraph

Complete the Paragraph   Write a spelling word from the box to fill each blank in the story.

My favorite __12.__ is horseback riding.
Sometimes I ride through the __13.__ . When I return,
I like to __14.__ my experiences to my friends and
__15.__ my thoughts in my diary. A horseback rider
__16.__ to carry as little as possible. That is __17.__ the
more you __18.__ the harder it is for your horse. A
rider should go __19.__ with a respect for nature. He
or she should disturb neither animals __20.__ plants,
so they will still be there for all to enjoy.

| forth |
| ought |
| sport |
| record |
| forest |
| because |
| report |
| nor |
| haul |

Replace the Words
1.
2.
3.
4.
5.
6.
7.

Use the Clues
8.
9.
10.
11.

Complete the Paragraph
12.
13.
14.
15.
16.
17.
18.
19.
20.

Spelling ^{and} Writing

Proofread a Story

Six words are not spelled correctly in this story. Write those words correctly.

Some Fun!

Sylvia went camping in the forist, a trip which oght to have been fun. She caught three fish and ate them for dinner. Then she had a good night's sleep.

Her trip home, however, was not pleasant bicause she fergot her compass and lost her way. Then she remembered what her mother had taugt her: Moss grows on the north side of trees. Home is south of here, she thot, so I should go in the opposite direction from the moss.

She did and learned an important lesson: Before going camping, check to see that you have all your supplies.

Proofreading Marks

 Make a capital.

 Make a small letter.

 Add something.

 Take out something.

 Add a period.

 New paragraph

SP Spelling error

Write a Story

Narrative Writing

Write a story from your imagination. Include all the information your reader will want to know. Be sure to tell

- the name of the main character.
- where the main character is.
- what he or she does.
- what happens and how the story ends.

Use as many spelling words as you can.

Proofread Your Writing During

Proofread your writing for spelling errors as part of the editing stage in the writing process. Be sure to check each word carefully. Use a dictionary to check spelling if you are not sure.

Writing Process

Prewriting

⇩

Drafting

⇩

Revising

⇩

Editing

⇩

Publishing

VOCABULARY CONNECTIONS

Strategy Words

Review Words

1. _____
2. _____
3. _____
4. _____
5. _____

Preview Words

6. _____
7. _____
8. _____
9. _____
10. _____

Review Words: Vowel Sounds /ôr/, /ô/

Write a word from the box that matches each clue.

before	form	morning
north	story	

1. an antonym of **south**
2. an antonym of **after**
3. a synonym of **tale**
4. a synonym of **shape**
5. what follows **night**

Preview Words: Vowel Sounds /ôr/, /ô/

Write the word from the box that fits each blank.

audience	author	enormous
important	launch	

Crowds gathered early in the __6.__ hall. They were there to __7.__ the sale of the new book. Many __8.__ public figures sat in the __9.__. Everyone seemed very pleased to see such a crowd. After the __10.__ spoke, she autographed copies of the book for those who bought them.

Content Words

Science: Plants

Write a word from the box to complete each sentence.

blossom	petals	nectar	pollen	orchard

1. One by one, the flower dropped its _____.
2. The _____ had rows and rows of fruit trees.
3. Birds and bees sip _____ from flowers.
4. That plant will not _____ until June.
5. Tiny grains of _____ from the flower stuck to the bee's legs.

Social Studies: Transportation

Write a word from the box for each clue.

airport	railway	cargo	stock	depot

6. another word for **freight**
7. where you might get a bus
8. where you might catch a plane
9. a supply; inventory
10. where you might find tracks and a locomotive

Apply the Spelling Strategy

Circle the letters that spell the /ôr/ sound in two of the Content Words you wrote.

Word Study

Word Roots

The word root **aud** comes from the old Latin word **audire,** which meant "to hear." Write the Strategy Word that has this root and means "a group of listeners."

Science: Plants

1. _____
2. _____
3. _____
4. _____
5. _____

Social Studies: Transportation

6. _____
7. _____
8. _____
9. _____
10. _____

Word Roots

1. _____

ear or eer

1. _____
2. _____
3. _____
4. _____
5. _____
6. _____
7. _____
8. _____
9. _____

er

10. _____
11. _____
12. _____
13. _____
14. _____
15. _____

ir or ur

16. _____
17. _____
18. _____
19. _____
20. _____

Spelling and Thinking

READ THE SPELLING WORDS

1.	near	*near*	I was **near** enough to touch the president.
2.	steer	*steer*	He is learning to **steer** his unicycle.
3.	certain	*certain*	Are you **certain** of the answer?
4.	return	*return*	My **return** address is on the card.
5.	tear	*tear*	The child wiped a **tear** from his eye.
6.	thirst	*thirst*	The heat of the day increased our **thirst**.
7.	perfect	*perfect*	He threw a nearly **perfect** pitch.
8.	fear	*fear*	Those who **fear** failure should try anyway.
9.	term	*term*	The first school **term** is over.
10.	cheer	*cheer*	They came to **cheer** for our team.
11.	turkey	*turkey*	We will eat **turkey** on Thanksgiving.
12.	firm	*firm*	Once on **firm** ground, I was safe.
13.	ear	*ear*	I held the seashell up to my **ear**.
14.	burst	*burst*	The soap bubble **burst** in the air.
15.	rear	*rear*	We marched at the **rear** of the parade.
16.	serve	*serve*	The waiter came to **serve** our party.
17.	year	*year*	A **year** is twelve months long.
18.	person	*person*	The price was $5 per **person**.
19.	clear	*clear*	We expect **clear** and sunny weather.
20.	herd	*herd*	In the field was a **herd** of cows.

SORT THE SPELLING WORDS

1.–9. Write the spelling words that spell the /îr/ sound **ear** or **eer**.

10.–15. Write the spelling words that spell the /ûr/ sound **er**.

16.–20. Write the spelling words that spell the /ûr/ sound **ir** or **ur**.

REMEMBER THE SPELLING STRATEGY

Remember that the **r**-controlled vowel sound you hear in **near** (/îr/) can be spelled in different ways: **ear** in **near** and **eer** in **cheer**.

The **r**-controlled vowel sound you hear in **firm** (/ûr/) can be spelled in different ways: **ir** in **firm**, **er** in **herd**, or **ur** in **burst**.

Spelling and Vocabulary

Word Meanings

Write a spelling word that has the same meaning as each word or phrase.

1. come back
2. a need for liquid
3. a period of time; reign
4. break open suddenly
5. offer food
6. a group of animals

Phonics

7. Write the spelling word that has only three letters.

8.–13. Write spelling words that rhyme with the word you just wrote and that spell the /îr/ sound the same way.

Word Math

Follow the directions to write spelling words.

14. certify – ify + ain = _____
15. perhaps – haps + son = _____
16. first – st + m = _____
17. perplex – plex + fect = _____
18. turban – ban + key = _____

USING THE Dictionary

Find these homographs in your **Spelling Dictionary**. Beside each word write the number of the definition and the letter that tells what part of speech it is.

19. steer
20. cheer

Dictionary Check Be sure to check the part of speech in your **Spelling Dictionary**.

Word Meanings
1. _____
2. _____
3. _____
4. _____
5. _____
6. _____

Phonics
7. _____
8. _____
9. _____
10. _____
11. _____
12. _____
13. _____

Word Math
14. _____
15. _____
16. _____
17. _____
18. _____

Using the Dictionary
19. _____
20. _____

near   steer   certain   return   tear
thirst   perfect   fear   term   cheer
turkey   firm   ear   burst   rear
serve   year   person   clear   herd

Complete the Sentences Write two spelling words to complete each sentence.

1.–2. Whitney would like to _____ one _____ as the class president.

3.–4. Please wait _____ this bench until I _____.

5.–6. That _____ has a voice that is pleasing to the _____.

Group the Words Write the spelling word that goes with each group.

7. sparrow, crow, chicken, _____

8. shout, yell, _____

9. day, week, month, _____

10. solid, stiff, hard, _____

11. alarm, fright, horror, _____

12. drive, guide, operate, _____

13. sure, positive, definite, _____

14. correct, excellent, _____

15. liquid, droplet, _____

Solve the Analogies Write the spelling word that completes each analogy.

16. Food is to **hunger** as **water** is to _____.

17. Glass is to **break** as **balloon** is to _____.

18. Cloudy is to **overcast** as **sunny** is to _____.

19. Face is to **front** as **back** is to _____.

20. Birds are to **flock** as **cattle** are to _____.

Complete the Sentences

1. _____
2. _____
3. _____
4. _____
5. _____
6. _____

Group the Words

7. _____
8. _____
9. _____
10. _____
11. _____
12. _____
13. _____
14. _____
15. _____

Solve the Analogies

16. _____
17. _____
18. _____
19. _____
20. _____

Spelling and Writing

Proofread a Travel Report

Six words are not spelled correctly in this travel report. Write those words correctly.

San Diego in the Fall

San Diego is a great city to visit any time of the yeer. My family chose fall and was not disappointed. The weather was bright and cleer in October. If you go, have no fear of public transportation. We rode all over the city, and even to Mexico and back, for $3 a pearson per day. Take a trolley, a bus, a boat. The sightseeing is purfect. We hope to make a riturn visit there. I am sertain you will want to revisit that city also.

Proofreading Marks

≡	Make a capital.
/	Make a small letter.
∧	Add something.
ℓ	Take out something.
⊙	Add a period.
⌗	New paragraph
SP	Spelling error

Write a Travel Report

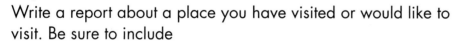

Descriptive Writing

Write a report about a place you have visited or would like to visit. Be sure to include

- the name of the place.
- what you like about it.
- the best time to visit it.
- how to get around there.
- what to see there.

Use as many spelling words as you can.

Writing Process

Prewriting
⇩
Drafting
⇩
Revising
⇩
Proofread Your Writing During ▶ Editing
⇩
Publishing

Proofread your writing for spelling errors as part of the editing stage in the writing process. Be sure to check each word carefully. Use a dictionary to check spelling if you are not sure.

VOCABULARY CONNECTIONS

Strategy Words

Review Words

1. _____
2. _____
3. _____
4. _____
5. _____

Preview Words

6. _____
7. _____
8. _____
9. _____
10. _____

Review Words:
r-Controlled Vowels /îr/, /ûr/

Write a word from the box for each clue.

curl	dirt	fur	heard	herself

1. a squirrel's soft, thick covering
2. a synonym of **coil**
3. the past tense of **hear**
4. something you can find on the ground
5. a pronoun that refers to a female

Preview Words:
r-Controlled Vowels /îr/, /ûr/

Write a word from the box for each definition.

appear	burnt	career	circulate	deserve

6. This word means "to show up."
7. This word means "to flow" or "to spread."
8. This word means "blazed."
9. This word means "be worthy of."
10. This word means "occupation."

Content Words

Health: Exercise

Write words from the box to complete the paragraph.

| injure | strain | jogging | stretching | risk |

If you like __1.__, you should always include __2.__ as part of your routine. If you do not, the __3.__ of the exercise could __4.__ you. Have fun at your sport, but do not __5.__ harming your body.

Social Studies: In Court

Write a word from the box for each clue.

| fact | jury | honor | justice | juror |

6. This names one person who considers trial evidence.
7. This is part of the title given to a judge.
8. This is the opposite of an opinion.
9. This group of citizens listens to evidence and makes legal decisions.
10. This is what our trial system is supposed to accomplish.

Apply the Spelling Strategy

Circle the two related words you wrote that have an **r**-controlled vowel sound.

Endings

In some words, the ending **-t** has the same meaning as **-ed**. For example, we say **kept,** not **keeped**. Write the Strategy Word that has the ending **-t** instead of **-ed**.

Health: Exercise

1. _____
2. _____
3. _____
4. _____
5. _____

Social Studies: In Court

6. _____
7. _____
8. _____
9. _____
10. _____

Endings

1. _____

Assessment and Review

Assessment Units 7–11

Each Assessment Word in the box fits one of the spelling strategies you have studied over the past five weeks. Read the spelling strategies. Then write each Assessment Word under the unit number it fits.

Unit 7

1.–4. The **long o** sound can be spelled in different ways: **o** in **pony, oa** in **goal,** and **ow** in **glow.**

Unit 8

5.–8. The vowel sound you hear in **true** and the vowel sound you hear in **few** can be spelled in different ways.

Unit 9

9.–12. The /**oi**/ sound can be spelled in different ways: **oi** in **coil** or **oy** in **joy.** The /**ou**/ sound can be spelled in different ways: **ou** in **mouth** or **ow** in **plow.**

Unit 10

13.–16. The **r**-controlled vowel sound you hear in **sport** (/ôr/) is spelled **or.** The vowel sound you hear in **haul** (/ô/) can be spelled in different ways: **au** in **haul, augh** in **caught,** and **ough** in **ought.**

Unit 11

17.–20. The **r**-controlled vowel sound you hear in **near** (/îr/) can be spelled in different ways: **ear** in **near** and **eer** in **cheer.** The **r**-controlled vowel sound you hear in **firm** (/ûr/) can be spelled in different ways: **ir** in **firm, er** in **herd,** or **ur** in **burst.**

clothing
value
whom
pointed
conserve
thrown
vault
beard
oyster
gear
haunt
blouse
ruin
mown
moan
inform
tune
growl
scorn
fern

 **Review**   **Unit 7: Long o Spelled o, oa, ow**

clothes	hello	moment	pillow	coast
grown	also	poem	obey	shown

Write the spelling word that completes each sentence.

1. Hang your _____ in the closet.
2. Here is another _____ for your bed.
3. I'll be right there in a _____.
4. Say _____ to your aunt for me.
5. The lighthouse is on the _____.
6. I cannot teach that dog to _____ commands.
7. When Joan is fully _____, she will be very tall.
8. Joe will be very tall, _____.
9. A spring day makes me want to write a _____.
10. He has to be _____ how to do that problem.

 **Review**   **Unit 8: Vowel Sounds /yo͞o/, /o͞o/**

few	lose	used	whose	music
true	fruit	human	tube	rule

Write the spelling word that completes each sentence.

11.–12. Is it _____ that there are just a _____ seats left?
13. Apples, bananas, and oranges are _____.
14. Who left the top off the _____ of toothpaste?
15. It's a club _____ that no food is allowed inside.
16. Do you know _____ books were left outside?
17. I'll be in trouble if I _____ my homework.
18. You can get a good price on a _____ bike.
19. All people are _____ beings.
20. We sang three songs in _____ class.

Unit 7
1.
2.
3.
4.
5.
6.
7.
8.
9.
10.
Unit 8
11.
12.
13.
14.
15.
16.
17.
18.
19.
20.

1.		
2.		
3.		
4.		
5.		
6.		
7.		
8.		
9.		
10.		

11.
12.
13.
14.
15.
16.
17.
18.
19.
20.

Review   Unit 9: Vowel Diphthongs /oi/, /ou/

amount	choice	flower	moist	however
enjoy	mouth	power	vowel	crowd

Write the spelling word that fits each meaning.

1. slightly damp
2. many people
3. not a consonant
4. strength or force
5. quantity or sum
6. where your teeth are
7. to have a good time
8. a selection
9. a bloom or blossom
10. anyway

Review   Unit 10: Vowel Sounds /ôr/, /ô/

because	brought	caught	thought	sort
forest	record	bought	report	nor

Find each misspelled word. Write the word correctly.

11. Neither my sister nur I will be able to go to the play.
12. The weather repoort promises a fine day.
13. I brawght the book with me.
14. Mom caut five trout.
15. Please sourt the clean socks.
16. I'll be late becauze our car has a flat tire.
17. I really thout that was the right answer.
18. The teacher will recored our test grades.
19. There are tall pines in that fourist.
20. We bawte new tires for our car.

 **Review** Unit 11: r-Controlled Vowels /îr/, /ûr/

certain	return	tear	year	cheer
person	firm	near	fear	clear

Write the spelling word that has the opposite meaning.

1. go
2. uncertain
3. far
4. soft
5. foggy
6. sadness

Write the spelling word for each meaning.

7. to be afraid
8. water in the eye
9. a human being
10. twelve months

Unit 11

1. _____
2. _____
3. _____
4. _____
5. _____
6. _____
7. _____
8. _____
9. _____
10. _____

 **Spelling Study Strategy**

Sorting by Spelling Pattern

One good way to practice spelling is to place words into groups according to some spelling pattern. Here is a way to practice some of the words you studied in the past few weeks.

 Write each of the spelling patterns for Units 7 through 11 at the top of its own long strip of paper. For example, for Unit 7 you will need three strips of paper: **long o spelled o; long o spelled oa; long o spelled ow**.

Then sort your spelling words and write each one in the column for that spelling pattern. Try to add other words that fit the pattern, too.

Grammar, Usage, and Mechanics

Common and Proper Nouns

A common noun names any person, place, or thing.

> That **student** goes to my **school**.

> The **building** is in a **city**.

A proper noun names a particular person, place, or thing.
A proper noun begins with a capital letter.

> **Carl Hansen** goes to **Roosevelt School**.

> The **Empire State Building** is in **New York City**.

Practice

A. What kind of noun is underlined in each sentence? Write **common** or **proper**.

1. My friend <u>Alice</u> will bring oranges.
2. Is one <u>horse</u> Black Beauty?
3. My family moved here from <u>Florida</u>.
4. The store is somewhere on <u>State Street</u>.
5. Our <u>principal</u> is Ms. Everson.

B. Write a proper noun that could replace each underlined common noun in these sentences. Be sure to begin your proper noun with a capital letter.

6. <u>She</u> lives across the street.
7. I always enjoy visiting the <u>city</u>.
8. We saw the <u>memorial</u> on our visit to Washington, D.C.
9. There is no school on a <u>holiday</u>.
10. We bought a recording of <u>my favorite singing group</u>.

A.
1.
2.
3.
4.
5.
B.
6.
7.
8.
9.
10.

WORKSHOP

One Sentence at a Time!

Good writers always proofread their work for spelling errors. Here's a strategy you can use to proofread your papers.

Instead of reading your entire paper, look at one sentence at a time. Make sure that the first word starts with a capital letter. Then make sure that the last word is followed by a punctuation mark.

Looking at your paper this way helps you think about details—capital letters and punctuation—instead of ideas. It may sound strange, but it works. Try it!

Electronic Spelling

Computer Terms

Computers have changed life in many ways. They have also changed our language. Today, we use many new words that didn't even exist fifty years ago. We also use older words in new ways. For instance, once a **notebook** was just a book that you could fill with paper. Today, a **notebook** is also a small computer.

Spell checkers may not catch these newer words, so you need to know how to spell them. Many of them are compound words—words made up of two shorter words. For example, **notebook** is made from **note** and **book**. To spell a compound word, first break it into two smaller words. Then spell each part.

One part of each compound word below is misspelled. Write the compound word correctly.

1. artwerk
2. skreensaver
3. passwurd
4. tulebox
5. laptopp
6. keybord

Electronic Spelling

1. _____
2. _____
3. _____
4. _____
5. _____
6. _____

/är/

1. _____
2. _____
3. _____
4. _____
5. _____
6. _____
7. _____
8. _____
9. _____
10. _____
11. _____
12. _____

/âr/

13. _____
14. _____
15. _____
16. _____
17. _____
18. _____
19. _____
20. _____

Spelling and Thinking

READ THE SPELLING WORDS

1.	share	*share*	I will do my **share** of the work.
2.	cart	*cart*	The horse pulled a heavy **cart**.
3.	beware	*beware*	We must **beware** of poison ivy.
4.	march	*march*	Drummers will **march** in the parade.
5.	rare	*rare*	A cold day in July is **rare**.
6.	army	*army*	The **army** set up camp near here.
7.	charge	*charge*	Put the **charge** on my bill.
8.	stare	*stare*	We tried not to **stare** at the movie stars.
9.	market	*market*	We bought food at the **market**.
10.	compare	*compare*	Do not **compare** apples and oranges.
11.	mark	*mark*	Please **mark** that date on your calendar.
12.	alarm	*alarm*	That noise will **alarm** the baby.
13.	parent	*parent*	Take this note to your **parent**.
14.	chart	*chart*	Did you **chart** your progress?
15.	spare	*spare*	Can you **spare** a pencil for me?
16.	smart	*smart*	You made a **smart** play today.
17.	charm	*charm*	The dancers have grace and **charm**.
18.	scare	*scare*	The dark does not **scare** me.
19.	apart	*apart*	He took the alarm clock **apart**.
20.	spark	*spark*	Strike a **spark** to start a fire.

SORT THE SPELLING WORDS

1.–12. Write the spelling words that spell the /är/ sound **ar**.

13.–20. Write the spelling words that spell the /âr/ sound **are**.

REMEMBER THE SPELLING STRATEGY

Remember that the **r**-controlled vowel sound you hear in **cart** (/är/) is spelled **ar**. The **r**-controlled vowel sound you hear in **spare** (/âr/) is spelled **are**.

Word Meanings ━━━━━━━━━━

Write the spelling word that matches each definition.

1. to examine two things for similarities and differences
2. a father or mother
3. to be careful of; to guard against
4. extra; more than is needed
5. a tiny piece of fire
6. intelligent
7. frighten or terrify

Word Clues ━━━━━━━━━━

Write a spelling word for each clue.

8. a synonym of **uncommon**
9. a homonym of **stair**
10. an antonym of **hoard**
11. begins with a vowel and rhymes with **harm**
12. ends with a **long e** sound
13. found in the word **apartment**

Write each group of spelling words in alphabetical order.

14.–16. mark, march, market

17.–20. cart, chart, charm, charge

◆ ◆ ◆

Dictionary Check Be sure to check the alphabetical order of the words in your **Spelling Dictionary**.

Word Meanings

1. _____
2. _____
3. _____
4. _____
5. _____
6. _____
7. _____

Word Clues

8. _____
9. _____
10. _____
11. _____
12. _____
13. _____

Using the Dictionary

14. _____
15. _____
16. _____
17. _____
18. _____
19. _____
20. _____

Complete the Facts

1. _____
2. _____
3. _____
4. _____
5. _____
6. _____
7. _____
8. _____

Complete the Opinions

9. _____
10. _____
11. _____
12. _____
13. _____
14. _____
15. _____

Solve the Analogies

16. _____
17. _____
18. _____
19. _____
20. _____

share	cart	beware	march	rare
army	charge	stare	market	compare
mark	alarm	parent	chart	spare
smart	charm	scare	apart	spark

Complete the Facts   Statements that can be checked and proven are facts. Write the spelling word that completes each fact.

1. A _____ is used to record a patient's progress over time.
2. The navy, marines, coast guard, and _____ are branches of our armed services.
3. You can make a _____ by striking flint on steel.
4. A _____ may have two or four wheels.
5. We can buy many different items in a _____.
6. Bands often _____ onto the football fields.
7. A smoke _____ in the house can warn us of fires.
8. Wolves are _____ in most of our states.

Complete the Opinions   Statements that cannot be proven are opinions. Write the spelling word that completes each opinion.

9. Every adult wants to be a _____.
10. It is simple to take _____ all machines.
11. We should _____ of making too many friends.
12. Playing video games is a _____ way to pass time.
13. I should be in _____ of this club.
14. The most important quality a person can possess is _____.
15. It is easy to _____ brands of canned goods.

Solve the Analogies   Write a spelling word to complete each analogy.

16. **Start** is to **continue** as **look** is to _____.
17. **Knife** is to **cut** as **pencil** is to _____.
18. **Selfish** is to **hoard** as **generous** is to _____.
19. **Tall** is to **stall** as **care** is to _____.
20. **Large** is to **small** as **extra** is to _____.

Spelling and Writing

Proofread a Thank-You Note

Six words are not spelled correctly in this thank-you note. Write those words correctly.

Dear Aunt Sue and Uncle Bob,

This is just a short note to thank you for my presents and the surprise birthday party you gave me. It was nice of you to shair your home with an army of my pals. It was smert to tell me I was coming to help clean out your spair room. I was shocked to compair the fun with the expected work, and that was part of the chaerm. It was a rair treat that I will never forget. Thanks for a great birthday!

Love,
Bruce

Proofreading Marks

☰ Make a capital.

╱ Make a small letter.

∧ Add something.

℘ Take out something.

⊙ Add a period.

⌗ New paragraph

⑤⑨ Spelling error

Write a Thank-You Note

Expository Writing

Write a thank-you note for a real or imagined treat. Be sure to include

- what the treat was.
- who provided it for you.
- what you liked best about it.
- how it made you feel.
- what you most appreciate about the treat giver.

Use as many spelling words as you can.

Proofread Your Writing During → Editing

Proofread your writing for spelling errors as part of the editing stage in the writing process. Be sure to check each word carefully. Use a dictionary to check spelling if you are not sure.

Writing Process

Prewriting

⇩

Drafting

⇩

Revising

⇩

Editing

⇩

Publishing

VOCABULARY CONNECTIONS

Strategy Words

Review Words

1. _____
2. _____
3. _____
4. _____
5. _____

Preview Words

6. _____
7. _____
8. _____
9. _____
10. _____

Strategy Words

Review Words: r-Controlled Vowels /âr/, /är/

Write a word from the box that fits each clue.

bare	fare	hare	large	partly

1. a synonym of **rabbit**
2. a synonym of **empty**
3. an antonym of **small**
4. an antonym of **completely**
5. a homophone of **fair**

Preview Words: r-Controlled Vowels /âr/, /är/

Write a word from the box that fits each clue.

argue	aware	carpet	declare	pardon

6. You can walk all over me.
7. I should beg this when I have done something wrong.
8. People sometimes do this when they have an important disagreement.
9. My brothers and sisters are **say, tell,** and **announce**.
10. This is what I am when I am awake and paying attention to things around me.

Content Words

Social Studies: Boats

Write a word from the box that matches each clue.

barge	skiff	ferry	tugboat	schooner

1. This is a boat that pushes or tows larger boats.
2. This is a little boat.
3. This is a ship with sails and at least two masts.
4. This is a boat that tows goods.
5. This is a boat that carries people and sometimes cars from one place to another.

Math: Measurement

Write a word from the box that matches each definition.

centimeter	kilometer	decimeter	millimeter	kilogram

6. one thousandth of a meter
7. one hundredth of a meter
8. one tenth of a meter
9. one thousand meters
10. one thousand grams

Apply the Spelling Strategy

Circle the letters that spell the /är/ sound in one of the Content Words you wrote.

Word Study

Idioms

An **idiom** is a saying that doesn't mean what the words in it say. For example, the idiom **keep your chin up** means "be brave" or "have courage." Write the Content Word that finishes this saying, which means "to interrupt": ____ **in.**

Social Studies: Boats
1. _____
2. _____
3. _____
4. _____
5. _____

Math: Measurement
6. _____
7. _____
8. _____
9. _____
10. _____

Idioms
1. _____

short a or short e

1. _____
2. _____
3. _____
4. _____
5. _____
6. _____
7. _____
8. _____
9. _____
10. _____
11. _____
12. _____

short i or short u

13. _____
14. _____
15. _____
16. _____
17. _____
18. _____
19. _____
20. _____

Spelling and Thinking

READ THE SPELLING WORDS

1.	meant	*meant*	I **meant** to return the library book.
2.	build	*build*	Shall we **build** a tree house?
3.	flood	*flood*	The **flood** was caused by heavy rain.
4.	laugh	*laugh*	I had to **laugh** at your funny story.
5.	breakfast	*breakfast*	I like **breakfast** better than lunch.
6.	enough	*enough*	One ball game a day is **enough** for me.
7.	sweater	*sweater*	Wear a **sweater** when it is cool.
8.	rough	*rough*	Sandpaper is **rough,** not smooth.
9.	bread	*bread*	Do you want **bread** or crackers?
10.	touch	*touch*	Silk feels soft when you **touch** it.
11.	spread	*spread*	The young bird **spread** its wings.
12.	tough	*tough*	Old corn can be **tough** and chewy.
13.	already	*already*	The sun has **already** risen.
14.	built	*built*	My grandparents **built** a log cabin.
15.	ready	*ready*	I am **ready** to go to bed.
16.	death	*death*	That is not a life or **death** matter.
17.	young	*young*	Both **young** and old enjoyed the show.
18.	instead	*instead*	Amy played the part **instead** of Sue.
19.	heavy	*heavy*	Can you carry that **heavy** bundle?
20.	ahead	*ahead*	I will go **ahead** and meet you there.

SORT THE SPELLING WORDS

1.–12. Write the spelling words with the **short a** or the **short e** sound. Circle the letters that spell this sound.

13.–20. Write the spelling words with the **short i** or the **short u** sound. Circle the letters that spell this sound.

REMEMBER THE SPELLING STRATEGY

Remember that some words have more vowel letters than vowel sounds.

Spelling and Vocabulary

Word Meanings

Write a spelling word that has the same meaning as each definition.

1. the first meal of the day
2. by this time; before
3. in place of
4. a knitted garment worn on the upper part of the body

Phonics

Change one letter at the beginning of each word to write a spelling word.

5. dread
6. guild
7. blood
8. quilt

Add one letter at the end of each word to write a spelling word.

9. mean
10. read

Antonyms

Write the spelling word that is an antonym of each word.

11. cry
12. smooth
13. tender
14. life
15. light
16. gather

USING THE Thesaurus

Write a spelling word to complete each synonym set.

17. adequate, ample, sufficient, _____
18. feel, handle, stroke, _____
19. before, forward, _____
20. juvenile, youthful, _____

◆ ◆ ◆

Thesaurus Check Be sure to check the synonyms in your **Writing Thesaurus**.

Word Meanings
1. _____
2. _____
3. _____
4. _____

Phonics
5. _____
6. _____
7. _____
8. _____
9. _____
10. _____

Antonyms
11. _____
12. _____
13. _____
14. _____
15. _____
16. _____

Using the Thesaurus
17. _____
18. _____
19. _____
20. _____

meant	build	flood	laugh	breakfast
enough	sweater	rough	bread	touch
spread	tough	already	built	ready
death	young	instead	heavy	ahead

Replace the Words Replace the underlined adjective in each sentence with a spelling word that has the same meaning.

1. Please help me lift this <u>weighty</u> box.
2. The tire went flat on the <u>bumpy</u> road.
3. That <u>youthful</u> student enjoys writing about animals.
4. We need a <u>strong</u> bag to hold the trash.
5. Be <u>prepared</u> to leave for the zoo at noon.

Complete the Sequences Write a spelling word to complete each group of words.

6. giggle, chuckle, _____
7. vest, coat, jacket, _____
8. dinner, lunch, _____
9. overflow, spillover, _____
10. see, hear, smell, taste, _____

Complete the Sentences Write a spelling word to complete each sentence.

11. To make toast, you start with a slice of _____.
12. Katrina doesn't have _____ orange paint to finish the job.
13. Mandy Lee can _____ a tree house in the backyard.
14. Every news station reported the _____ of the famous author.
15. We can _____ this tablecloth on the ground for our picnic.
16. Did you know what that word _____?
17. Our school was _____ more than fifty years ago.
18. Let's read a book _____ of watching television.
19. Alex has _____ finished his homework.
20. We will go on _____ if they are late.

Replace the Words

1.
2.
3.
4.
5.

Complete the Sequences

6.
7.
8.
9.
10.

Complete the Sentences

11.
12.
13.
14.
15.
16.
17.
18.
19.
20.

Spelling and Writing

Proofread a Book Review

Six words are not spelled correctly in this book review. Write those words correctly.

Bobby Baseball
by Robert Kimmel Smith

Bobby Ellis is a yung boy who loves baseball. He knows alredy that he wants to be a pitcher. But his father, the coach, wants him to be a second baseman insted. How can Bobby go ahead with his plans when he cannot please Dad, who is so tuff he expects his son to be perfect? Will Bobby be able to laff off his father's interference, or will it be the deth of his dream? Read to find out. It is a great book.

Proofreading Marks

≡ Make a capital.

/ Make a small letter.

∧ Add something.

℘ Take out something.

⊙ Add a period.

⌗ New paragraph

(SP) Spelling error

Write a Book Review

Expository Writing

Write a book review about a book you have read. Be sure to include

- the title of the book.
- the name of the author.
- what the story is about.
- what problem the main character has.
- whether you would recommend the book and why or why not.

Use as many spelling words as you can.

Proofread Your Writing During

Writing Process

Prewriting

Drafting

Revising

Editing

Publishing

Proofread your writing for spelling errors as part of the editing stage in the writing process. Be sure to check each word carefully. Use a dictionary to check spelling if you are not sure.

VOCABULARY CONNECTIONS

Strategy Words

Review Words

1. _____
2. _____
3. _____
4. _____
5. _____

Preview Words

6. _____
7. _____
8. _____
9. _____
10. _____

Review Words: More Letters Than Sounds

Write a word from the box that spells each sound in the following way.

heat	board	friend	great	weigh

1. the **long e** sound spelled **ea**
2. the **long a** sound spelled **ea**
3. the **long a** sound spelled **eigh**
4. the **short e** sound spelled **ie**
5. the /ô/ sound spelled **oa**

Preview Words: More Letters Than Sounds

Write words from the box by adding missing letters.

plaid	pleasant	pleasure	subhead	sweatshirt

6. ple __ __ __ re
7. s __ bh __ __ d
8. pl __ __ d
9. sw __ __ tsh __ rt
10. plea __ __ __ t

Content Words

Health: Medicine

Write words from the box to complete the paragraph.

headache	discover	cause	science	cure

Modern __1.__ has searched for years to find a __2.__ for the common cold, but scientists have only learned how to make cold sufferers more comfortable. Today's cold remedies can merely relieve your __3.__ and stuffy nose. Doctors know that germs are the __4.__ of the illness, but they have not found the remedy. Maybe you will become the first scientist to __5.__ that remedy.

Health: Being Me

Write a word from the box to match each clue.

height	temper	mood	well-being	strength

6. a state of mind; rhymes with **food**
7. how tall someone or something is
8. how strong someone or something is
9. a state of feeling good
10. one's usual state of mind; one's disposition

Apply the Spelling Strategy

Circle the two-letter spelling of the **short e** sound and the **long i** sound in two of the Content Words you wrote.

Word Study

Prefixes

The prefix **dis-** means "opposite." **Dishonest** is the opposite of **honest**. Write the Content Word that contains this prefix and means the opposite of "cover up" or "hide."

Health: Medicine

1. _____

2. _____

3. _____

4. _____

5. _____

Health: Being Me

6. _____

7. _____

8. _____

9. _____

10. _____

Prefixes

1. _____

Spelling and Thinking

READ THE SPELLING WORDS

1.	often	often	We **often** call our grandparents.
2.	knot	knot	I have a **knot** in my shoelace.
3.	wring	wring	We **wring** the water from our wet socks.
4.	island	island	You can reach the **island** by ferry.
5.	lamb	lamb	A **lamb** is a young sheep.
6.	answer	answer	Please **answer** the question.
7.	knee	knee	He hurt his **knee** climbing a cliff.
8.	written	written	They have **written** many letters.
9.	though	though	He could read, **though** he was not six.
10.	knock	knock	You should **knock** before entering.
11.	echo	echo	Call and you will hear an **echo**.
12.	known	known	Her address is not **known**.
13.	comb	comb	Wait until I **comb** my hair.
14.	wrong	wrong	No question that you ask is **wrong**.
15.	limb	limb	The bird sat on the **limb** of the tree.
16.	knife	knife	On the table were a **knife** and fork.
17.	listen	listen	You must **listen** to each question.
18.	honest	honest	Please give me an **honest** answer.
19.	doubt	doubt	I do not **doubt** your story.
20.	calm	calm	The sea was **calm** after the storm.

SORT THE SPELLING WORDS

1.–13. Write each spelling word that begins or ends with one or more silent consonants. Underline those consonants.

14.–20. Write the spelling words with one or more silent consonants within the word. Underline those consonants.

REMEMBER THE SPELLING STRATEGY

Remember that some words are spelled with silent consonants: **k** in **knot** and **s** in **island**.

silent consonants begin or end word

1. _____
2. _____
3. _____
4. _____
5. _____
6. _____
7. _____
8. _____
9. _____
10. _____
11. _____
12. _____
13. _____

silent consonants in middle

14. _____
15. _____
16. _____
17. _____
18. _____
19. _____
20. _____

Word Meanings

Write a spelling word for each definition.

1. frequently
2. quiet; peaceful
3. a young sheep
4. to be unsure
5. a reply to a question
6. a large branch of a tree
7. the joint where thigh and lower leg connect
8. to send back a sound
9. a tool with teeth; used to arrange hair

Alphabetical Order

Write each group of spelling words in alphabetical order.

10.–12. wring, wrong, written

13.–16. knot, knock, known, knife

17.–19. island, listen, honest

USING THE Dictionary

A conjunction can join two sentences or two parts of one sentence. Look up the following words in your **Spelling Dictionary**. Write the one that can be used as a conjunction.

20. often, honest, though, echo

◆ ◆ ◆

Dictionary Check Be sure to check the parts of speech in your **Spelling Dictionary**.

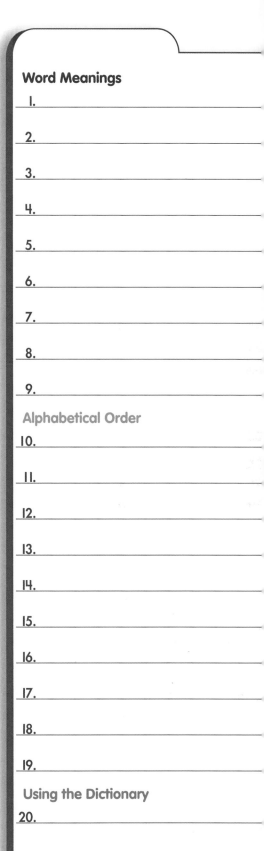

Word Meanings

1. _____
2. _____
3. _____
4. _____
5. _____
6. _____
7. _____
8. _____
9. _____

Alphabetical Order

10. _____
11. _____
12. _____
13. _____
14. _____
15. _____
16. _____
17. _____
18. _____
19. _____

Using the Dictionary

20. _____

93

often	knot	wring	island	lamb
answer	knee	written	though	knock
echo	known	comb	wrong	limb
knife	listen	honest	doubt	calm

Use the Clues

1. _____
2. _____
3. _____
4. _____
5. _____
6. _____
7. _____
8. _____
9. _____

Solve the Analogies

10. _____
11. _____
12. _____
13. _____
14. _____

Write the Antonyms

15. _____
16. _____
17. _____
18. _____
19. _____
20. _____

Use the Clues   Write a spelling word for each clue.

1. I can make your shoelaces hard to untie.
2. I am your voice sent back to you.
3. I can mean "to search carefully."
4. I rhyme with **low** and can be a conjunction.
5. I am surrounded by water.
6. I am an arm, a leg, a flipper, or a wing.
7. I am something you do on a door.
8. I am a form of the word **know**.
9. I am a form of the word **write**.

Solve the Analogies   Write the missing spelling word to complete each analogy.

10. **Cow** is to **calf** as **sheep** is to _____.
11. **Loaves** is to **loaf** as **knives** is to _____.
12. **Arm** is to **elbow** as **leg** is to _____.
13. **Not** is to **knot** as **ring** is to _____.
14. **See** is to **watch** as **hear** is to _____.

Write the Antonyms   Write the spelling word that is an antonym for each underlined word or phrase.

15. Are you sure this answer is <u>correct</u>?
16. An <u>untruthful</u> person will have many friends.
17. I <u>am sure</u> that Katera will come with us.
18. Please write the <u>question</u> on the chalkboard.
19. The sea was <u>rough</u> after the storm.
20. We <u>rarely</u> go shopping in the city.

Spelling and Writing

Proofread a Letter

Six words are not spelled correctly in this letter of complaint. Write those words correctly.

Dear Sir or Madam:

    I have been billed the rong amount for a pair of slacks I purchased. Since I ofen shop at your store, I am sure this was an honist mistake and, since your good reputation is well known, I do not dout that you will correct the error. The price of the slacks was $23.42, not $32.42, as charged. I would appreciate a writen anser to this letter. Thank you.

                Sincerely,

                Thomas R. Whitman

Proofreading Marks

≡ Make a capital.

/ Make a small letter.

∧ Add something.

ℓ Take out something.

⊙ Add a period.

⌗ New paragraph

ⓢⓟ Spelling error

Write a Letter

Expository Writing

Write a letter of complaint about a real or imaginary problem. Be polite. Include

- the name of the person to whom you are writing.
- complete information about the problem.
- how you would like the problem to be solved.
- your name.

Use as many spelling words as you can.

Writing Process

Prewriting
⬇
Drafting
⬇
Revising
⬇

Proofread Your Writing During → **Editing**
⬇
Publishing

Proofread your writing for spelling errors as part of the editing stage in the writing process. Be sure to check each word carefully. Use a dictionary to check spelling if you are not sure.

VOCABULARY CONNECTIONS

►Strategy Words◄

Review Words: Silent Consonants

Write a word from the box that matches each clue.

half	hourly	knew	knight	wrap

1. It is a past tense verb.
2. It begins with a silent **h**.
3. It is a homophone of **night**.
4. It contains a silent **l**.
5. It begins with a silent **w**.

Preview Words: Silent Consonants

Write a word from the box that matches each clue.

beret	design	frighten	knapsack	thorough

6. This describes what horror movies do.
7. It contains the word **sign**.
8. It contains the word **rough**.
9. This is something you wear on your head. It's popular in France.
10. This is something you might wear on your back. You could put books in it.

Review Words

1. _____
2. _____
3. _____
4. _____
5. _____

Preview Words

6. _____
7. _____
8. _____
9. _____
10. _____

Content Words

Social Studies: Crafts

Add and subtract letters to form words from the box.

crafts	sewing	handmade	weaving	knitting

1. c + rafting – ing + s = _____
2. know – ow + it + tin + g = _____
3. h + and + making – king + de = _____
4. send – nd + win + get – et = _____
5. wear – r + v + ink – k + g = _____

Math: Operations

Write a word from the box for each clue.

answers	subtraction	numeral	zero	problem

6. I have plenty of nothing.
7. Are you taking it away?
8. Questions need these.
9. Each one of these is an example: 3, 72, 108.
10. This needs a solution.

Apply the Spelling Strategy

Circle the silent consonant that begins one of the Content Words you wrote. Circle the silent consonant in the second syllable in another Content Word you wrote.

Word Study

Changes in Pronunciation

In very old English, **comb** ended with a /b/ sound, and **knitting** began with a /k/ sound. Over time, the **b** and the **k** became silent, but the spellings of these words remained the same. Write the Strategy Word that once was pronounced /kuh-ny-cht/.

Social Studies: Crafts
1. _____
2. _____
3. _____
4. _____
5. _____

Math: Operations
6. _____
7. _____
8. _____
9. _____
10. _____

Changes in Pronunciation
1. _____

Spelling and Thinking

qu
1. _____
2. _____
3. _____
4. _____
5. _____
6. _____
7. _____
8. _____
9. _____
10. _____
11. _____
12. _____
13. _____
14. _____

squ
15. _____
16. _____
17. _____
18. _____
19. _____
20. _____

READ THE SPELLING WORDS

1.	quick	quick	She is **quick** to learn her lessons.
2.	quarter	quarter	I ate dinner at **quarter** till seven.
3.	squint	squint	We had to **squint** in the bright light.
4.	quiz	quiz	There will be a math **quiz** tomorrow.
5.	squeeze	squeeze	I **squeeze** oranges for juice.
6.	quote	quote	We would like to **quote** what you said.
7.	quit	quit	I **quit** the game when I got tired.
8.	squash	squash	We grew **squash** in our garden.
9.	queen	queen	The king and **queen** rode in a carriage.
10.	squirm	squirm	A worm will **squirm** in your hand.
11.	quilt	quilt	A heavy **quilt** covered the bed.
12.	quart	quart	I will buy bread and a **quart** of milk.
13.	squeal	squeal	Children at play **squeal** with joy.
14.	quake	quake	My cats **quake** with fear during storms.
15.	quill	quill	A porcupine's **quill** is sharp.
16.	quarrel	quarrel	A **quarrel** among friends is not serious.
17.	square	square	A **square** has four sides.
18.	quite	quite	It is not **quite** seven o'clock.
19.	question	question	That **question** is easy to answer.
20.	quiet	quiet	Thank-you for being **quiet** while I study.

SORT THE SPELLING WORDS

1.–14. Write the spelling words that begin with **qu**.

15.–20. Write the spelling words that begin with **squ**.

REMEMBER THE SPELLING STRATEGY

Remember that the /**kw**/ sound is spelled **qu**: **quiz**, **squint**.

Spelling and Vocabulary

Word Meanings

Write a spelling word for each definition.

1. a sentence that asks something
2. a coin worth twenty-five cents
3. an argument
4. to turn and twist the body
5. to look at with partly opened eyes
6. to compress; press together hard
7. a heavy bed covering
8. a rectangle with four equal sides

Rhymes

Write a spelling word that rhymes with each of these words.

9. whiz
10. wash
11. take
12. short

13. pill
14. green
15. tight
16. wit

Write the spelling word that is a synonym for these words.

17. swift
18. recite

19. cry
20. silent

◆ ◆ ◆

Thesaurus Check Be sure to check the synonyms in your **Writing Thesaurus**.

Word Meanings

1. _____
2. _____
3. _____
4. _____
5. _____
6. _____
7. _____
8. _____

Rhymes

9. _____
10. _____
11. _____
12. _____
13. _____
14. _____
15. _____
16. _____

Using the Thesaurus

17. _____
18. _____
19. _____
20. _____

Spelling <small>and</small> Reading

quick	quarter	squint	quiz	squeeze
quote	quit	squash	queen	squirm
quilt	quart	squeal	quake	quill
quarrel	square	quite	question	quiet

Answer the Questions Write the spelling word that answers each question.

1. Which word means "to argue or fight"?
2. Which word means "a fourth of something"?
3. Which word refers to an open space surrounded by streets?
4. For what can quotation marks be a clue?
5. What do you answer?
6. What can keep you warm at night?
7. Which word means "to shake or vibrate"?
8. Which word names a vegetable?
9. Which is the wife of a king?
10. Which used to be part of a pen?

Complete the Story Write spelling words from the box to complete the story.

Last night it was very __11.__ in my house. I was studying for a math __12.__. I decided to take a __13.__ break for a glass of milk. As I removed the __14.__ of milk from the refrigerator, I heard a loud __15.__ outside. It was so dark, I had to __16.__ to see better. As my eyes focused, I saw our smallest piglet trying to __17.__ through a hole in the fence. He had gotten caught, so I rescued him. He surely did __18.__ around in my arms when I picked him up! He __19.__ struggling and ran when I put him down. After being stuck, he seemed __20.__ happy to be inside the fence again.

squeal
squint
squeeze
squirm
quite
quart
quick
quiz
quit
quiet

Answer the Questions
1.
2.
3.
4.
5.
6.
7.
8.
9.
10.

Complete the Story
11.
12.
13.
14.
15.
16.
17.
18.
19.
20.

Spelling and Writing

Proofread a Diary Entry

Six words are not spelled correctly in this diary entry. Write those words correctly.

July 17

I went out to the farm today to visit Grandfather Howard. It was qwite a trip. Although he is a qwiet man, he knows a lot, and he patiently answered each questshun I asked. We looked at the sqwash he had planted and listened to the squeel of the pigs. I helped him weed, and we quit only for lunch. When we finished, he gave me a dollar and a qwarter for my work.

Proofreading Marks

≡ Make a capital.

/ Make a small letter.

∧ Add something.

℮ Take out something.

⊙ Add a period.

⌗ New paragraph

SP Spelling error

Write a Diary Entry

Narrative Writing

Write a diary entry about an experience you had. Be sure to include

- where you were.
- what you did.
- whom you were with.
- what you liked or disliked.

Use as many spelling words as you can.

Writing Process

Prewriting
⇩
Drafting
⇩
Revising
⇩
Editing
⇩
Publishing

Proofread Your Writing During Editing

Proofread your writing for spelling errors as part of the editing stage in the writing process. Be sure to check each word carefully. Use a dictionary to check spelling if you are not sure.

101

VOCABULARY CONNECTIONS

Strategy Words

Review Words: qu, squ

Write a word from the box that fits each sentence.

equal	clock	fresh	grand	stitch

1. It begins with a **cl** consonant cluster.
2. You can make it by changing a consonant cluster in **stand**.
3. It has a **qu** spelling pattern.
4. It ends with an **sh** digraph.
5. It has the word **it** between two consonant clusters.

Preview Words: qu, squ

Write a word from the box that fits each sentence.

aquarium	quart	squirrel
square	unequal	

6. It begins with **qu**.
7. It begins with **squ** and rhymes with **stare**.
8. It has four syllables and a **qu** spelling pattern.
9. It begins with **squ** and has a double consonant.
10. It begins with a prefix that means "not."

Review Words

1. _____
2. _____
3. _____
4. _____
5. _____

Preview Words

6. _____
7. _____
8. _____
9. _____
10. _____

Content Words

Fine Arts: Instruments

Write the word from the box that solves each riddle.

quartet	piccolo	oboe	clarinet	bassoon

1. I am a woodwind instrument with a **net** in me.
2. I am a small flute with a double **c** in me.
3. I am a U-shaped woodwind whose name starts with the name of a fish.
4. I am a group of four musicians.
5. I am a thin woodwind instrument whose name ends in two vowels.

Science: Matter

Write the word from the box that fits each description.

airy	liquid	gas	solid	helium

6. It is an antonym of **hollow**.
7. It describes the state of water.
8. It lifts balloons.
9. It is a synonym of **breezy**.
10. It describes the state of steam.

Apply the Spelling Strategy

Circle the spelling of the /**kw**/ sound in two of the Content Words you wrote.

Word Study

Word Roots

The Latin word **aqua** meant "water." The color **aqua** looks like water. Write the Strategy Word that is related to water and means "a place to keep fish and other water animals and plants."

Fine Arts: Instruments

1. _____

2. _____

3. _____

4. _____

5. _____

Science: Matter

6. _____

7. _____

8. _____

9. _____

10. _____

Word Roots

1. _____

dge

1. _____
2. _____
3. _____
4. _____
5. _____
6. _____
7. _____

g followed by e, y, or i

8. _____
9. _____
10. _____
11. _____
12. _____
13. _____
14. _____
15. _____
16. _____
17. _____
18. _____
19. _____
20. _____

Spelling and Thinking

READ THE SPELLING WORDS

1.	badge	*badge*	She pinned the **badge** on her uniform.
2.	gym	*gym*	In **gym** we climb ropes and play ball.
3.	rigid	*rigid*	My teacher avoids **rigid** rules.
4.	gem	*gem*	A diamond is a precious **gem**.
5.	baggage	*baggage*	He checked his **baggage** at the airport.
6.	range	*range*	Their ages **range** from six to ten.
7.	dodge	*dodge*	In this game you must **dodge** the ball.
8.	package	*package*	The **package** was delivered yesterday.
9.	engine	*engine*	Oil keeps an **engine** from overheating.
10.	cottage	*cottage*	He built a **cottage** in six months.
11.	gigantic	*gigantic*	A **gigantic** wave crashed ashore.
12.	edge	*edge*	The **edge** of a ruler is straight.
13.	gentle	*gentle*	A calf is **gentle** and friendly.
14.	strange	*strange*	That book had a **strange** plot.
15.	ridge	*ridge*	Trees grew along the rocky **ridge**.
16.	cabbage	*cabbage*	A **cabbage** has a solid, round head.
17.	bridge	*bridge*	The **bridge** spanned the stream.
18.	hedge	*hedge*	He trimmed the **hedge** to lower it.
19.	village	*village*	The band played on the **village** green.
20.	judge	*judge*	The **judge** instructed the jury.

SORT THE SPELLING WORDS

1.–7. Write the spelling words that spell the /**j**/ sound **dge**.

8.–20. Write the spelling words that spell the /**j**/ sound **g** followed by **e, y,** or **i**.

REMEMBER THE SPELLING STRATEGY

Remember that the /**j**/ sound can be spelled in different ways: **g** followed by **e** in **gem** and **range**, **g** followed by **y** in **gym**, and **g** followed by **i** in **gigantic**. The /**j**/ sound can also be spelled **dge**: **edge**.

Word Meanings

Write a spelling word for each clue.

1. Take me on your trip.
2. I am very big.
3. Use me for sports.
4. I can be gift-wrapped.
5. I've got a green head.

Words and Letters

Follow the directions to write spelling words.

6. Drop one letter in **frigid**.
7. Drop one letter in **ledge**.
8. Change the first letter of **fudge**.
9. Change the first letter of **pottage**.
10. Change the last two letters of **villain**.
11. Change the last letter of **get**.
12. Add a letter at the start of **edge**.
13. Change the second letter in **budge**.
14. Add one letter to **ride**.
15. Add one letter to **bride**.
16. Drop one letter from **strangle**.

USING THE Dictionary

Write the spelling word that would be on the same page as these guide words.

17. decimeter • dye
18. eager • envelope
19. fourteenth • govern
20. radio • recheck

Word Meanings
1. _____
2. _____
3. _____
4. _____
5. _____

Words and Letters
6. _____
7. _____
8. _____
9. _____
10. _____
11. _____
12. _____
13. _____
14. _____
15. _____
16. _____

Using the Dictionary
17. _____
18. _____
19. _____
20. _____

badge	gym	rigid	gem	baggage
range	dodge	package	engine	cottage
gigantic	edge	gentle	strange	ridge
cabbage	bridge	hedge	village	judge

Find the Rhymes   Write the spelling word that rhymes with each of these words.

1. lentil
2. Atlantic
3. grim
4. bearskin

5. stem
6. lodge
7. strange

Replace the Words   Write the spelling word to replace each underlined word or phrase.

8. The wind did not damage the <u>unbending</u> flagpole.
9. All of our <u>luggage</u> was put onto the plane.
10. Did anyone deliver a <u>parcel</u> to 18 Locust Drive?
11. They live in a <u>place smaller than a town</u> in Ohio.
12. He trimmed the <u>fence of bushes</u> with his clippers.
13. She put stones around the <u>border</u> of her flower garden.
14. Sue boiled a <u>vegetable with a leafy head</u> for dinner.
15. The <u>person who presides over a court</u> wore a black robe.

Complete the Story   Write spelling words to complete the story.

Yesterday we came across a __16.__ scene. We saw a deserted __17.__ on a pine-covered mountain __18.__. No one knew who lived there. The sheriff pinned on his __19.__ and asked me to go with him. We rode across the __20.__ over the river and entered the house. There we found nothing but cobwebs—and a newspaper dated July 1, 1898.

| badge |
| cottage |
| strange |
| ridge |
| bridge |

Find the Rhymes
1.
2.
3.
4.
5.
6.
7.

Replace the Words
8.
9.
10.
11.
12.
13.
14.
15.

Complete the Story
16.
17.
18.
19.
20.

Spelling ᴬⁿᵈ Writing

Proofread a Letter

Six words are not spelled correctly in this letter asking about a job. Write those words correctly.

Dear Ms. Roget:

Please consider me for the job of clerk in your store. I am a hard worker who knows most of the people in our vilage. Sam King, owner of a jim where I worked before, is a good juje of my ability. I am sure he will give me a good recommendation. I have a range of talents and can sell anything from cabbige to baggije, and, I can wrap a gift pakage very well. I will be glad to come in and talk with you about the opening.

Sincerely,
Ima Pearl

Write a Letter

Persuasive Writing

Write a letter in which you ask for a job. Be sure to include
- what job you are applying for.
- what your abilities are.
- what experience, if any, you have had.
- who can recommend you.

Use as many spelling words as you can.

Proofread Your Writing During

Proofread your writing for spelling errors as part of the editing stage in the writing process. Be sure to check each word carefully. Use a dictionary to check spelling if you are not sure.

Proofreading Marks

☰ Make a capital.

╱ Make a small letter.

∧ Add something.

℘ Take out something.

⊙ Add a period.

⌗ New paragraph

🆂🅿 Spelling error

Writing Process

Prewriting
⬇
Drafting
⬇
Revising
⬇
Editing
⬇
Publishing

VOCABULARY CONNECTIONS

Strategy Words

Review Words: Consonant Sound /j/

Write the word from the box that matches each definition.

age	change	larger	largest	page

1. bigger
2. number of years old
3. sheet of paper
4. biggest
5. make different

Preview Words: Consonant Sound /j/

Write a word from the box to fit each description.

apology	average	general
imagine	judgment	

6. This word has two syllables.
7. This word has four syllables.
8. This word means "a high-ranking officer."
9. This word means "not great, not bad."
10. This word tells what fiction writers do.

Review Words

1. _____
2. _____
3. _____
4. _____
5. _____

Preview Words

6. _____
7. _____
8. _____
9. _____
10. _____

Content Words

Language Arts: Drama

Write words from the box to complete the paragraph.

outrage	tour	pity	wit	stage

Last week our family went on a guided __1.__ of a movie set. We even got to visit behind the __2.__ and talk with some of the actors and actresses. Then we saw a scene where a young boy felt __3.__ for a poor animal that had been hurt. In another scene, an actor showed his __4.__ over the misuse of national parks. That evening we saw a show in which a comedian made us laugh with his clever __5.__.

Math: Division

Write a word from the box that names each numbered part.

dividend	remainder	division	quotient	divisor

6.
7. 8.
9.

$$7 \; R2$$
$$8) \overline{58}$$

This is a __10.__ problem.

Apply the Spelling Strategy

Circle the **ge** spelling of the /**j**/ sound in two of the Content Words you wrote.

More Than One Meaning

Many words have more than one meaning. Write the one Strategy Word that can have these meanings:

- part of a book
- to call out a person's name on a loudspeaker

Language Arts: Drama
1. _____
2. _____
3. _____
4. _____
5. _____

Math: Division
6. _____
7. _____
8. _____
9. _____
10. _____

More Than One Meaning
1. _____

Assessment and Review

Assessment — Units 13–17

Each Assessment Word in the box fits one of the spelling strategies you have studied over the past five weeks. Read the spelling strategies. Then write each Assessment Word under the unit number it fits.

Unit 13

1.–4. The **r**-controlled vowel sound you hear in **cart** (/är/) is spelled **ar**. The **r**-controlled vowel sound you hear in **spare** (/âr/) is spelled **are**.

Unit 14

5.–8. Some words have more vowel letters than vowel sounds.

Unit 15

9.–12. Some words are spelled with silent consonants: **k** in **knot** and **s** in **island**.

Unit 16

13.–16. The /**kw**/ sound is spelled **qu: quiz, squint.**

Unit 17

17.–20. The /**j**/ sound can be spelled in different ways: **g** followed by **e** in **gem** and **range, g** followed by **y** in **gym,** and **g** followed by **i** in **gigantic.** The /**j**/ sound can also be spelled **dge: edge.**

starch
deaf
bomb
squab
flare
squad
wage
leather
fudge
writer
squawk
wreck
dread
carve
mare
steady
voyage
sword
queer
urge

Unit 13
1.
2.
3.
4.

Unit 14
5.
6.
7.
8.

Unit 15
9.
10.
11.
12.

Unit 16
13.
14.
15.
16.

Unit 17
17.
18.
19.
20.

 **Unit 13: r-Controlled Vowels /âr/, /är/**

apart	chart	parent	scare	market
compare	share	beware	mark	army

These spelling words are missing letters. Write the spelling words.

1. m __ rk
2. ch __ __ t
3. ap __ __ t
4. p __ __ ent
5. m __ __ ket
6. __ __ my

Write the spelling word that completes each sentence.

7. When you finish, _____ your answers with those in the book.
8. The sign told us to _____ of the dog.
9. Please _____ your paper with me.
10. That movie didn't _____ me.

 **Unit 14: More Letters Than Sounds**

built	instead	meant	ready	enough
young	breakfast	already	build	touch

Write the spelling word that completes each sentence.

11. Now, I am _____ to go.
12. You have taken more than _____ time.
13. Did you have a good _____ this morning?
14. That child is too _____ to play with us.
15. Have you ever _____ a sandcastle?
16. I plan to _____ a castle on the beach today.
17. Lee wants to build a sand city _____ of a castle.
18. I'm sorry, but that was not what I _____ to say.
19. If you stretch, can you _____ the top of the door?
20. I have read that book _____.

Unit 13

1. _____
2. _____
3. _____
4. _____
5. _____
6. _____
7. _____
8. _____
9. _____
10. _____

Unit 14

11. _____
12. _____
13. _____
14. _____
15. _____
16. _____
17. _____
18. _____
19. _____
20. _____

 **Review** Unit 15: Silent Consonants

answer	honest	often	listen	known
though	island	knee	wrong	calm

Add the missing silent consonants to write the spelling words.

1. ans __ er
2. i __ land
3. __ nee
4. __ rong
5. lis __ en
6. __ nown
7. of __ en
8. __ onest
9. thou __ __
10. ca __ m

 **Review** Unit 16: qu, squ

quiet	quit	quite	square	quarter
squeeze	question	queen	quilt	quick

Write the spelling word that rhymes with the underlined word in each clue.

11. These flowers will <u>wilt</u>, but they'll stay fresh in the _____.
12. This doll will <u>sneeze</u> if you give her a _____.
13. The shape of the <u>fair</u> was set up in a _____.
14. That tall person has _____ a great <u>height</u>.
15. This delicious <u>bean</u> soup is fit for a _____.
16. John played the mail <u>sorter</u>, and stamps were just a _____.

Write the spelling word that has the opposite meaning of each word.

17. noisy
18. answer
19. slow
20. continue

Review Unit 17: Consonant Sound /j/

baggage	gem	judge	strange	village
edge	engine	range	dodge	bridge

1.–3. Write the spelling words that have two syllables.

4.–7. Write the spelling words that spell the /j/ sound **dge**.

8. Write the spelling word that means the opposite of **familiar**.

9. Write the spelling word that means "a precious stone."

10. Write the spelling word that can mean "a kitchen stove" or "open grazing country for cattle."

 **Spelling Study Strategy**

 Play Circle Dot

Practicing spelling words can be fun if you make it into a game.

1. Choose a partner. Each of you should write a list of twenty spelling words that you find hard to spell. Trade your list with your partner. Ask your partner to read your list aloud. Give help with any words the partner finds hard to read.

2. Then, your partner should read one word from your list aloud. You write that word on a piece of paper. When you finish, your partner should spell the word out loud, one letter at a time.

3. As your partner says each letter, make a dot under the correct letter on your page. If you have a letter that is not correct, draw a circle under it. If you have left out a letter, make a little circle to show where it should have been.

4. The circles will show where you have trouble. Write the word again and check the spelling.

5. Take turns as you play **Circle Dot**.

Unit 17

1. _____
2. _____
3. _____
4. _____
5. _____
6. _____
7. _____
8. _____
9. _____
10. _____

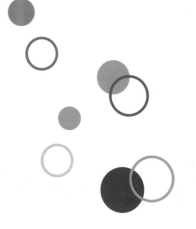

WRITER'S

Grammar, Usage, and Mechanics

Linking Verbs

A linking verb links the subject with words that tell what the subject is like. For example, in the sentence, "The carpet was dirty," **was** is a linking verb. It links **carpet** and **dirty**. **Dirty** tells what the carpet is like. Linking verbs include **am, is, are, was, were, become,** and **seem**.

The swans **are** beautiful!

The icicles **were** cold.

Suddenly the room **became** warm.

I **am** happy.

The football player **is** injured.

The coaches **seem** proud.

Practice Activity

A. Write the linking verb in each sentence.

   1. My school bus was late this morning.

   2. That new girl seems friendly.

   3. Today I am cold and tired.

   4. The twins were happy about the party.

   5. After the storm, the ground soon became dry again.

B. Find the linking verb in each sentence. Then write the word in each sentence that comes after the linking verb and tells what the subject is like.

   6. That picture seems strange.

   7. Everyone was calm during the storm.

   8. Last year those kittens were young.

   9. You are wrong about that!

  10. The ripe oranges tasted sweet.

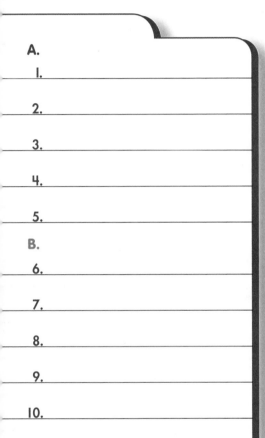

A.
1.
2.
3.
4.
5.
B.
6.
7.
8.
9.
10.

WORKSHOP

Proofreading Strategy

Work With a Partner!

Good writers always proofread their writing for spelling errors. Here's a strategy you can use to proofread your papers.

Instead of proofreading all alone, work with a partner. Ask your partner to read your work aloud. Ask the person to read slowly. While your partner reads, you look at each word and think about each sentence. Are the words spelled correctly? Does the sentence make sense?

This strategy helps you focus on spelling and meaning. Try it!

Electronic Spelling

Spell Checkers and Homophones

Many computers have spell checkers that can help you proofread. But even the best spell checker cannot do it all. You still need to think about the spelling of some words.

Sometimes you type one word and mean another. For example, do you write letters on **stationery** or **stationary**? Both words are spelled correctly because they are homophones. However, the one you write letters on contains an **e**.

A computer checked the spelling of the words in these sentences. Find the incorrect homophone the computer missed in each sentence. Write it correctly.

Electronic Spelling

1. _____
2. _____
3. _____
4. _____
5. _____
6. _____

1. Put the boxes hear, please.
2. We have ate pencils left.
3. Our principle decides when to close school.
4. I would like plane milk with nothing in it.
5. We will leave in an our.
6. The tree has begun to lose it's leaves.

Spelling and Thinking

READ THE SPELLING WORDS

1. bottle	*bottle*	They bought a **bottle** of juice.
2. pebble	*pebble*	A **pebble** is smaller than a rock.
3. single	*single*	I have only a **single** pencil left.
4. jumble	*jumble*	A **jumble** of papers lay on his desk.
5. tickle	*tickle*	When you **tickle** me, I have to laugh.
6. rattle	*rattle*	Keys **rattle** when we unlock the door.
7. middle	*middle*	She is in **middle** school.
8. bubble	*bubble*	Angie blew a huge soap **bubble**.
9. sample	*sample*	Taste a **sample** of my cooking.
10. cattle	*cattle*	They raise **cattle** on the prairie.
11. snuggle	*snuggle*	I **snuggle** under warm blankets.
12. kettle	*kettle*	The hot **kettle** was whistling.
13. jungle	*jungle*	He photographs many **jungle** animals.
14. ankle	*ankle*	She wore a silver **ankle** bracelet.
15. giggle	*giggle*	A laugh often follows a **giggle**.
16. simple	*simple*	I am learning to tie **simple** knots.
17. settle	*settle*	They came here to **settle** the land.
18. temple	*temple*	We attend a **temple** on Main Street.
19. battle	*battle*	The **battle** was fought at sea.
20. mumble	*mumble*	When you **mumble**, I cannot hear you.

double consonants

1.
2.
3.
4.
5.
6.
7.
8.
9.
10.
11.

no double consonants

12.
13.
14.
15.
16.
17.
18.
19.
20.

SORT THE SPELLING WORDS

1.–11. Write the spelling words that have double consonants. Draw a line between the syllables of each word.

12.–20. Write the words that do not have double consonants. Circle the words that have a **short u** sound in the first syllable.

REMEMBER THE SPELLING STRATEGY

Remember that the second syllable in each of this week's spelling words ends in **le**.

Spelling and Vocabulary

Word Meanings

Write a spelling word for each definition.

1. a small stone
2. to touch lightly to produce laughter
3. a building for worship
4. a wild, tropical land
5. a small laugh
6. the joint that connects the leg to the foot
7. a container usually made of glass or plastic
8. a round film of liquid

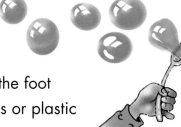

Phonics

Follow the directions to write spelling words.

9.–11. Change the first letter in **tattle** to write spelling words.

12.–13. Change the first letter in **nettle** to write spelling words.

14.–15. Change the first letter in **bumble** to write spelling words.

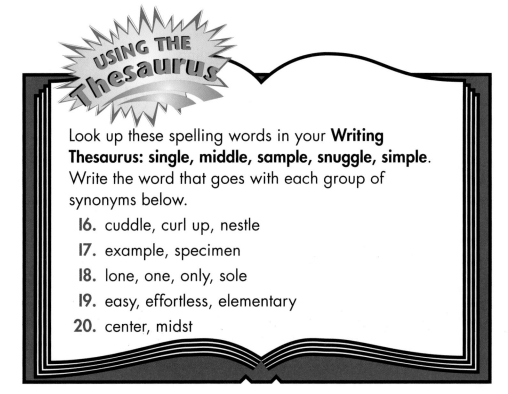

USING THE Thesaurus

Look up these spelling words in your **Writing Thesaurus: single, middle, sample, snuggle, simple**. Write the word that goes with each group of synonyms below.

16. cuddle, curl up, nestle
17. example, specimen
18. lone, one, only, sole
19. easy, effortless, elementary
20. center, midst

Word Meanings

1. _____
2. _____
3. _____
4. _____
5. _____
6. _____
7. _____
8. _____

Phonics

9. _____
10. _____
11. _____
12. _____
13. _____
14. _____
15. _____

Using the Thesaurus

16. _____
17. _____
18. _____
19. _____
20. _____

bottle	pebble	single	jumble	tickle
rattle	middle	bubble	sample	cattle
snuggle	kettle	jungle	ankle	giggle
simple	settle	temple	battle	mumble

Complete the Sentences Write the spelling word that best completes each sentence.

1. The wind is making the window _____.
2. Boots and an umbrella will help us _____ the storm.
3. Do all _____ have horns and hoofs?
4. It is hard to _____ down after all that excitement.
5. All our jackets are on the bed in a _____.
6. The _____ is whistling merrily on the stove.
7. Did she _____ that she was sorry?

Replace the Words There is one form of a spelling word in each sentence. Find that form and write the spelling word it came from.

8. The workers in the dairy are bottling milk.
9. The water will start bubbling when it boils.
10. Sarah was reading the comics and giggling.
11. Timmy enjoys snuggling up with a good book.
12. We will be sampling different fruits today.
13. The fur on my collar is tickling my chin.

Solve the Analogies Write the spelling word that completes each analogy.

14. **Two** is to **double** as **one** is to _____.
15. **Hard** is to **difficult** as **easy** is to _____.
16. **Large** is to **boulder** as **small** is to _____.
17. **Deer** is to **forest** as **monkey** is to _____.
18. **Education** is to **school** as **religion** is to _____.
19. **Side** is to **edge** as **center** is to _____.
20. **Hand** is to **wrist** as **foot** is to _____.

Complete the Sentences

1. _____
2. _____
3. _____
4. _____
5. _____
6. _____
7. _____

Replace the Words

8. _____
9. _____
10. _____
11. _____
12. _____
13. _____

Solve the Analogies

14. _____
15. _____
16. _____
17. _____
18. _____
19. _____
20. _____

Spelling and Writing

Proofread a Letter

Six words are not spelled correctly in this letter to a newspaper editor. Write those words correctly.

Dear Editor:

I am writing to say that I am alarmed at the way our land is disappearing. Our catle are grazing on less grass. Our jungel animals have fewer trees. Our children are caught in the midle with hardly any space to play. The solution seems simpel. Set aside more land for parks and wildlife refuges. A singel park can be used for both humans and animals. Ask your readers to battel for open space. Let us not settle for houses, stores, and huge parking lots.

Yours truly,

Lee Jamison

Proofreading Marks

☰ Make a capital.

/ Make a small letter.

∧ Add something.

℘ Take out something.

⊙ Add a period.

⌗ New paragraph

ⓢⓟ Spelling error

Write a Letter

Persuasive Writing

Write a letter about something that concerns you. Be sure to include

- what your concerns are about.
- what you think should be done.
- the reasons for keeping or changing something.
- what the reader can do to make a difference.

Use as many spelling words as you can.

Writing Process

Prewriting

Drafting

Revising

Editing

Publishing

Proofread Your Writing During ▶ **Editing**

Proofread your writing for spelling errors as part of the editing stage in the writing process. Be sure to check each word carefully. Use a dictionary to check spelling if you are not sure.

VOCABULARY CONNECTIONS

Strategy Words

Review Words

1. _____
2. _____
3. _____
4. _____
5. _____

Preview Words

6. _____
7. _____
8. _____
9. _____
10. _____

Review Words: Final le

Write a word from the box to complete each sentence.

| circle | couple | maple | people | uncle |

1. We get syrup from _____ trees.
2. My mother's brother is my _____.
3. Form a _____ to play dodge ball.
4. We speak of one person or many _____.
5. A _____ is a pair.

Preview Words: Final le

Write a word from the box that fits each clue.

| bicycle | needle | principle | syllable | triangle |

6. It names a part of a word. There are three of them in this word.
7. It names something to sew with.
8. It names something with two wheels that you might ride in the park.
9. It names a three-sided figure.
10. It names a rule, a truth, or a law and is a homophone for a person in charge of a school.

Content Words

Math: Geometry

Write the word from the box that fits each definition.

curves	rectangle	length	width	polygon

1. how long something is
2. a figure with three or more sides
3. bends smoothly and gradually
4. how wide something is
5. a four-sided figure with right angles

Language Arts: Humor

Write the word that best completes each sentence.

pun	chuckle	silly	laughter	witty

6. Sometimes the funniest jokes are foolish and _____.
7. The purpose of jokes is to bring forth _____.
8. Playing with words is the fun part of a _____.
9. A clever and humorous person can be described as _____.
10. A small laugh that is like a giggle is a _____.

Apply the Spelling Strategy

Circle the **le** ending in two of the Content Words you wrote.

Word Study

Related Words

Words such as **circus, circuit,** and **circulate** are related by the root **circ,** which means "ring." Write the Strategy Word that is also related to these words.

Math: Geometry

1. _____
2. _____
3. _____
4. _____
5. _____

Language Arts: Humor

6. _____
7. _____
8. _____
9. _____
10. _____

Related Words

1. _____

Spelling and Thinking

le endings

1. _____
2. _____
3. _____
4. _____
5. _____
6. _____
7. _____
8. _____

en endings

9. _____
10. _____
11. _____
12. _____
13. _____
14. _____
15. _____
16. _____
17. _____
18. _____
19. _____
20. _____

READ THE SPELLING WORDS

1.	stumble	*stumble*	It is easy to **stumble** in the dark.
2.	trouble	*trouble*	When in **trouble** you need a friend.
3.	eagle	*eagle*	An **eagle** builds a huge nest.
4.	harden	*harden*	The candy will **harden** as it cools.
5.	brighten	*brighten*	Your kindness will **brighten** my day.
6.	thicken	*thicken*	Use flour to **thicken** the sauce.
7.	wrinkle	*wrinkle*	Try not to **wrinkle** your clothes.
8.	soften	*soften*	The sun will **soften** the ice.
9.	lighten	*lighten*	Two helpers will **lighten** the load.
10.	table	*table*	The children set the **table**.
11.	dampen	*dampen*	Before ironing, **dampen** the cloth.
12.	moisten	*moisten*	Please **moisten** the sponge with water.
13.	double	*double*	Twins are **double** the pleasure.
14.	weaken	*weaken*	Lack of exercise can **weaken** you.
15.	tighten	*tighten*	I must **tighten** a bolt on my bike.
16.	example	*example*	He set a good **example** for others.
17.	darken	*darken*	Rain clouds will **darken** the sky.
18.	tremble	*tremble*	The dog began to **tremble** with cold.
19.	fasten	*fasten*	Be sure to **fasten** your seat belt.
20.	blacken	*blacken*	Factory soot can **blacken** homes.

SORT THE SPELLING WORDS

1.–8. Write the words that end with **le**.

9.–20. Write the words that end with **en**.

REMEMBER THE SPELLING STRATEGY

Remember that the words on this week's list end in **le** or **en**. Final **en** usually means "to make" or "to become." The word **brighten** means "to become bright."

Spelling and Vocabulary

Word Meanings

The suffix **-en** means "to make" or "to become." Write the spelling word that goes with each meaning.

1. to make light
2. to make moist
3. to become weak
4. to become dark
5. to become hard
6. to make black
7. to make thick
8. to make damp

Word Structure

Read the following words and write the spelling word that each came from.

9. softener
10. fastener
11. brightener
12. tightener

Syllables ending with a vowel sound are called **open syllables**. Those ending with a consonant sound are called **closed syllables**. Find the following spelling words in your **Spelling Dictionary**. Write each word. Then write **o** if the first syllable is open or **c** if the first syllable is closed.

13. table
14. stumble
15. wrinkle
16. example
17. eagle
18. tremble
19. double
20. trouble

Word Meanings

1. _____
2. _____
3. _____
4. _____
5. _____
6. _____
7. _____
8. _____

Word Structure

9. _____
10. _____
11. _____
12. _____

Using the Dictionary

13. _____
14. _____
15. _____
16. _____
17. _____
18. _____
19. _____
20. _____

Spelling ᴬⁿᵈ Reading

stumble	trouble	eagle	harden	brighten
thicken	wrinkle	soften	lighten	table
dampen	moisten	double	weaken	tighten
example	darken	tremble	fasten	blacken

Complete the Sentences   Write the spelling word that best completes each sentence.

1. Do not _____ over the rug in the dark hallway.

2. We _____ our safety belts as soon as we get in the car.

3. This bread dough will soon _____ in size.

4. If I do not hang up this shirt, it will _____.

5. Leah's helmet strap is loose; please ask her to _____ it.

6. She took three of his books to _____ his heavy load.

7. The sun will soon _____ this cheerless, gray day.

8. We watched the magnificent _____ swoop over the hills.

9.–10. Storm clouds are about to _____ and _____ the bright sky.

11. If I don't wash this glue off my fingers, it will _____.

12. Please do not let her remarks _____ your wonderful high spirits.

13. Did the heavy rain further _____ the loose, rickety fence?

Complete the Story   Write spelling words to complete the story.

Seth has often helped his neighbor, Mabel, work on projects on a __14.__ in the basement. Mabel has made useful items. For __15.__, she made a powder to help __16.__ the sparse grass in her yard. She also made a cream to __17.__ and __18.__ dry, rough skin.

Mabel's inventions were not always useful. Seth remembers when he tried a new food she had created. He knew he was in __19.__ when his mouth began to twitch and __20.__.

thicken
moisten
trouble
tremble
example
soften
table

Complete the Sentences

1. _____
2. _____
3. _____
4. _____
5. _____
6. _____
7. _____
8. _____
9. _____
10. _____
11. _____
12. _____
13. _____

Complete the Story

14. _____
15. _____
16. _____
17. _____
18. _____
19. _____
20. _____

Spelling and Writing

Proofread a Letter

Six words are not spelled correctly in this friendly letter. Write those words correctly.

Dear Eva,

    I am planning to change my room decorations. For exampel, I want to lightin the color of my walls and briten my bed with a new red and blue spread. I think a new lampshade should sofen the glare on my tabel and also dubble the amount of light I get.

    I can hardly wait to show you the results. If it is no trouble, why not plan to visit next weekend? I miss you.

              Your best friend,

              Becky

Proofreading Marks

- ≡ Make a capital.
- / Make a small letter.
- ∧ Add something.
- ℓ Take out something.
- ⊙ Add a period.
- ⌗ New paragraph
- SP Spelling error

Write a Letter

Narrative Writing

Write a friendly letter to someone you know. Be sure to include
- the name of the person you are writing to.
- what you are doing or have done.
- when you would like to see or hear from the person.
- a closing that includes your relationship with the person and your name.

Use as many spelling words as you can.

Writing Process

Prewriting
⇩
Drafting
⇩
Revising
⇩
Editing
⇩
Publishing

Proofread Your Writing During ▷ Editing

Proofread your writing for spelling errors as part of the editing stage in the writing process. Be sure to check each word carefully. Use a dictionary to check spelling if you are not sure.

VOCABULARY CONNECTIONS

Strategy Words

Review Words

1. _____
2. _____
3. _____
4. _____
5. _____

Preview Words

6. _____
7. _____
8. _____
9. _____
10. _____

Review Words: Final le, Final en

Write the word from the box that matches each clue.

kitten	mitten	open	sudden	women

1. something you wear
2. more than one woman
3. a young cat
4. an antonym of **close**
5. a synonym of **quick**

Preview Words: Final le, Final en

Write a word from the box to complete each sentence.

angle	chosen	forgotten	lengthen	straighten

6. I must _____ this short pair of pants in order to make them fit properly.
7. The driver has _____ the way back to town so now we are lost.
8. Please fasten the top button of your shirt and _____ your tie.
9. The road makes a sharp _____ to the right just before our house.
10. Have you _____ some heavy, warm clothes for the trip to the mountains?

Content Words

Social Studies: Time

Write the word from the box for each clue.

century	triple	decade	twice	months

1. three times as many
2. twelve in a year
3. ten years
4. one hundred years
5. two times as many

Science: Astronomy

Write a word from the box for each clue.

comet	orbit	explode	planet	meteor

6. It is the path of one body traveling around another.
7. It is a solid fragment from space that falls into the earth's atmosphere and burns.
8. It looks like a star but has a trail of light.
9. It is a synonym of **burst**.
10. It is one of nine in our solar system.

Apply the Spelling Strategy

Circle the **le** spelling of the /l/ sound in one of the Content Words you wrote.

Word Study

Word History

An old Greek word, **planasthai,** meant "to wander." When the Greeks looked up in the sky and saw certain lights "wandering," they named them with a word that meant "wanderer." Write the Content Word that has this Greek history.

Social Studies: Time

1. _____
2. _____
3. _____
4. _____
5. _____

Science: Astronomy

6. _____
7. _____
8. _____
9. _____
10. _____

Word History

1. _____

Spelling and Thinking

READ THE SPELLING WORDS

1. gather	*gather*	Let us **gather** the ripe apples.
2. winter	*winter*	This **winter** is colder than last.
3. master	*master*	I will **master** my fear of heights.
4. tractor	*tractor*	The **tractor** pulled a plow.
5. shower	*shower*	I felt cool and clean after my **shower**.
6. major	*major*	The hail caused no **major** damage.
7. danger	*danger*	There is no **danger** of being late.
8. enter	*enter*	I will **enter** a drawing contest.
9. whether	*whether*	I must decide **whether** to go or stay.
10. water	*water*	Drink **water** when you are thirsty.
11. thunder	*thunder*	I heard **thunder** and saw lightning.
12. eager	*eager*	She is **eager** to see her aunt again.
13. bitter	*bitter*	That fruit has a **bitter** taste.
14. silver	*silver*	Kim wore **silver** earrings.
15. minor	*minor*	That was only a **minor** mistake.
16. neither	*neither*	She eats **neither** fish nor fowl.
17. wonder	*wonder*	I **wonder** where I left my pen.
18. either	*either*	We will elect **either** John or Maria.
19. rather	*rather*	I would **rather** swim than dive.
20. together	*together*	We can study the lesson **together**.

SORT THE SPELLING WORDS

1.–17. Write the spelling words in which the **schwa-r** sound is spelled **er**.

18.–20. Write the spelling words in which the **schwa-r** sound is spelled **or**.

REMEMBER THE SPELLING STRATEGY

Remember that the **schwa-r** sound is spelled in different ways: **er** in **water** and **or** in **major**.

er
1.
2.
3.
4.
5.
6.
7.
8.
9.
10.
11.
12.
13.
14.
15.
16.
17.
or
18.
19.
20.

Spelling and Vocabulary

Word Meanings

Write a spelling word for each definition.

1. somewhat; to a certain extent; instead
2. less important
3. having a harsh, unpleasant taste
4. to bring together in a group
5. to go into
6. excitedly wanting or expecting
7. the season between autumn and spring
8. one or the other of two
9. not one or the other

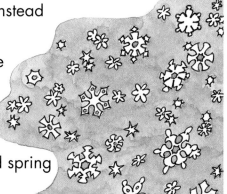

Base Words

The suffix **-ous** means "full of" or "having." Write the spelling word that is the base word for each of the following words.

10. wondrous
11. dangerous
12. thunderous

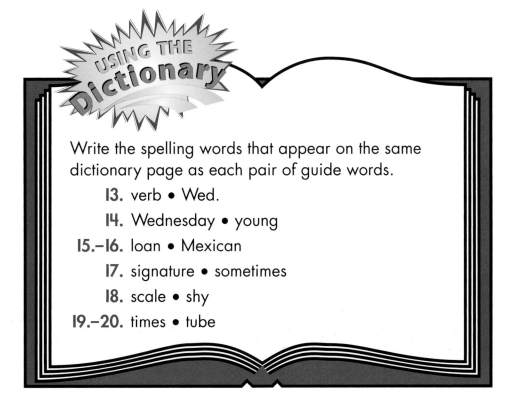

USING THE Dictionary

Write the spelling words that appear on the same dictionary page as each pair of guide words.

13. verb • Wed.
14. Wednesday • young
15.–16. loan • Mexican
17. signature • sometimes
18. scale • shy
19.–20. times • tube

Word Meanings

1. _____
2. _____
3. _____
4. _____
5. _____
6. _____
7. _____
8. _____
9. _____

Base Words

10. _____
11. _____
12. _____

Using the Dictionary

13. _____
14. _____
15. _____
16. _____
17. _____
18. _____
19. _____
20. _____

Spelling **and** Reading

gather	winter	master	tractor	shower
major	danger	enter	whether	water
thunder	eager	bitter	silver	minor
neither	wonder	either	rather	together

Complete the Rhymes

I.

2.

3.

4.

5.

6.

Complete the Sentences

7.

8.

9.

10.

11.

12.

13.

14.

15.

16.

Solve the Analogies

17.

18.

19.

20.

Complete the Rhymes Write the spelling word that rhymes with the underlined word and completes the sentence.

1. I _____ what is <u>under</u> the blanket.

2. Use the <u>center</u> door to _____ the store.

3. Sandy got a <u>splinter</u> while chopping firewood for the _____.

4. That beautiful <u>flower</u> soaked up the rain _____.

5. The park <u>ranger</u> talked about the _____ of hiking alone.

6. I could not tell _____ the suitcase was made of plastic or <u>leather</u>.

Complete the Sentences Write two spelling words to complete each sentence.

7.–8. If we study _____, we can help each other _____ the words.

9.–10. Shannon was not _____ to begin _____ of her two chores.

11.–12. In the story, _____ of the baby squirrels knew how to _____ nuts.

13.–14. She would _____ have a _____ dollar than a dollar bill.

15.–16. When we proofread, we correct the _____ errors as well as the _____ mistakes.

Solve the Analogies Write a spelling word to complete each analogy.

17. **Feel** is to **rough** as **taste** is to _____.

18. **Eat** is to **food** as **drink** is to _____.

19. **Street** is to **car** as **field** is to _____.

20. **See** is to **lightning** as **hear** is to _____.

Spelling and Writing

Proofread a Description

Six words are not spelled correctly in this description. Write those words correctly.

Reflections on a Lake

While camping in the forest, I got up early one day and wandered down to the lake. The sun was shining on the watter, turning it a beautiful silvor color. The wintir had been long. I was enjoying the warmth of spring.

As I watched the lake, I began to wunder about the fish that lived in it and the animals that drank from it. I was in no dangir from the wildlife, so I was not eger to return to camp. I would rather stay where I was.

Write a Description

Descriptive Writing

Write a description about something you experienced. Be sure to include

- where you were.
- the season of the year and the time of the day.
- what you saw and what you did.
- what thoughts you had.

Use as many spelling words as you can.

Proofread Your Writing During

Proofread your writing for spelling errors as part of the editing stage in the writing process. Be sure to check each word carefully. Use a dictionary to check spelling if you are not sure.

Writing Process

Prewriting

⇩

Drafting

⇩

Revising

⇩

Editing

⇩

Publishing

VOCABULARY CONNECTIONS

Strategy Words

Review Words: Schwa -r Spelled er, or

Write a word from the box for each clue.

colors	father	later	mother	never

1. It means "not ever."
2. It names a male parent.
3. It is an antonym of **earlier**.
4. Red, green, orange, and blue are these.
5. It names a female parent.

Preview Words: Schwa -r Spelled er, or

Write a word from the box to fill each blank in the story.

alligator	bother	differ	passenger	professor

An elderly ___6.___ was a ___7.___ aboard a small boat sailing down the Mississippi River. Everything seemed quiet and calm when suddenly he saw an ___8.___.

"Oh, it will not ___9.___ you. This animal is harmless," someone said.

The old man frowned. "I beg to ___10.___ with you," he replied. "If you don't mind, I will stay away from the water."

Review Words

1. _____
2. _____
3. _____
4. _____
5. _____

Preview Words

6. _____
7. _____
8. _____
9. _____
10. _____

Content Words

Math: Fractions

Write the word from the box that completes each sentence.

denominator	mixed	equally	numerator	fraction

1. This number—¼—is a _____.
2. The **one** in this fraction is the _____.
3. The **four** in this fraction is the _____.
4. This number—1¾—is called a _____ number.
5. The number **ten** can be divided _____ in half.

Social Studies: Geography

Write words from the box to complete the paragraph.

altitude	summit	crag	timber	evergreen

We climbed to the __6.__ of the mountain. At that high __7.__, we were above the __8.__ line. The view was magnificent. There, on a rugged __9.__, we stood and looked down at the tops of __10.__ trees.

Apply the Spelling Strategy

Circle the spelling of the final **schwa-r** sound in three of the Content Words you wrote.

Word Study

Words From Other Languages

The name for this reptile came from the Spanish term **el lagarto,** which means "the lizard." Write the Strategy Word that names the reptile.

Math: Fractions

1. _____
2. _____
3. _____
4. _____
5. _____

Social Studies: Geography

6. _____
7. _____
8. _____
9. _____
10. _____

Words From Other Languages

1. _____

-er

1. _____
2. _____
3. _____
4. _____
5. _____
6. _____
7. _____
8. _____
9. _____
10. _____

-est

11. _____
12. _____
13. _____
14. _____
15. _____
16. _____
17. _____
18. _____
19. _____
20. _____

Spelling and Thinking

READ THE SPELLING WORDS

1.	cuter	cuter	I think kittens are **cuter** than cats.
2.	nearer	nearer	The house is **nearer** than the store.
3.	thinnest	thinnest	That is the **thinnest** tree I ever saw!
4.	kinder	kinder	Mel seems **kinder** than Homer.
5.	easiest	easiest	Jogging is the **easiest** thing I do.
6.	funnier	funnier	That joke was **funnier** than the other.
7.	nearest	nearest	The Pells are our **nearest** neighbors.
8.	happier	happier	I could not be **happier** for you.
9.	kindest	kindest	She did the **kindest** deed of the week.
10.	thinner	thinner	My dog is **thinner** than before.
11.	quietest	quietest	Monday is the **quietest** weekday.
12.	funniest	funniest	That is the **funniest** program on TV.
13.	safer	safer	You will be **safer** wearing a helmet.
14.	quieter	quieter	Babies are **quieter** at night.
15.	safest	safest	This is the **safest** smoke alarm.
16.	quicker	quicker	The hand is **quicker** than the eye.
17.	cutest	cutest	She has the **cutest** puppy in town.
18.	easier	easier	Studying is **easier** when we are quiet.
19.	quickest	quickest	Which is the **quickest** way home?
20.	happiest	happiest	This is the **happiest** day of my life.

SORT THE SPELLING WORDS

1.–10. Write the spelling words with the **-er** suffix. Circle the suffix. Note if the spelling of the base word changes.

11.–20. Write the spelling words with the **-est** suffix. Circle the suffix. Note if the spelling of the base word changes.

REMEMBER THE SPELLING STRATEGY

Remember that suffixes such as **-er** and **-est** are added to the ends of words to make new words: **kind, kinder, kindest**.

Spelling ᵃⁿᵈ Vocabulary

Word Meanings

Write the correct form of the underlined word in each sentence.

1. We are the <u>quiet</u> of all the students in the school.
2. A whisper is <u>quiet</u> than a screech.
3. That was the <u>quick</u> fire drill of the three we had.
4. Beth is <u>quick</u> than the runner behind her.
5. Of all the ways to play the game, this is the <u>safe</u> way.

Phonics

Write the spelling word that does not belong in each group.

6. safest, funnier, nearest, quietest
7. safer, easier, kinder, cutest
8. safer, quickest, nearest, funniest

Antonyms

Write the spelling word that is the antonym of each word.

9. farther
10. thickest
11. meanest
12. hardest
13. thicker
14. saddest

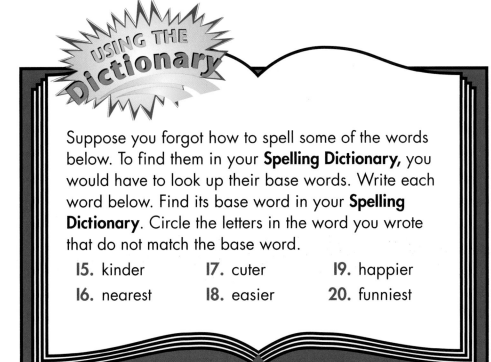

USING THE Dictionary

Suppose you forgot how to spell some of the words below. To find them in your **Spelling Dictionary,** you would have to look up their base words. Write each word below. Find its base word in your **Spelling Dictionary**. Circle the letters in the word you wrote that do not match the base word.

15. kinder
16. nearest
17. cuter
18. easier
19. happier
20. funniest

Spelling ᴬⁿᵈ Reading

cuter	nearer	thinnest	kinder	easiest
funnier	nearest	happier	kindest	thinner
quietest	funniest	safer	quieter	safest
quicker	cutest	easier	quickest	happiest

Replace the Words   Write a spelling word to replace each underlined group of words.

1. Your cat is <u>more cute</u> than mine.
2. You drew the <u>most cute</u> picture of all.
3. You are the <u>most kind</u> person I have ever met.
4. Her comic book is <u>more funny</u> than mine.
5. Here is the <u>most thin</u> wire I could find.
6. Mrs. Crosby is <u>more happy</u> working outside the house than in it.
7. Your house is <u>more near</u> the school than mine.
8. The crosswalk is the <u>most safe</u> place to cross the street.
9. Use the <u>more thin</u> board for the sign.
10. The library is the <u>most quiet</u> room in the school.

Complete the Sentences   Write a spelling word to complete each sentence.

11. Wearing a seat belt while riding in a car is _____ than riding without one.
12. I find math to be _____ than science.
13. Crickets are _____ in the daytime than at night.
14. The baby smiles and acts _____ when he is being held.
15. It would be _____ to say nothing than to say something mean.
16. The _____ library is three blocks from here.
17. That was the _____ joke I have ever heard!
18. We are in no hurry, so we do not need to go the _____ way.
19. That test was easy. In fact, it was the _____ test I ever took.
20. Sending this message by e-mail is _____ than sending a letter, which will take at least a day to arrive.

Replace the Words

1. _____
2. _____
3. _____
4. _____
5. _____
6. _____
7. _____
8. _____
9. _____
10. _____

Complete the Sentences

11. _____
12. _____
13. _____
14. _____
15. _____
16. _____
17. _____
18. _____
19. _____
20. _____

Spelling and Writing

Proofread Instructions

Six words are not spelled correctly in these instructions. Write those words correctly.

How to Enjoy Backyard Camping

The qwickest way to get started is to set up a tent in your backyard. Pick a spot nearist the house if you feel you will be happyier within shouting distance of your parents. The safist place is a level area away from tree branches that could fall during a storm.

To make eating easer, stock the tent with goodies. Add two sleeping bags, a flashlight, and your funniest books.

Now invite a friend. This could be your happyest experience as you eat, chat, and read.

Proofreading Marks

≡	Make a capital.
/	Make a small letter.
∧	Add something.
ℰ	Take out something.
⊙	Add a period.
⌗	New paragraph
SP	Spelling error

Write Instructions

Expository Writing

Write instructions to tell someone how to do something. Be sure to include

- a brief description of the activity.
- step-by-step instructions.
- the advantages of doing as instructed.
- safety warnings, if necessary.
- comfort hints.

Use as many spelling words as you can.

Writing Process

Prewriting
⇩
Drafting
⇩
Revising
⇩
Editing
⇩
Publishing

Proofread Your Writing During Editing

Proofread your writing for spelling errors as part of the editing stage in the writing process. Be sure to check each word carefully. Use a dictionary to check spelling if you are not sure.

VOCABULARY CONNECTIONS

Review Words

1. _____
2. _____
3. _____
4. _____
5. _____

Preview Words

6. _____
7. _____
8. _____
9. _____
10. _____

Review Words: Suffixes -er, -est

Write the words from the box to complete the paragraph.

closer	hotter	reddest	sharper	widest

We were crossing the __1.__ desert I had ever seen. The sun above us was the biggest, __2.__, and hottest I had experienced. The wind grew __3.__, hurling sand particles like knives against our skin. The __4.__ we got to our destination, the __5.__ the temperature seemed to get. Would we ever make it alive?

Preview Words: Suffixes -er, -est

Read the words in the box. Write each word to complete the patterns below.

calmest	slimmer	slimmest	sunnier	wiser

wise, __6.__, wisest

calm, calmer, __7.__

sunny, __8.__, sunniest

slim, __9.__, __10.__

Content Words

Language Arts: Cities

Write the word from the box that fits each clue.

dense	smog	noise	taxicab	skyline

1. smoke + fog
2. a ride for hire
3. thick
4. an outline of buildings against the sky
5. the opposite of **quiet**

Social Studies: Ranching

Write the word from the box that matches each definition.

auction	livestock	barn	ranch	corral

6. animals on a farm
7. a pen for horses
8. a sale in which people bid
9. a large farm with animals such as horses and cows
10. a home for cattle

Apply the Spelling Strategy

Circle the Content Word you wrote that is the base word for the words **denser** and **densest**.

Compound Words

A **compound word** is made of two or more smaller words. For example, the compound word **skyline** is made of the words **sky** and **line**. Write the Content Word that is a compound word for a kind of transportation.

Language Arts: Cities
1. _____
2. _____
3. _____
4. _____
5. _____

Social Studies: Ranching
6. _____
7. _____
8. _____
9. _____
10. _____

Compound Words
1. _____

consonant cluster

1. _____
2. _____
3. _____
4. _____
5. _____
6. _____

single consonant

7. _____
8. _____
9. _____
10. _____
11. _____
12. _____
13. _____
14. _____
15. _____
16. _____
17. _____
18. _____
19. _____
20. _____

Spelling and Thinking

READ THE SPELLING WORDS

1.	lone	_lone_	There was a **lone** clerk in the store.
2.	break	_break_	Lift but do not **break** the cover.
3.	waist	_waist_	Around his **waist** he wore a belt.
4.	passed	_passed_	We **passed** a school crossing.
5.	sore	_sore_	I hiked until my feet were **sore**.
6.	cellar	_cellar_	In the **cellar** was an old chest.
7.	roll	_roll_	Would you like a muffin or a **roll**?
8.	died	_died_	The flower **died** from lack of water.
9.	past	_past_	My father drove **past** your house.
10.	steak	_steak_	He likes his **steak** well-done.
11.	role	_role_	What **role** did he play in the movie?
12.	steel	_steel_	Aluminum is lighter than **steel**.
13.	loan	_loan_	They needed a **loan** to buy the house.
14.	dyed	_dyed_	The feather had been **dyed** yellow.
15.	seller	_seller_	The buyer gave the **seller** money.
16.	brake	_brake_	Step on the **brake** to stop.
17.	soar	_soar_	Eagles **soar** across the sky.
18.	steal	_steal_	Do not **steal** or damage goods.
19.	stake	_stake_	A **stake** supports each plant.
20.	waste	_waste_	Recycling does not **waste** material.

SORT THE SPELLING WORDS

1.–6. Write the pairs of spelling words that begin with a consonant cluster and that are pronounced the same but have different spellings and meanings.

7.–20. Write the pairs of spelling words that begin with a single consonant and that are pronounced the same but have different spellings and meanings.

REMEMBER THE SPELLING STRATEGY

Remember that **homophones** are words that sound the same but have different spellings and meanings: **roll** and **role**.

Spelling and Vocabulary

Word Meanings

Write the spelling word that goes with each meaning.

1. without company; by itself or oneself
2. a slice of beef
3. the middle part of the body
4. colored with dye
5. the part played by an actor
6. earlier than the present time
7. to come apart

Homophones

Write the spelling word that is a homophone for each word.

8. break
9. role
10. lone
11. past

12. dyed
13. stake
14. waist

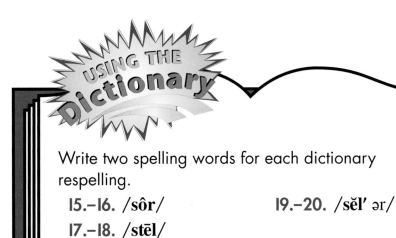

USING THE Dictionary

Write two spelling words for each dictionary respelling.

15.–16. /sôr/

19.–20. /sĕl′ ər/

17.–18. /stēl/

◆ ◆ ◆

Dictionary Check Be sure to check the respellings in your **Spelling Dictionary**.

Word Meanings
1.
2.
3.
4.
5.
6.
7.

Homophones
8.
9.
10.
11.
12.
13.
14.

Using the Dictionary
15.
16.
17.
18.
19.
20.

lone	break	waist	passed	sore
cellar	roll	died	past	steak
role	steel	loan	dyed	seller
brake	soar	steal	stake	waste

Choose the Homophones

1.

2.

3.

4.

5.

6.

7.

8.

9.

10.

11.

12.

Complete the Sentences

13.

14.

15.

16.

17.

18.

19.

20.

Choose the Homophones Choose the correct homophone for each sentence.

1. Please pass me a (roll, role) to eat.
2. Look at those seagulls (soar, sore) over the waves.
3. We try not to (waist, waste) the paper.
4. We need one more (steak, stake) to secure this tent.
5. She is playing the (roll, role) of the princess in the school play.
6. These paintings are on (lone, loan) from the museum.
7. Pele's knee was (sore, soar) after he fell.
8. He ate the soup before the (steak, stake).
9. A (lone, loan) horse stood in the field.
10. Please (brake, break) the seal to open the jar.
11. The dress with the black belt at the (waste, waist) looks nice.
12. When I go sledding, I use my foot as a (break, brake).

Complete the Sentences Write a homophone pair to complete each sentence.

13.–14. I remember that on our _____ trips we _____ that farmhouse.
15.–16. Why would anyone want to _____ a truckload of _____?
17.–18. The _____ showed us what was for sale in her _____.
19.–20. The flower _____ when the florist _____ it green.

Spelling and Writing

 **Proofread a Postcard**

Six words are not spelled correctly on this postcard. Write those words correctly.

Hi Folks,

   Greetings from the passed. I'm in historic Williamstown, where a plate of stake and eggs once cost a few cents. We pay more than that today for a buttered role. I may need a lone from you when I get back, since my waist is bigger than my wallet. But, seriously, I'm having fun, although my feet are soar from walking. This was a great brake from my studies. See you soon.

                    Love,
                    Ted

Proofreading Marks

☰ Make a capital.

／ Make a small letter.

∧ Add something.

ℓ Take out something.

⊙ Add a period.

⌗ New paragraph

🆂🅿 Spelling error

 Write a Postcard — *Narrative Writing*

Write a postcard about a place you have visited or can imagine. Be sure to mention

- where you are.
- what you have seen.
- what you have been doing.
- what you like or dislike about your trip.

Use as many spelling words as you can.

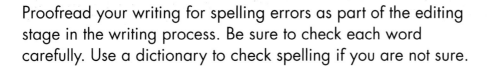 **Proofread Your Writing During** ▶ Editing

Proofread your writing for spelling errors as part of the editing stage in the writing process. Be sure to check each word carefully. Use a dictionary to check spelling if you are not sure.

Writing Process

Prewriting

Drafting

Revising

Editing

Publishing

VOCABULARY CONNECTIONS

Strategy Words

Review Words

1. _____

2. _____

3. _____

4. _____

5. _____

Preview Words

6. _____

7. _____

8. _____

9. _____

10. _____

Review Words: Homophones

Write words from the box to complete this paragraph about the Santos family.

| its | it's | there | their | they're |

The Santos family has helped the school for years. I think ___1.___ time to honor ___2.___ good works. I know ___3.___ going to be surprised when they get ___4.___ and see what we have planned. I am going to present them with a trophy and read ___5.___ inscription to the audience.

Preview Words: Homophones

Write the word from the box that fits each clue.

| capital | capitol | vain | vane | vein |

6. It carries blood to the heart.

7. It tells what kind of letter begins a sentence.

8. It is on top of many buildings and shows which way the wind is moving.

9. It is an antonym of **modest**.

10. It is a building in which a state legislature meets and decides on laws.

Content Words

Art: On Canvas

Write the word from the box that solves each riddle.

landscape	print	painting	scene	pastel

1. I begin with **p** and am a soft, pale color.
2. I am made up of two words and show the outdoors.
3. I begin with **p** and am a copy of a picture.
4. I am a little word, but I can be a big picture.
5. I begin with **p** and am made with brushes.

Language Arts: Word Play

Write words from the box to replace the underlined words.

toot	trap	loop	sees	level

6. We tried to <u>catch</u> the mouse.
7. Once we got down to <u>flat</u> ground, the walking was easier.
8. The train began to <u>sound its whistle</u> as it neared town.
9. He <u>views</u> the plane coming in.
10. The electrician took a <u>coil</u> of wire from her toolbox.

Apply the Spelling Strategy

Circle the Content Word you wrote that is a homophone for **seen**. Underline the Content Word you wrote that is a homophone for **seas**.

Writer's Tip

Good writers need to use words correctly when they write. The word **their** is a possessive word and means that something belongs to **them**. Write the Strategy Word that is often confused with **their** and means "they are."

Art: On Canvas

1. _____
2. _____
3. _____
4. _____
5. _____

Language Arts: Word Play

6. _____
7. _____
8. _____
9. _____
10. _____

Writer's Tip

1. _____

Assessment and Review

Assessment — Units 19–23

Each Assessment Word in the box fits one of the spelling strategies you have studied over the past five weeks. Read the spelling strategies. Then write each Assessment Word under the unit number it fits.

Unit 19

1.–6. The second syllable in some words ends in **le**.

Unit 20

7.–8. Words often end with **le** or **en**. Final **en** usually means "to make" or "to become."

Unit 21

9.–12. The **schwa-r** sound is spelled in different ways: **er** in **water** and **or** in **major**.

Unit 22

13.–16. Suffixes such as **-er** and **-est** are added to the ends of words to make new words: **kind, kinder, kindest**.

Unit 23

17.–20. **Homophones** are words that sound the same but have different spellings and meanings.

paddle
driven
heir
janitor
driest
trimmer
clever
handle
forever
aisle
saddle
dozen
juggle
sunniest
candle
throne
isle
anger
humble
smaller

Unit 19
1.
2.
3.
4.
5.
6.

Unit 20
7.
8.

Unit 21
9.
10.
11.
12.

Unit 22
13.
14.
15.
16.

Unit 23
17.
18.
19.
20.

 **Review** Unit 19: Final le

middle	sample	simple	single	cattle
jungle	tickle	battle	bottle	settle

These spelling words are missing letters. Write the spelling words.

1. j __ n __ le
2. cat __ __ e
3. s __ n __ le
4. bo __ __ le
5. ti __ __ le

6. mi __ dl __
7. __ et __ le
8. sam __ __ e
9. ba __ tl __
10. si __ p __ e

 **Review** Unit 20: Final le, Final en

moisten	example	fasten	trouble	brighten
harden	table	lighten	darken	double

Write the spelling word that completes each sentence.

11. Drink some water to _____ your mouth.
12. Put four chairs around the _____.
13. Pull the shades down to _____ the room.
14. The sailor will _____ the boat to the dock with rope.
15. We will need to _____ the box of books before I can carry it.
16. The coach's hard work set a good _____ for his team.
17. Cold weather caused the water to _____ into ice.
18. We are having _____ with our television.
19. The morning sun began to _____ the room.
20. If you _____ five, you will get ten.

Unit 19

1. _____
2. _____
3. _____
4. _____
5. _____
6. _____
7. _____
8. _____
9. _____
10. _____

Unit 20

11. _____
12. _____
13. _____
14. _____
15. _____
16. _____
17. _____
18. _____
19. _____
20. _____

Unit 21

1.

2.

3.

4.

5.

6.

7.

8.

9.

10.

Unit 22

11.

12.

13.

14.

15.

16.

17.

18.

19.

20.

Review — Unit 21: Schwa-r er, or

| together | tractor | whether | wonder | either |
| water | rather | winter | neither | silver |

Write a spelling word for each clue.

1. It is an antonym for **apart**.
2. It begins with a **long e** sound spelled **ei**.
3. Add one letter to your answer for number 2.
4. You will find one of these on most farms.
5. Change one letter in **gather** to make this word.
6. It comes before spring.
7. A homophone for this word is **weather**.
8. Use this with soap.
9. The word **won** can be found in this word.
10. Some coins contain this.

Review — Unit 22: Suffixes -er, -est

| cuter | easier | funniest | quietest | kindest |
| safest | happier | nearer | kinder | nearest |

Write the spelling word that completes each group of words.

11. happy, ____, happiest
12. near, nearer, ____
13. safe, safer, ____
14. funny, funnier, ____
15. kind, ____, kindest
16. cute, ____, cutest
17. kind, kinder, ____
18. easy, ____, easiest
19. quiet, quieter, ____
20. near, ____, nearest

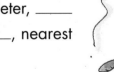

Review — Unit 23: Homophones

| break | past | steel | waste | roll |
| passed | brake | waist | role | steal |

Write the homophone that completes each sentence.

1. We (passed, past) the school on our way to the game.
2. In the (passed, past), it took weeks to cross the ocean.
3. One should never (waist, waste) food.
4. The cook tied an apron around her (waist, waste).
5. If you drop the glass, it will surely (brake, break).
6. Use the (brake, break) to stop your bicycle.
7. Heavy trucks cross the river on a (steal, steel) bridge.
8. Put your money where no one can (steal, steel) it.
9. What is your (role, roll) in the play?
10. We watched the huge snowball (role, roll) down the hill.

 **Spelling Study Strategy**

Sorting by Endings

One good way to practice spelling is to place words into groups according to some spelling pattern. Here is a way to practice some of the words you studied in the past few weeks.

1. Make five columns on a large piece of paper or on the chalkboard.

2. Write one of the following words at the top of each column: **apple, soften, sailor, power,** and **simplest.**

3. Have a partner choose a spelling word from Units 19 through 22 and say it aloud.

4. Write the spelling word under the word with the same ending.

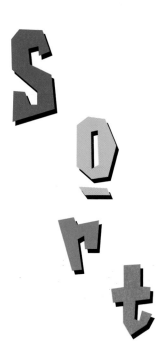

149

Grammar, Usage, and Mechanics

Pronouns

Personal pronouns include the words **I, me, you, we, us, he, him, she, her, they, them,** and **it**. These words can be used in place of names for people and things.

Ida is here. **She** came early.

Possessive pronouns include the words **my, your, his, her, its, their,** and **our**. These pronouns show ownership.

Call **Guy**. **His** tickets are here.

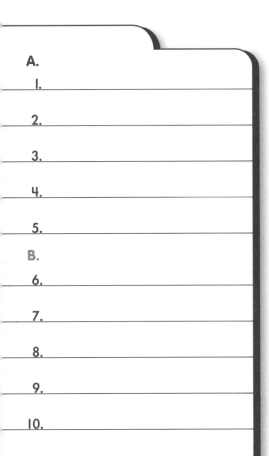

A.

1.

2.

3.

4.

5.

B.

6.

7.

8.

9.

10.

A. Write the boldfaced word in each sentence that is a pronoun.

   1. The bird **is** carrying food to **its** babies.

   2. **The** players are tired, so **they** want to stop.

   3. Bart and **he** are co-captains **of** the men's team.

   4. The lifeguard **put** sunscreen on **her** nose.

   5. The vase of **colorful** flowers made **their** table look pretty.

B. Replace the underlined word or words with pronouns from the box.

them	he	we	its	their	she	our

   6. All the cattle are waiting for <u>the cattle's</u> water.

   7. Eric is late, so <u>Eric</u> may lose this seat.

   8. Did you bring the lunches that <u>you and I</u> packed?

   9. Mom is still at work, but <u>Mom</u> will be home soon.

  10. The playful kitten tumbled around with <u>the kitten's</u> ball of yarn.

WORKSHOP

Circle and Check

Good writers always proofread their writing for spelling errors. Here's a strategy that you should try to proofread your papers.

Instead of reading your whole paper, look at just the first three or four words. Are they spelled correctly? If you are sure that they are correct, go on and check the next three or four words. If you are unsure of a word's spelling, circle the word and keep going. Look at your whole paper this way—one small group of words at a time.

When you are done looking, get a dictionary and check the spelling of all the circled words. Looking up the words later keeps you focused on the task of proofreading. It's also faster to look up several words at once. Try it!

Electronic Spelling

Spell Checkers and Similar Words

A spell checker can help you with spelling, but it can't do the whole job. Many times writers confuse two words. They write one when they mean to write another. For example, don't **axis** and **axes** sound alike? Yet the earth does not revolve around an axes. Axes cut down trees.

Spell checkers are not as smart as you are. They can't tell which word belongs in a sentence. You need to know the spelling of words that are easy to confuse.

Practice on the sentences below. Find the misspelled word in each sentence. Write it correctly.

1. The artist drew a picture of an angle with wings.
2. Travelers in the dessert must carry plenty of water.
3. You may chose any seat on the bus.
4. Witch jacket did you bring?
5. Please weight until Leslie can join us.
6. Josh past right by us on the way to school.

Electronic Spelling

1. _____
2. _____
3. _____
4. _____
5. _____
6. _____

Spelling and Thinking

READ THE SPELLING WORDS

will, not, or us

1.	he'd	*he'd*	We thought **he'd** been on vacation.
2.	you're	*you're*	When **you're** ready, let us know.
3.	wasn't	*wasn't*	I **wasn't** prepared for a storm.
4.	she'd	*she'd*	She said **she'd** call her friend.
5.	they'll	*they'll*	After dinner, **they'll** walk the dog.
6.	aren't	*aren't*	Why **aren't** you shopping with Mom?
7.	let's	*let's*	When we get tired, **let's** rest.
8.	I'd	*I'd*	He thought **I'd** know his address.
9.	she'll	*she'll*	If you play the piano, **she'll** sing.
10.	we've	*we've*	Did you know **we've** been calling you?
11.	you'd	*you'd*	If you had won, **you'd** know it.
12.	he'll	*he'll*	He said **he'll** tell what happened.
13.	I've	*I've*	I forgot to tell you that **I've** moved.
14.	hasn't	*hasn't*	The cat **hasn't** eaten yet.
15.	they'd	*they'd*	Each summer **they'd** visit each other.
16.	you'll	*you'll*	After I bat, **you'll** be up.
17.	haven't	*haven't*	Sorry, I **haven't** any change.
18.	we'll	*we'll*	If you want to see us, **we'll** visit you.
19.	you've	*you've*	Tell me when **you've** finished reading.
20.	hadn't	*hadn't*	I **hadn't** yet thought of a good plan.

SORT THE SPELLING WORDS

1.–11. Write the spelling words in which **will, not,** or **us** has been shortened.

12.–20. Write the spelling words in which **have, had, would,** or **are** has been shortened.

REMEMBER THE SPELLING STRATEGY

Remember that a **contraction** is a shortened form of two words: **you're** means **you are.** An apostrophe (') shows where letters have been left out.

---

will, not, or us

1. _____
2. _____
3. _____
4. _____
5. _____
6. _____
7. _____
8. _____
9. _____
10. _____
11. _____

have, had, would, or are

12. _____
13. _____
14. _____
15. _____
16. _____
17. _____
18. _____
19. _____
20. _____

Spelling ᴬⁿᵈ Vocabulary

Word Meanings

Write the spelling words that are contractions of these words.

1. I had *or* I would
2. let us
3. he will
4. he had *or* he would
5. we will
6. you are
7. I have
8. we have
9. they had *or* they would
10. she will

Opposites

Write the spelling word that means the opposite of the underlined word in each sentence.

11. Did you forget that we <u>had</u> bought our tickets?
12. I <u>have</u> ridden in a hot air balloon.
13. I could tell that this <u>was</u> your first ride.
14. We <u>are</u> afraid to ride in a helicopter.
15. This bus company <u>has</u> lost many suitcases.

Write the spelling word for each dictionary respelling.

16. /shēd/
17. /yo͞ol/ or /yo͝ol/
18. /yo͞ov/
19. /yo͞od/
20. /thāl/

◆ ◆ ◆

Dictionary Check Be sure to check your answer in the **Spelling Dictionary**.

Word Meanings
1.
2.
3.
4.
5.
6.
7.
8.
9.
10.

Opposites
11.
12.
13.
14.
15.

Using the Dictionary
16.
17.
18.
19.
20.

Complete the Sentences

1.
2.
3.
4.
5.
6.
7.
8.
9.
10.
11.
12.
13.
14.

Complete the Story

15.
16.
17.
18.
19.
20.

he'd	you're	wasn't	she'd	they'll
aren't	let's	I'd	she'll	we've
you'd	he'll	I've	hasn't	they'd
you'll	haven't	we'll	you've	hadn't

Complete the Sentences   Write the spelling words that best complete each sentence.

1.–2. Since you _____ been to the seashore, _____ have to ask directions.

3.–4. Sara says _____ find someone else to ride with if we _____ going.

5.–6. Jason's report card _____ arrived in the mail yet, so _____ have to go to the school to get it.

7.–8. Your grandmother would have written if _____ found the picture that _____ looking for.

9. In our class, _____ been studying early American explorers.

10. My parents were sure that they _____ forgotten their car keys.

11. Jesse and his sister say _____ be moving next week.

12.–13. We know _____ been waiting for us, but if you wait a little more, _____ both walk you home.

14. Our play is soon, so _____ practice our lines.

Complete the Story   Write the spelling word that fits in each blank in the story.

Our school held a costume party. The guests dressed as something __15.__ like to be. I guess __16.__ be surprised at how many people dressed as cats! One boy said that __17.__ love to be a cat because they sleep so much.

I think __18.__ rather be a fish. I love to swim, and __19.__ spent hours watching the fish in my tank. So I dressed as a goldfish. There __20.__ another fish at the party!

| I've |
| they'd |
| I'd |
| you'd |
| he'd |
| wasn't |

Spelling and Writing

Proofread a Letter

Six words are not spelled correctly in this letter of appeal. Write those words correctly.

Dear Paul,

    Why not consider joining our club? I think youd love it. So far weave got fourteen members, and I know they'ed like to include you. We'll play games, put on a play for our parents, and have holiday parties. Let's get together to talk about it when youve got the time.

    Mark is our president. He says he'l be glad to tell you more about our activities when your ready.

               Your pal,

               Jacob

Proofreading Marks

≡	Make a capital.
/	Make a small letter.
∧	Add something.
ℓ	Take out something.
⊙	Add a period.
⌗	New paragraph
SP	Spelling error

Write a Letter — Persuasive Writing

Write an appeal for money, members, or support for a group. Be sure to include

- what you want your reader to do or give.
- why the reader should do or give what you ask for.
- what the reader can expect to get in return.

Use as many spelling words as you can.

Writing Process

Prewriting

Drafting

Revising

Editing

Publishing

Proofread Your Writing During ▶ Editing

Proofread your writing for spelling errors as part of the editing stage in the writing process. Be sure to check each word carefully. Use a dictionary to check spelling if you are not sure.

VOCABULARY CONNECTIONS

Strategy Words

Review Words: Contractions

Write the word from the box that fits each definition or clue.

can't	didn't	doesn't	I'll	I'm

1. It means "not able to."
2. It combines a pronoun and the word **will**.
3. It combines a past tense verb with **not**.
4. It combines a pronoun and the word **am**.
5. It is the opposite of **does**.

Preview Words: Contractions

Write the word from the box that is the contraction for each pair of words.

couldn't	weren't	we'd	who's	who've

6. were not
7. who have
8. could not
9. we would *or* we had
10. who is

Review Words

1. _____
2. _____
3. _____
4. _____
5. _____

Preview Words

6. _____
7. _____
8. _____
9. _____
10. _____

WHO'S

Content Words

Language Arts: Parts of a Letter

Write words from the box to complete this paragraph about the parts of a letter.

closing	heading	envelope	signature	greeting

  To write and send a letter, you must first write the __1.__, which gives the date and your address. Then you write a __2.__, such as "Dear Friend." After you complete the body, where you write whatever you want, you add the __3.__ and your __4.__. Address and stamp the __5.__, and your letter is ready to send.

Social Studies: Civics

Write the word from the box that matches each clue.

election	taxes	govern	vote	statehood

6. what we do when we cast our ballot
7. what we pay to support the government
8. what territories had to apply for
9. what elected officials do
10. what we hold to choose officials

Word Study

Related Words

Words such as **governor, government,** and **governess** are related by the word part **gov**. Write the Content Word that is also related to these words.

Language Arts: Parts of a Letter
1. _____
2. _____
3. _____
4. _____
5. _____

Social Studies: Civics
6. _____
7. _____
8. _____
9. _____
10. _____

Related Words
1. _____

Spelling and Thinking

READ THE SPELLING WORDS

1.	unlucky	*unlucky*	What an **unlucky** choice of seats!
2.	review	*review*	Let us **review** what we learned.
3.	preschool	*preschool*	The young child is in **preschool**.
4.	unfair	*unfair*	He took **unfair** advantage of us.
5.	reheat	*reheat*	They will **reheat** the vegetables.
6.	prepay	*prepay*	You must **prepay** your trip.
7.	untie	*untie*	I cannot **untie** the knot.
8.	recover	*recover*	We will **recover** the lost sock.
9.	preview	*preview*	They saw a **preview** of the movie.
10.	unhappy	*unhappy*	The lost child is **unhappy**.
11.	rewrite	*rewrite*	Please **rewrite** the letter in ink.
12.	pretest	*pretest*	A **pretest** prepares us for the test.
13.	rebuild	*rebuild*	Will you **rebuild** the damaged shed?
14.	uncover	*uncover*	We have to **uncover** the pan.
15.	recheck	*recheck*	Let me **recheck** that answer.
16.	unlock	*unlock*	Use this key to **unlock** the door.
17.	preheat	*preheat*	We **preheat** the oven before baking.
18.	unsafe	*unsafe*	Biking without a helmet is **unsafe**.
19.	reread	*reread*	I must **reread** the instructions.
20.	unpack	*unpack*	They will **unpack** after their trip.

SORT THE SPELLING WORDS

1.–8. Write the spelling words with the **un-** prefix.

9.–15. Write the spelling words with the **re-** prefix.

16.–20. Write the spelling words with the **pre-** prefix.

REMEMBER THE SPELLING STRATEGY

Remember that prefixes, like **un-**, **re-**, and **pre-**, are added to the beginnings of words to make new words: **pack, unpack; write, rewrite; pay, prepay**.

un-
1.
2.
3.
4.
5.
6.
7.
8.

re-
9.
10.
11.
12.
13.
14.
15.

pre-
16.
17.
18.
19.
20.

Spelling and Vocabulary

Word Meanings

The prefix **un-** means "not." The prefix **re-** means "again." The prefix **pre-** means "before." Write the spelling word that fits each definition.

1. to cover again
2. to look at before
3. to not be lucky
4. to read again
5. to heat beforehand
6. not fair
7. to build again
8. to pay beforehand
9. to write again
10. a place for children to go before they go to school
11. to check again

Synonyms

Write the spelling word that is a synonym for each word.

12. unlace
13. dangerous
14. reveal
15. sad
16. study
17. open

USING THE Dictionary

Guide words in a dictionary help you find a word easily. If the word you are looking for belongs alphabetically between a pair of guide words, then the word belongs on that page. Write the spelling word that would be found on the page in your **Spelling Dictionary** with these guide words.

18. player • print
19. record • ridge
20. Tues. • useless

unlucky	review	preschool	unfair	reheat
prepay	untie	recover	preview	unhappy
rewrite	pretest	rebuild	uncover	recheck
unlock	preheat	unsafe	reread	unpack

Complete the Sequences   A word in each series is missing a prefix. Write the spelling word to complete the sequence.

1. to wrap, to bake, to _____cover, to eat
2. to pack, to travel, to _____pack
3. to lock, to travel, to return, to _____lock
4. to cook, to cool, to _____heat, to eat
5. to build, to fall apart, to _____build
6. to put on, to tie, to _____tie, to take off
7. to write, to proofread, to _____write
8. to catch a cold, to be ill, to _____cover

Replace the Words   Replace the underlined words with a spelling word with the same meaning.

9. I will <u>read</u> those directions <u>again</u>.
10. Please <u>look over and study</u> your notes again.
11. I will <u>pay ahead</u> for the book I ordered.
12. I have been <u>having bad luck</u> lately.
13. I am going to <u>check</u> my answers <u>again</u>.

Complete the Sentences   Write the spelling word that best completes each sentence.

14. The cook will _____ the oven before he bakes the potatoes.
15. We are going to _____ our home movies before we show them to friends.
16. My four-year-old brother goes to _____.
17. What was your score on the spelling _____?
18. I will be _____ when my best friend moves.
19. Using a tool before you are taught how to use it is _____.
20. It is _____ to borrow a book and not return it.

Complete the Sequences

1. _____
2. _____
3. _____
4. _____
5. _____
6. _____
7. _____
8. _____

Replace the Words

9. _____
10. _____
11. _____
12. _____
13. _____

Complete the Sentences

14. _____
15. _____
16. _____
17. _____
18. _____
19. _____
20. _____

Spelling and Writing

Proofread a List

Six words are not spelled correctly in this list. Write those words correctly.

> ## Things to Do This Week
>
> 1. Study for the math preatest.
> 2. Make a list of unnsafe activities for social studies.
> 3. Rereed *Everywhere*, revue plot, and prepare book report.
> 4. Finish writing story *Unlucky Me* by Wednesday.
> 5. Help Dad rebild doghouse this weekend.
> 6. Recheck my school supplies.
> 7. Ask Mom for money to preapay this week's lunches.

Proofreading Marks

≡ Make a capital.

/ Make a small letter.

∧ Add something.

℘ Take out something.

⊙ Add a period.

⌗ New paragraph

(SP) Spelling error

Write a List

Narrative Writing

Write a list of things to do. Be sure to include

- what time period your list covers.
- what you want to remember.
- when something must be done.
- why you need to do something or buy some items.

Use as many spelling words as you can.

Proofread Your Writing During →

Proofread your writing for spelling errors as part of the editing stage in the writing process. Be sure to check each word carefully. Use a dictionary to check spelling if you are not sure.

Writing Process

Prewriting

⇩

Drafting

⇩

Revising

⇩

Editing

⇩

Publishing

VOCABULARY CONNECTIONS

Strategy Words

Review Words

1. _____
2. _____
3. _____
4. _____
5. _____

Preview Words

6. _____
7. _____
8. _____
9. _____
10. _____

Review Words: Prefixes un-, re-, pre-

Write the word from the box that fits each description.

preslice	preplan	regroup
rename		unkind

1. It means "to group again."
2. It is an antonym of **kind**.
3. It means "to plan ahead of time."
4. It means "to slice beforehand."
5. It means "to name again."

Preview Words: Prefixes un-, re-, pre-

Write a word from the box to complete each sentence.

prehistoric	prerecorded	reform
refresh		unknown

6. Although the word was _____ to me, I figured out the meaning from the prefix and the base word.
7. The concert was _____ and then broadcast on the radio.
8. I do not remember your address; please _____ my memory.
9. Although we have no written records, fossils and other materials give us data about _____ times.
10. I know I keep my room messy, but I promise to _____ next year.

Content Words

Language Arts: Handwriting

Write words from the box to complete the paragraph.

| alphabet | letters | cursive | strokes | handwriting |

Our ___1.___ is made up of twenty-six ___2.___. Children usually learn ___3.___ ___4.___ after they have mastered printing. In this second kind of writing, the end ___5.___ of letters are connected to the beginning of the next ones.

Math: Addition

Write the word that completes each of these sentences.

| addend | facts | addition | total | arithmetic |

6. We use _____ to solve this problem: 5 + 4 = 9.
7. The 5 in this problem is an _____.
8. The _____ of the two numbers is 9.
9. 2 × 3 = 6 and 2 × 4 = 8 are multiplication _____.
10. Questions 6 through 9 refer to _____ problems.

Apply the Spelling Strategy

Circle the one Content Word you wrote to which you could add the prefix **re-** or **pre-**.

Word Study

Antonyms

Antonyms are words with opposite meanings. **Addition** and **subtraction** are antonyms. Write the Strategy Word that is an antonym for **famous**.

Language Arts: Handwriting
1. _____
2. _____
3. _____
4. _____
5. _____

Math: Addition
6. _____
7. _____
8. _____
9. _____
10. _____

Antonyms
1. _____

Spelling and Thinking

just add -er

1. _____
2. _____
3. _____
4. _____
5. _____
6. _____
7. _____
8. _____
9. _____
10. _____
11. _____
12. _____
13. _____
14. _____
15. _____
16. _____
17. _____

drop final e and add -er

18. _____
19. _____
20. _____

READ THE SPELLING WORDS

1.	farmer	*farmer*	The **farmer** milked his cows.
2.	skater	*skater*	She was judged the best **skater**.
3.	painter	*painter*	The **painter** stirred his paint.
4.	camper	*camper*	We met a **camper** in the forest.
5.	listener	*listener*	Drake is a good **listener**.
6.	banker	*banker*	We got a loan from the **banker**.
7.	owner	*owner*	Who is the **owner** of this farm?
8.	learner	*learner*	A good **learner** pays attention.
9.	hiker	*hiker*	Each **hiker** wore a backpack.
10.	catcher	*catcher*	The **catcher** signaled to the pitcher.
11.	speaker	*speaker*	That **speaker** was very entertaining.
12.	climber	*climber*	A rock **climber** needs good equipment.
13.	player	*player*	The team captain is a good **player**.
14.	reader	*reader*	This book will please any **reader**.
15.	baker	*baker*	Thanks to the **baker** for this bread.
16.	dreamer	*dreamer*	He is a **dreamer** who has great ideas!
17.	reporter	*reporter*	The **reporter** covered the fire.
18.	builder	*builder*	The house was planned by the **builder**.
19.	singer	*singer*	Each **singer** used the microphone.
20.	leader	*leader*	He is the **leader** of the band.

SORT THE SPELLING WORDS

1.–17. Write the spelling words in which the **-er** suffix is added without changing the base word.

18.–20. Write the spelling words in which the final **e** is dropped from the base word before the **-er** suffix is added.

REMEMBER THE SPELLING STRATEGY

Remember that the suffix **-er** means "one who." A **player** is "one who plays." A **singer** is "one who sings."

Spelling and Vocabulary

Word Meanings

The suffix **-er** can change a verb to a noun that means "someone who does something." Add the **-er** suffix to each underlined verb to write a noun that is a spelling word.

1. I often <u>hike</u> in the woods. I am a _____.

2. Missy will <u>play</u> goalie on a hockey team. She will be a _____.

3. I <u>listen</u> carefully. I am a good _____.

4. Walter likes to <u>speak</u> to large groups of people. He is a _____.

5. My cousin wants to <u>report</u> on sports for a newspaper. He wants to be a _____.

6. Mr. Brown can <u>farm</u> both his land and his father's. He is a successful _____.

Word Completion

Write a spelling word by adding the suffix that means "one who does something" to each of the following base words.

7. climb   **9.** own   **11.** dream

8. lead   **10.** paint   **12.** read

USING THE Dictionary

Write the spelling word for each of the following dictionary respellings.

13. /kăm′ pər/   **17.** /bā′ kər/

14. /băng′ kər/   **18.** /skā′ tər/

15. /sĭng′ ər/   **19.** /bĭl′ dər/

16. /kăch′ ər/   **20.** /lûr′ nər/

Word Meanings

1. _____

2. _____

3. _____

4. _____

5. _____

6. _____

Word Completion

7. _____

8. _____

9. _____

10. _____

11. _____

12. _____

Using the Dictionary

13. _____

14. _____

15. _____

16. _____

17. _____

18. _____

19. _____

20. _____

farmer	skater	painter	camper	listener
banker	owner	learner	hiker	catcher
speaker	climber	player	reader	baker
dreamer	reporter	builder	singer	leader

Solve the Riddles

1.
2.
3.
4.
5.
6.
7.
8.
9.
10.

Complete the Sentences

11.
12.
13.
14.
15.
16.
17.
18.
19.
20.

Solve the Riddles   Write the spelling word that solves each riddle.

1. I make fresh bread and rolls each day. Who am I?
2. I spend many nights in a tent. Who am I?
3. I study hard and learn my lessons. Who am I?
4. I am a box that sound comes from. What am I?
5. I take care of my animals and plow my fields. Who am I?
6. I spend all my spare time looking at words in books. Who am I?
7. I am looking for my lost dog. Who am I?
8. I see pictures in my sleep. Who am I?
9. I handle a lot of money every day. Who am I?
10. I go for long walks in the mountains. Who am I?

Complete the Sentences   Write a spelling word to complete each sentence.

11. A monkey is a natural tree ____.
12. The ____ captured the colors of the sunset.
13. She is a ____ on a baseball team.
14. Abraham Lincoln was a great ____.
15. That ____ is helping to put up the new shopping mall.
16. We went to the ice arena to watch the figure ____ perform.
17. A good ____ is as important as a good speaker.
18. The local television station sent its best news ____ to cover the mayor's speech.
19. She is a ____ with a beautiful soprano voice.
20. A pitcher and a ____ work together to strike out a batter.

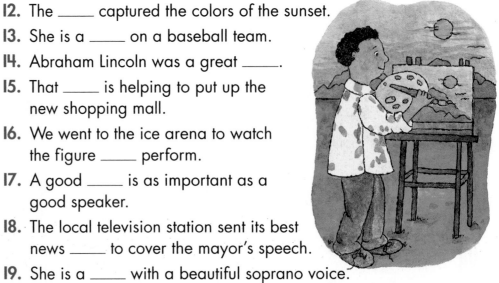

Spelling and Writing

Proofread a Description

Six words are not spelled correctly in this description. Write those words correctly.

A Lesson on Ice

No paintir could have produced such a colorful picture. No reporter could have imagined a more exciting show. Each skatr, wearing a splendid costume, glided onto the ice. The speeker roared the name of each star as he or she whipped around the arena, following the leeder of the group. The beautiful scene was the work of a dremer, and everyone in the audience became a leerner.

Write a Description

Descriptive Writing

Write a description of something you have seen. Be sure to include information such as

- where you were.
- what you saw.
- what you heard.
- how you felt.

Use as many spelling words as you can.

Writing Process

Prewriting
⬇
Drafting
⬇
Revising
⬇
 Editing
⬇
Publishing

Proofread Your Writing During Editing

Proofread your writing for spelling errors as part of the editing stage in the writing process. Be sure to check each word carefully. Use a dictionary to check spelling if you are not sure.

VOCABULARY CONNECTIONS

Strategy Words

Review Words

1. _____
2. _____
3. _____
4. _____
5. _____

Preview Words

6. _____
7. _____
8. _____
9. _____
10. _____

Review Words: Suffix -er

Write the word from the box that uses **-er** in each of the following ways.

ladder	teacher	redder	sadder	wider

1. The base word and the suffix **-er** mean "one who teaches."
2. The base word and the suffix **-er** mean "more sad."
3. The base word and the suffix **-er** mean "more red."
4. The base word and the suffix **-er** mean "more wide."
5. The **-er** is not a suffix. It is part of a word that means "a structure to climb on."

Preview Words: Suffix -er

Write the word from the box that fits each meaning.

commander	gardener	homemaker
pitcher	publisher	

6. one who pitches
7. one who gardens
8. one who publishes
9. one who commands
10. one who keeps or makes a home

Content Words

Social Studies: Pioneers

Write the word from the box that fits each description.

barter	hunter	blanket	pelt	feast

1. an animal skin
2. one who hunts
3. to trade without money
4. a cover; a quilt
5. a large meal

Science: Joints

Write the word from the box that completes each sentence.

elbow	socket	hinge	tendons	pivot

6. The _____ is the joint connecting the upper and lower arm.
7. Your jaw works like a _____.
8. When you turn on one foot, you _____.
9. An eye is set in a _____.
10. The muscles of your body are attached to the bones with _____.

Apply the Spelling Strategy

Circle the suffix that means "one who does something" in one of the Content Words you wrote.

Word Study

Word History

The old Greek word **klinein** meant "to incline." One of the Strategy Words comes from **klinein**. When you use this, you *lean* it against something. Write the Strategy Word.

Social Studies: Pioneers
1. _____
2. _____
3. _____
4. _____
5. _____

Science: Joints
6. _____
7. _____
8. _____
9. _____
10. _____

Word History
1. _____

-ful

1. _____
2. _____
3. _____
4. _____
5. _____
6. _____
7. _____
8. _____
9. _____
10. _____
11. _____
12. _____

-less

13. _____
14. _____
15. _____
16. _____
17. _____
18. _____
19. _____
20. _____

Spelling and Thinking

READ THE SPELLING WORDS

1.	joyful	*joyful*	She sang a **joyful,** happy song.
2.	helpless	*helpless*	We untangled the **helpless** butterfly.
3.	restful	*restful*	The quietness was **restful**.
4.	careless	*careless*	She tried not to be **careless**.
5.	useful	*useful*	A pen is a **useful** writing tool.
6.	thankless	*thankless*	Worry is a **thankless** activity.
7.	peaceful	*peaceful*	May your day be happy and **peaceful**.
8.	hopeless	*hopeless*	Finding the lost coin was **hopeless**.
9.	thankful	*thankful*	He is **thankful** for family and friends.
10.	cloudless	*cloudless*	The sky was **cloudless** and bright.
11.	powerful	*powerful*	Kindness is a **powerful** force.
12.	helpful	*helpful*	We try to be **helpful** at home.
13.	powerless	*powerless*	They felt **powerless** against the wind.
14.	careful	*careful*	Be **careful** not to slip on the tile.
15.	restless	*restless*	He was **restless** with nothing to do.
16.	wasteful	*wasteful*	Not recycling bottles is **wasteful**.
17.	cheerful	*cheerful*	We are **cheerful** most of the time.
18.	useless	*useless*	The toy is **useless** without a battery.
19.	playful	*playful*	Kittens are young, **playful** cats.
20.	thoughtful	*thoughtful*	The decision was a **thoughtful** one.

SORT THE SPELLING WORDS

1.–12. Write the spelling words with the suffix **-ful**.

13.–20. Write the spelling words with the suffix **-less**.

REMEMBER THE SPELLING STRATEGY

Remember that when you add **-ful** or **-less** to a word, you often do not need to change the spelling of the base word before adding the suffix: **help, helpful; rest, restless**.

Spelling and Vocabulary

Word Meanings

In each sentence, find and write a spelling word. It should describe the underlined word.

1. Tomorrow's party will be a joyful <u>celebration</u>.
2. JoAnn is a careful and hard-working <u>child</u>.
3. The <u>earthquake</u> was powerful enough to damage buildings.
4. Throwing away good food is a wasteful <u>act</u>.
5. The <u>people</u> were thankful for the rainfall.
6. <u>Humans</u> are powerless over the weather.
7. A <u>map</u> is useful when you take a long trip.
8. <u>People</u> who litter are careless.
9. She sent me a thoughtful <u>note</u> when I was sick.
10. My <u>teacher</u> is always helpful when I have a question.

Antonyms

Write the spelling word that is an antonym for each word below.

11. hopeful
12. calm
13. cheerless
14. cloudy
15. thankful
16. warlike
17. useful

USING THE Thesaurus

Write the following words. Beside each word, write the number of synonyms for it that are listed in your **Writing Thesaurus**.

18. restful
19. helpless
20. playful

◆ ◆ ◆

Thesaurus Check Be sure to check for synonyms in your **Writing Thesaurus**.

Word Meanings
1. _____
2. _____
3. _____
4. _____
5. _____
6. _____
7. _____
8. _____
9. _____
10. _____

Antonyms
11. _____
12. _____
13. _____
14. _____
15. _____
16. _____
17. _____

Using the Thesaurus
18. _____
19. _____
20. _____

joyful	helpless	restful	careless	useful
thankless	peaceful	hopeless	thankful	cloudless
powerful	helpful	powerless	careful	restless
wasteful	cheerful	useless	playful	thoughtful

Replace the Words Write the spelling word that is a synonym for each underlined word.

1. I am grateful that you offered to help.
2. I will never be a reckless driver.
3. A key without a lock is worthless.
4. Be cautious when crossing the street.
5. This flashlight may be handy tonight.
6. Although not ungrateful, she still refused my help.
7. He seemed to be impatient while he waited.
8. The shoppers were good-humored and friendly.
9. Without help the army was lacking the strength to attack.

Complete the Sentences Write the spelling word that best completes each sentence.

10. A thrifty person is not _____.
11. That nation will not wage war; it is a _____ country.
12. Sending a get-well card was very _____ of you.
13. The sky was clear and _____.
14. The lost climbers felt _____ until they saw the search plane.

Complete the Comparisons Choose a spelling word from the box that best completes each comparison.

15. A kitten with a ball is as _____ as a baby with a rattle.
16. The little lost puppy was as _____ as a newborn baby.
17. Your map was more _____ than mine.
18. The dinner was as _____ as a holiday celebration.
19. The engine in that machine is as _____ as the engine in a locomotive.
20. A ten-minute nap is not as _____ as a night's sleep.

helpless
restful
helpful
powerful
joyful
playful

Replace the Words
1.
2.
3.
4.
5.
6.
7.
8.
9.

Complete the Sentences
10.
11.
12.
13.
14.

Complete the Comparisons
15.
16.
17.
18.
19.
20.

Spelling and Writing

Proofread a Paragraph

Six words are not spelled correctly in this paragraph. Write those words correctly.

ANIMAL SHELTER

Last night we went to the animal shelter, and I got a plaiful white kitten. She was afraid of us at first, and she seemed so helples. But she soon learned that we were friendly and carefil, and she began to explore the house. We tried to keep her in the kitchen, but it was usless. She ran so fast! We were powerless to stop her. It was very late when she settled down for a restfull nap. The house was finally peacful again.

Proofreading Marks

≡ Make a capital.

/ Make a small letter.

∧ Add something.

℮ Take out something.

⊙ Add a period.

⌗ New paragraph

(SP) Spelling error

Write a Paragraph

Narrative Writing

Write a paragraph about getting a pet, either your own or someone else's. Try to include information about

- where the pet came from.
- how the pet acted at first.
- how you or the pet's owner felt.
- how the pet changed.

Use as many spelling words as you can.

Writing Process

Prewriting

⇩

Drafting

⇩

Revising

⇩

Proofread Your Writing During ➤ **Editing**

⇩

Publishing

Proofread your writing for spelling errors as part of the editing stage in the writing process. Be sure to check each word carefully. Use a dictionary to check spelling if you are not sure.

VOCABULARY CONNECTIONS

Strategy Words

Review Words

1. _____
2. _____
3. _____
4. _____
5. _____

Preview Words

6. _____
7. _____
8. _____
9. _____
10. _____

Review Words: Suffixes -ful, -less

Write the word from the box that fits each description.

airless	lawful	landless	loveless	hurtful

1. having no land
2. obeying the law
3. causing pain or injury
4. having no air
5. having no love

Preview Words: Suffixes -ful, -less

Write a word from the box to complete each sentence.

awful	beautiful	homeless	senseless	weightless

6. After the fire, the family was temporarily _____.
7. We saw a _____ sight as the sun disappeared over the ocean.
8. It is _____ to blame me for the windy and rainy weather.
9. The _____ astronauts floated around in their space capsule.
10. Because of delays and lost luggage, we had an _____ trip.

Content Words

Health: Injuries

Write words from the box to complete the paragraph.

ache	painful	aspirin	swollen	clinic

My older brother always seems to have his shoelaces untied. Well, this morning, he tripped and hurt his ankle. It was __1.__ and __2.__ , so my father took him to the __3.__ to see the doctor. She said that nothing was broken, but his ankle would __4.__ for a while. My father asked if he could give him __5.__ for the pain. Then the doctor told him to keep his shoes tied!

Social Studies: Fishing

Write the word from the box that matches each clue.

Canada	haddock	fishery	trawler	flounder

6. It is a fishing boat.
7. It is a country.
8. This is a fish with a **dock** in its name.
9. It is a place where fish are caught.
10. This is a flat fish with both eyes on top of its head.

Apply the Spelling Strategy

Circle the suffix that means "full of" in one of the Content Words you wrote.

Word Study

Synonyms

Synonyms are words with meanings that are the same or almost the same. **Attractive, gorgeous,** and **handsome** are synonyms. Write the Strategy Word that is an overused synonym for these words.

Health: Injuries

1. _____
2. _____
3. _____
4. _____
5. _____

Social Studies: Fishing

6. _____
7. _____
8. _____
9. _____
10. _____

Synonyms

1. _____

one syllable
1. _____
2. _____
3. _____

two syllables
4. _____
5. _____
6. _____
7. _____
8. _____
9. _____
10. _____
11. _____
12. _____

three or more syllables
13. _____
14. _____
15. _____
16. _____
17. _____
18. _____
19. _____
20. _____

Spelling and Thinking

READ THE SPELLING WORDS

1.	January	*January*	The new year begins on **January** 1.
2.	February	*February*	Valentine's Day is **February** 14.
3.	March	*March*	**March** is named for the god Mars.
4.	April	*April*	**April** is a month with thirty days.
5.	May	*May*	Mother's Day is celebrated in **May**.
6.	June	*June*	School vacation begins in **June**.
7.	July	*July*	**July** Fourth is Independence Day.
8.	August	*August*	Many people vacation in **August**.
9.	September	*September*	Thirty days has **September**.
10.	October	*October*	**October** ends with Halloween.
11.	November	*November*	Elections are held in **November**.
12.	December	*December*	**December** ends the year.
13.	calendar	*calendar*	Mark today's date on the **calendar**.
14.	Sunday	*Sunday*	**Sunday** begins a new week.
15.	Monday	*Monday*	On **Monday** we go back to school.
16.	Tuesday	*Tuesday*	**Tuesday** comes early in the week.
17.	Wednesday	*Wednesday*	**Wednesday** falls in midweek.
18.	Thursday	*Thursday*	Thanksgiving falls on **Thursday**.
19.	Friday	*Friday*	**Friday** ends the work week.
20.	Saturday	*Saturday*	School is not held on **Saturday**.

SORT THE SPELLING WORDS

1.–3. Write the spelling words with one syllable.

4.–12. Write the spelling words with two syllables.

13.–20. Write the spelling words with three or more syllables.

REMEMBER THE SPELLING STRATEGY

Remember that it is important to learn to spell the names of the months of the year and the days of the week. These words always begin with a capital letter.

Word Meanings

Write the name of the month that completes each sentence.

1. In ____ we celebrate Independence Day.
2. I will wear a costume on the thirty-first day of ____.
3. Mom will try to fool me on the first day of ____.
4. I will send you a valentine in ____.
5. In ____ we will have a Memorial Day picnic.
6. When spring begins, in ____, I will fly my kite.
7. In the Northern Hemisphere, summer begins late in the month of ____.
8. The month before the last month of the year is ____.
9. Labor Day always falls on the first Monday of ____.

Word Structure

Unscramble the letters to write spelling words. Begin the names of the months with a capital letter.

10. auyjnar
11. utgsua
12. eembrcde
13. alncedra

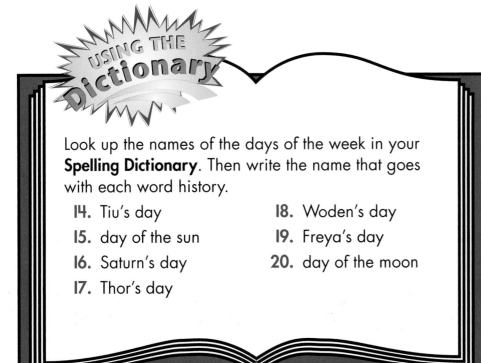

USING THE Dictionary

Look up the names of the days of the week in your **Spelling Dictionary**. Then write the name that goes with each word history.

14. Tiu's day
15. day of the sun
16. Saturn's day
17. Thor's day
18. Woden's day
19. Freya's day
20. day of the moon

Word Meanings

1. ____
2. ____
3. ____
4. ____
5. ____
6. ____
7. ____
8. ____
9. ____

Word Structure

10. ____
11. ____
12. ____
13. ____

Using the Dictionary

14. ____
15. ____
16. ____
17. ____
18. ____
19. ____
20. ____

January	February	March	April	May
June	July	August	September	October
November	December	calendar	Sunday	Monday
Tuesday	Wednesday	Thursday	Friday	Saturday

Complete the Sentences   Write a spelling word to complete each sentence.

1. After all the yard work I did last weekend, I was glad to go back to school on _____.

2. With three days on either side of it, _____ is the middle of the week.

3. Thanksgiving falls on the fourth _____ of November.

4. _____ is the last weekday but the first day of the weekend.

5. The last day of school each week is _____.

6. The first day of the week on many calendars is _____.

7. _____ is the day that follows Monday.

8. Jim writes the date of every away game in his _____.

Complete the Poem   Write the names of the months to complete this poem.

In __9.__ the new year starts.

__10.__ brings Valentine hearts.

In __11.__ the winds will come and go.

In __12.__ we usually don't see snow.

In __13.__ the green grass grows, and soon

School will end in the month of __14.__.

And maybe we'll watch a parade go by

On our own most special Fourth of __15.__.

__16.__ is usually hot, not cool.

__17.__ sees us back in school.

In __18.__ the leaves turn gold,

And in __19.__ the weather turns cold.

So now let's give a little cheer

For __20.__, which ends the year.

Complete the Sentences

1. _____
2. _____
3. _____
4. _____
5. _____
6. _____
7. _____
8. _____

Complete the Poem

9. _____
10. _____
11. _____
12. _____
13. _____
14. _____
15. _____
16. _____
17. _____
18. _____
19. _____
20. _____

Spelling and Writing

Proofread a Paragraph

Six words are not spelled correctly in this paragraph of gardening hints. Write those words correctly.

Gardening Hints

Mark your calender for January 1. This is a good month to buy seed. In Febuary, check that you have all your supplies. Start your seeds indoors. Take a Saterday to plan your garden. Hardy crops may be planted in Aprel or May. Know which plants like the heat of July and Augist. You may be able to harvest crops as late as Septembir or October. Happy gardening!

Proofreading Marks

≡ Make a capital.

/ Make a small letter.

∧ Add something.

℮ Take out something.

⊙ Add a period.

New paragraph

(SP) Spelling error

Write a Paragraph

Expository Writing

Write a paragraph of hints about how to make or do something. Explain

- what you are advising the reader to make or do.
- what steps the reader should follow.
- the time involved in or between steps.
- the things to be aware of.
- the advantages of following your advice.

Use as many spelling words as you can.

Writing Process

Prewriting
⇩
Drafting
⇩
Revising
⇩
Editing
⇩
Publishing

Proofread Your Writing During ▶

Proofread your writing for spelling errors as part of the editing stage in the writing process. Be sure to check each word carefully. Use a dictionary to check spelling if you are not sure.

VOCABULARY CONNECTIONS

◄ Strategy Words ►

Review Words
1. _____
2. _____
3. _____
4. _____
5. _____

Preview Words
6. _____
7. _____
8. _____
9. _____
10. _____

Review Words: Calendar Words

Write the word from the box that matches each description.

month	monthly	spring	summer	sunshine

1. happening on a regular schedule, about thirty days apart
2. the season that comes between spring and fall
3. light from the sun
4. a period of time, usually a little more than 4 weeks
5. the season noted for showers, flowers, and warming weather

Preview Words: Calendar Words

Write the word from the box that completes each sentence.

bimonthly	biweekly	daily
twenty-seven	up-to-date	

6. Since I happen every day, you can say I am a _____ event.

7. I am a magazine that is published once every two weeks, so you can call me a _____ magazine.

8. I am a hyphenated word that means "modern; timely." You could say I am _____.

9. I am a meeting that is held once every two months. Everyone calls me the _____ meeting.

10. My nearest whole-number neighbors are twenty-six and twenty-eight. You know my name as _____.

Content Words

Language Arts: Research

Write a word from the box for each clue.

define	library	dictionary	paperback	entry

1. I am a book of definitions and words.
2. I am a book with a soft cover.
3. I am what you do when you write the meanings of words.
4. I am the word and everything about it in the dictionary.
5. I am a collection of books, magazines, and reference materials.

Social Studies: Pioneers

Write the word from the box that matches each definition.

colony	provide	cranberry	pumpkin	pilgrim

6. a thick, round, orange fruit with seeds
7. to supply or furnish something that is needed or useful
8. a group of settlers in a new land, still subject to rule by the parent country
9. a tart, edible berry that grows on a vine
10. a traveler in search of something sacred

Apply the Spelling Strategy

Circle the Content Words you wrote that could make you think of Thanksgiving.

Word Study

More Than One Meaning

Some words have more than one meaning. Write the one Strategy Word that fits these meanings:

- season of the year
- coil
- water source
- to jump up

Language Arts: Research

1. _____
2. _____
3. _____
4. _____
5. _____

Social Studies: Pioneers

6. _____
7. _____
8. _____
9. _____
10. _____

More Than One Meaning

1. _____

Unit 25

1.

2.

3.

4.

Unit 26

5.

6.

7.

8.

9.

Unit 27

10.

11.

12.

13.

Unit 28

14.

15.

16.

17.

18.

Unit 29

19.

20.

Assessment and Review

Assessment   Units 25–29

Each Assessment Word in the box fits one of the spelling strategies you have studied over the past five weeks. Read the spelling strategies. Then write each Assessment Word under the unit number it fits.

Unit 25

1.–4. A contraction is a shortened form of two words: **you're** means **you are**. An apostrophe (') shows where letters have been left out.

Unit 26

5.–9. Prefixes, like **un-**, **re-**, and **pre-**, are added to the beginnings of words to make new words: **pack, unpack; write, rewrite; pay, prepay**.

Unit 27

10.–13. The suffix **-er** means "one who." A **player** is "one who plays." A **singer** is "one who sings."

Unit 28

14.–18. When you add **-ful** or **-less** to a word, you often do not need to change the spelling of the base word before adding the suffix: **help, helpful; rest, restless**.

Unit 29

19.–20. It is important to learn to spell the names of the months of the year and the days of the week.

preset
would've
biker
painless
could've
endless
yearly
kicker
unload
retell
keeper
harmful
mightn't
unemployed
weekly
should've
adventurer
glassful
preflight
blissful

Review Unit 25: Contractions

| haven't | let's | wasn't | you're | aren't |
| he'd | I'd | we'll | you'll | I've |

Write the spelling words that are contractions for each pair of words below.

1. I would
2. he would
3. we will
4. you will
5. I have

6. you are
7. are not
8. was not
9. have not
10. let us

Review Unit 26: Prefixes un-, re-, pre-

| preschool | reread | rewrite | untie | prepay |
| unlock | recover | unfair | unhappy | uncover |

Write the spelling word that fits the meaning.

11. before school
12. pay in advance
13. read again
14. get well
15. write again

16. not fair
17. not happy
18. take the cover off
19. open the lock
20. undo the knot or bow

Unit 25
1. _____
2. _____
3. _____
4. _____
5. _____
6. _____
7. _____
8. _____
9. _____
10. _____
Unit 26
11. _____
12. _____
13. _____
14. _____
15. _____
16. _____
17. _____
18. _____
19. _____
20. _____

Review — Unit 27: Suffix -er

builder	listener	reporter	speaker	reader
painter	player	owner	leader	farmer

Write the spelling word that completes each sentence.

1. If you farm, you are a _____.
2. If you build things, you are a _____.
3. If you have a role in a game, you are a _____.
4. If you own a bike, you are its _____.
5. If you can read, you are a _____.
6. If you direct a band, you are its _____.
7. If you listen to a speaker, you are a _____.
8. If you report stories for a newspaper, you are a _____.
9. If you paint pictures or houses, you are a _____.
10. If you give a speech, you are a _____.

Review — Unit 28: Suffixes -ful, -less

careless	thoughtful	useless	useful	helpful
cheerful	peaceful	careful	helpless	powerful

Write the spelling word that is the opposite of each of these words.

11. careful
12. powerless
13. useful
14. useless
15. helpful
16. helpless
17. cheerless
18. thoughtless
19. careless
20. warlike

 **Review** Unit 29: Calendar Words

April	February	Saturday	Wednesday	Sunday
Friday	July	Monday	March	June

Write the spelling word for each clue.

1. This word ends with a **long e** sound.

2. This word has an **r**-controlled vowel.

3. This word begins with a **long a** sound.

4. This word has a **vowel-consonant-e** spelling pattern.

5. This word ends with a **long i** sound.

6.–10. List the five spelling words that name days according to their order in the week.

 **Spelling Study Strategy**

Word Swap

Practicing spelling words can be fun if you make it into a game. Here's an idea you can try with a friend.

1. Swap spelling lists with a partner. Ask your partner to read your list and tell you if there are any words she or he doesn't know how to say. Say those words for your partner.

2. Ask your partner to read the first word on your list. Write the word on a piece of scrap paper.

3. Ask your partner to check your spelling. If you spelled the word correctly, your partner should say the next word on your list. If you did not spell the word correctly, ask your partner to spell the word out loud for you. Write the correct spelling.

4. Keep going until you have practiced five words. Then trade roles. You will say the first word on your partner's list, and your partner will try to write the word correctly.

5. Keep taking turns until you and your partner have practiced all the words on your lists.

Grammar, Usage, and Mechanics

Adjectives

An adjective usually describes a noun or a pronoun. It tells what the noun or pronoun is like. Adjectives can tell what kind, how many, or which one.

- what kind:

    The **friendly** dog wagged its **bushy** tail.

- how many:

    We ate **three** pizzas in **one** hour!

- which one:

    This computer cannot solve **that** problem.

A. Write the adjective in each sentence.

  1. Tara looked for the correct key.

  2. Don't use a dull pencil.

  3. Yesterday was a chilly day for a picnic.

  4. What a delicious drink you made!

  5. I snuggled in the soft blanket.

B. Fill in the blank with other adjectives from the spelling lists in Units 25–29.

  6. Jon wore a _____ smile.

  7. One _____ act could ruin the project.

  8. A _____ storm damaged trees and buildings.

  9. Throw out that _____ lamp.

  10. I appreciate your _____ act of kindness.

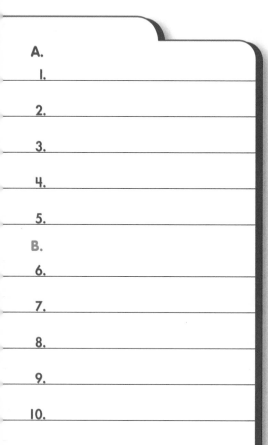

A.
1.
2.
3.
4.
5.
B.
6.
7.
8.
9.
10.

One at a Time!

Good writers always proofread their writing for spelling mistakes. Here's a strategy that you can use to proofread your papers.

Focus on one kind of mistake at a time. First, skim your paper and look for only one kind of problem, such as word endings. Then, look for another kind of problem, such as words that sound alike or contractions.

It will take only a few minutes to check for each problem, so this method does not take long. And you'll be surprised by how easy it is to find problems when you look for only one kind. Try it!

Electronic Spelling

Graphics

Computers allow you to make graphics quickly and easily. You can make a chart or a timetable in just a few seconds, and it will look good and help your readers understand certain kinds of information.

Your readers will not understand your charts, though, if the heads are misspelled. The heads are the words that explain what each row or column contains. Make sure you double-check the spelling of these. Look at the chart heads below. Which have misspelled words? Write the words correctly. Write **OK** if a head is correct.

1. Name of Playor
2. Wednsday Classes
3. Morning Speaker
4. Pet's Owner
5. Games in Febuary
6. Weakly Jobs

Electronic Spelling

1. _____
2. _____
3. _____
4. _____
5. _____
6. _____

-s to base word

1. _____
2. _____
3. _____
4. _____
5. _____
6. _____
7. _____
8. _____

-es to base word

9. _____
10. _____
11. _____
12. _____
13. _____
14. _____

y to i before -es added

15. _____
16. _____
17. _____
18. _____
19. _____
20. _____

Spelling and Thinking

READ THE SPELLING WORDS

1. monkeys	*monkeys*	I like to watch **monkeys** at the zoo.
2. babies	*babies*	We have to feed **babies** often.
3. teams	*teams*	Both **teams** ran onto the field.
4. lunches	*lunches*	Does the school serve hot **lunches**?
5. factories	*factories*	Some items are made in **factories**.
6. scratches	*scratches*	Our cat **scratches** on a padded post.
7. trays	*trays*	They served **trays** of cookies.
8. libraries	*libraries*	Most **libraries** lend books.
9. members	*members*	There are thirty **members** in the club.
10. ladies	*ladies*	Three **ladies** hosted the luncheon.
11. slippers	*slippers*	My bathrobe and **slippers** are warm.
12. coaches	*coaches*	The soccer team has two **coaches**.
13. armies	*armies*	Both **armies** sent in troops.
14. friends	*friends*	Amy, Paul, and I are good **friends**.
15. patches	*patches*	We sewed **patches** on the worn spots.
16. adults	*adults*	Children and **adults** like to read.
17. pennies	*pennies*	I have more **pennies** than dimes.
18. holidays	*holidays*	My sister is home for the **holidays**.
19. stitches	*stitches*	That cut required fourteen **stitches**.
20. sandwiches	*sandwiches*	We ate **sandwiches** at the picnic.

SORT THE SPELLING WORDS

Write the spelling words that form their plural by

1.–8. adding **-s** to the base word.

9.–14. adding **-es** to the base word.

15.–20. changing the final **y** to **i** before adding **-es**.

REMEMBER THE SPELLING STRATEGY

Remember that plural nouns name more than one person, place, or thing. Plurals are formed in different ways: add **-s** (**trays**), add **-es** (**lunches**), or change final **y** to **i** and add **-es** (**pennies**).

Spelling *and* Vocabulary

Word Meanings

Write the spelling word that goes with each meaning.

1. very young children; infants
2. grown-ups
3. animals that have long tails
4. women
5. people one knows and likes
6. places where books and reference materials are kept
7. days on which people celebrate an event or honor a person
8. players on the same side in a game

Word Structure

The **-es** ending added to singular nouns forms a plural noun and also creates a new syllable. Write the spelling words by adding the syllables.

9. scratch + es = _____
10. sand + wich + es = _____
11. stitch + es = _____
12. coach + es = _____
13. lunch + es = _____
14. patch + es = _____

USING THE Dictionary

Write the plural form of the words with the following meanings:

15. a large group of soldiers
16. a person belonging to a group
17. a low, comfortable shoe
18. a place where goods are manufactured
19. one cent
20. a flat, shallow holder with a low rim

Word Meanings
1. _____
2. _____
3. _____
4. _____
5. _____
6. _____
7. _____
8. _____

Word Structure
9. _____
10. _____
11. _____
12. _____
13. _____
14. _____

Using the Dictionary
15. _____
16. _____
17. _____
18. _____
19. _____
20. _____

monkeys	babies	teams	lunches	factories
scratches	trays	libraries	members	ladies
slippers	coaches	armies	friends	patches
adults	pennies	holidays	stitches	sandwiches

Complete the Sentences

Complete the Sentences   The endings **-s** and **-es** can also be added to verbs. Add **-s** or **-es** to each word in parentheses to make the verb that completes the sentence.

I. Grandmother often _____ my torn clothes. (patch)

2. This old sewing machine still _____ well. (stitch)

3. My pet rooster always _____ in the dirt. (scratch)

4. Mr. Harris _____ a very successful team. (coach)

5. Aunt Ruth often _____ with her friends. (lunch)

Complete the Groups

Complete the Groups   Write the spelling word that belongs in each of the following groups.

6. infants, tots, _____

7. soups, salads, _____

8. squads, crews, _____

9. camels, zebras, _____

10. boots, shoes, _____

II. dimes, nickels, _____

12. Sundays, weekends, _____

13. plates, platters, _____

14. gentlemen, women, _____

15. air forces, navies, _____

16. mills, plants, _____

Complete the Paragraph

Complete the Paragraph   Write the spelling words that best complete the paragraph.

Besides providing books to borrow, many _**17.**_ offer interesting activities and convenient meeting places for both children and _**18.**_. Preschoolers can enjoy story hours, and students can meet their _**19.**_ to work on projects together. People can become _**20.**_ of book clubs, computer societies, and drama groups. Do you know what activities your library offers?

Complete the Sentences
I.
2.
3.
4.
5.

Complete the Groups
6.
7.
8.
9.
10.
II.
12.
13.
14.
15.
16.

Complete the Paragraph
17.
18.
19.
20.

Spelling and Writing

Proofread a Story

Six words are not spelled correctly in this story. Write those words correctly.

A Garage Circus

My frends and I were always looking for something to do during summer vacation. Once, we had a new idea. Why not have a circus in our garage? We invited all the adultes who were home and charged them a few pennys for admission. The ladys came, with their dogs and babys. Some members of our circus performed tricks, while others sold the lemonade and sandwichs we had made. We had fun and made some money, too!

Write a Story

Narrative Writing

Write a story about something you and your friends did. Be sure to include information about

- the people who were there.
- what you and your friends did.
- why you did it.
- how successful the idea was.
- whether you would do it again.

Use as many spelling words as you can.

Writing Process

Prewriting
⇩
Drafting
⇩
Revising
⇩
Editing
⇩
Publishing

Proofread Your Writing During ⟩ Editing

Proofread your writing for spelling errors as part of the editing stage in the writing process. Be sure to check each word carefully. Use a dictionary to check spelling if you are not sure.

VOCABULARY CONNECTIONS

Strategy Words

Review Words: Plurals

Write the word from the box that matches each description.

| apples | branches | drums | flags | inches |

1. They are musical instruments played by striking them with sticks.
2. They are small units of measure.
3. We fly them on holidays, such as the Fourth of July.
4. We eat these raw or cooked.
5. Found on trees; leaves and flowers grow on them.

Preview Words: Plurals

Write the word from the box that matches each definition.

| envelopes | essays | heroes | pianos | valleys |

6. brave people
7. paper wrappers you put letters into
8. a plural word for one kind of musical instrument
9. short written compositions
10. a plural word naming the kind of land you might find between mountains

---

Review Words

1. _____
2. _____
3. _____
4. _____
5. _____

Preview Words

6. _____
7. _____
8. _____
9. _____
10. _____

Content Words

Science: Volcanoes

Write the word from the box that matches each definition.

ashes	magma	cinders	volcano	lava

1. melted rock inside the earth's crust
2. melted rock that flows out of a mountain
3. pieces of partly burned coal or wood
4. material left after wood burns
5. an opening in the earth from which molten rock and gases flow

Math: Multiplication

Study the following problem. Then write the word from the box that completes each sentence.

factor	product	groups	times	multiplication

$$8 \times 3 = 24$$

6. This is a _____ problem.
7. 24 is the _____.
8. The $\times$ means _____.
9. 8 is a _____ of 24.
10. 24 is 3 _____ of 8.

Apply the Spelling Strategy

Circle the plural endings in three of the nouns you wrote.

Word Study

Word History

Vulcan was the old Latin name for the god of fire. Write the Content Word that comes from this name.

Science: Volcanoes

1. _____
2. _____
3. _____
4. _____
5. _____

Math: Multiplication

6. _____
7. _____
8. _____
9. _____
10. _____

Word History

1. _____

Spelling and Thinking

READ THE SPELLING WORDS

1.	farmer's	*farmer's*	We brought in the **farmer's** crops.
2.	poets'	*poets'*	The **poets'** haikus were read.
3.	group's	*group's*	They finished the **group's** work.
4.	calf's	*calf's*	A **calf's** legs are long and weak.
5.	watches'	*watches'*	The **watches'** faces were identical.
6.	fish's	*fish's*	That **fish's** tail is forked.
7.	poem's	*poem's*	The **poem's** last line was a surprise.
8.	calves'	*calves'*	The **calves'** mothers watch over them.
9.	brother's	*brother's*	This is my **brother's** book.
10.	herd's	*herd's*	The **herd's** pasture is on the hill.
11.	couples'	*couples'*	We accepted the **couples'** ideas.
12.	mother's	*mother's*	Anna is my **mother's** best friend.
13.	wives'	*wives'*	They listened to their **wives'** ideas.
14.	child's	*child's*	Read a **child's** book to youngsters.
15.	fathers'	*fathers'*	The coach liked the **fathers'** plans.
16.	daughter's	*daughter's*	Her **daughter's** name is Pamela.
17.	sisters'	*sisters'*	The **sisters'** reunion was a success.
18.	children's	*children's*	We heard the **children's** laughter.
19.	wife's	*wife's*	He appreciated his **wife's** gift.
20.	sons'	*sons'*	All his **sons'** names begin with **J**.

SORT THE SPELLING WORDS

1.–12. Write the spelling words that end with an apostrophe **s** (**-'s**).

13.–20. Write the spelling words that end with an **s** apostrophe (**-s'**).

REMEMBER THE SPELLING STRATEGY

Remember that possessive nouns show ownership. Add an apostrophe and **s** (**'s**) to show possession when a noun is singular: **calf's**. Add an apostrophe (**'**) to show ownership when a plural noun ends in **-s: calves'**. When a noun is plural and does **not** end in **-s**, add an apostrophe and **s** (**'s**) to show ownership: **children's**.

-'s

1. _____
2. _____
3. _____
4. _____
5. _____
6. _____
7. _____
8. _____
9. _____
10. _____
11. _____
12. _____

-s'

13. _____
14. _____
15. _____
16. _____
17. _____
18. _____
19. _____
20. _____

Spelling and Vocabulary

Word Meanings

Write a possessive noun to complete the equation.

1. The tail of one calf = one _____ tail.
2. A playground for more than one child = a _____ playground.
3. The fields of one farmer = one _____ fields.
4. The bands of three watches = the _____ bands.

Plural Possessives

Each word below is the singular possessive form of a noun. Write the spelling word that is the plural possessive form of the same noun.

5. calf's   7. poet's   9. son's   11. sister's

6. wife's   8. couple's   10. father's

Singular Possessives

Each word below is the plural possessive form of a noun. Write the word that is the singular possessive form of the same noun.

12. herds'   14. groups'   16. children's   18. brothers'

13. wives'   15. poems'   17. mothers'   19. daughters'

20. Which spelling word can be used as a singular possessive and a plural possessive? Check your answer by finding the base word and a plural form of the word in your **Spelling Dictionary**.

Dictionary Check Be sure to check the plural form of the word in your **Spelling Dictionary**.

Word Meanings
1.
2.
3.
4.

Plural Possessives
5.
6.
7.
8.
9.
10.
11.

Singular Possessives
12.
13.
14.
15.
16.
17.
18.
19.

Using the Dictionary
20.

farmer's	poets'	group's	calf's	watches'
fish's	poem's	calves'	brother's	herd's
couples'	mother's	wives'	child's	fathers'
daughter's	sisters'	children's	wife's	sons'

Complete the Sentences

1.
2.
3.
4.
5.
6.
7.
8.
9.
10.
11.
12.

Complete the Sentences Complete each sentence by writing the correct possessive form of each of the words in parentheses.

1. This is the spotted _____ collar. (calf)
2. All the _____ names are on this list. (father)
3. The farmer painted the _____ barn. (herd)
4. Thursday was the sick _____ last day of school. (child)
5. Three _____ works were read at the library program. (poet)
6. All the _____ bands are made of the same material. (watch)
7. Both of my _____ rooms are decorated differently. (sister)
8. His only _____ birthday is in June. (daughter)
9. I laughed at my _____ joke when he told it. (brother)
10. My _____ car is in the driveway. (mother)
11. Her two _____ toys were neatly put away. (son)
12. My mom and dad went to the _____ picnic. (couple)

Form the Possessives

13.
14.
15.
16.
17.
18.
19.
20.

Form the Possessives Write the spelling word that is the possessive form of each word.

13. the lines of the poem; the _____ lines
14. the project of the group; the _____ project
15. the idea of the wife; the _____ idea
16. the crop of the farmer; the _____ crop
17. the feed for the calves; the _____ feed
18. the faces of the children; the _____ faces
19. the fins of the fish; the _____ fins
20. the meeting of the wives; the _____ meeting

Spelling and Writing

Proofread an Ad

Six words are not spelled correctly in this advertisement from a bookstore. Write those words correctly.

Inexpensive Travel

Got the winter doldrums? Don't know how to spend the long, dark nights? Why not curl up with a good book? Reading is a farmers' escape, a wifes tropical trip, a childs' adventure. Between the covers of a book lie a poems appeal and a mothers tender tale. Best Books has it all—even a childrens' section and two poets' corners.

Proofreading Marks

≡ Make a capital.

/ Make a small letter.

∧ Add something.

℮ Take out something.

⊙ Add a period.

⌗ New paragraph

ⓈⓅ Spelling error

Write an Ad

Persuasive Writing

Write an ad for something. Be sure to include

- what you are selling.
- advantages to the reader of buying your product.
- advantages to the reader of buying it from you.
- how you can save the reader money.

Use as many spelling words as you can.

Writing Process

Prewriting

⇩

Drafting

⇩

Revising

⇩

Editing

⇩

Publishing

Proofread Your Writing During

Proofread your writing for spelling errors as part of the editing stage in the writing process. Be sure to check each word carefully. Use a dictionary to check spelling if you are not sure.

VOCABULARY CONNECTIONS

Strategy Words

Review Words: Possessives

For each phrase, write the correct possessive form of a word from the box.

city	geese	grandmother	grandfather	pies

1. our _____ mayor
2. the _____ crusts
3. my _____ dress
4. your _____ beard
5. the _____ nests

Preview Words: Possessives

Write the singular or plural possessive form, as indicated, of the words in the box.

actor	artist	company	youth	tourist

6. an item owned by one youth
7. one item owned by a group of actors
8. items owned by more than one tourist
9. an item owned by one artist
10. many items owned by a single company

Review Words

1. _____
2. _____
3. _____
4. _____
5. _____

Preview Words

6. _____
7. _____
8. _____
9. _____
10. _____

Content Words

Health: Illnesses

Write a word from the box that matches each definition.

disease	infect	hospital	virus	immune

1. a condition that can result from infection
2. to transmit a disease
3. resistant to disease
4. a tiny substance that can carry disease
5. a place for treatment of the sick and injured

Science: Conductivity

Write a word from the box that matches each definition.

acid	crystal	antenna	metal	battery

6. an element that can carry heat
7. an aerial that sends and receives signals
8. a device that makes and stores electricity
9. a chemical that can "burn"
10. a body, such as quartz, used in an electronic circuit

Apply the Spelling Strategy

Circle the Content Words you wrote that could be written as possessive words.

Suffixes

The suffix **-ist** is used to make words that mean "a person who does or makes." A **chemist** works with chemicals. Write the Strategy Word that means "a person who enjoys going on tours."

Health: Illnesses

1. _____
2. _____
3. _____
4. _____
5. _____

Science: Conductivity

6. _____
7. _____
8. _____
9. _____
10. _____

Suffixes

1. _____

199

-ness

1. _____
2. _____
3. _____
4. _____
5. _____
6. _____
7. _____
8. _____
9. _____
10. _____
11. _____

-ment

12. _____
13. _____
14. _____
15. _____
16. _____
17. _____
18. _____
19. _____
20. _____

Spelling and Thinking

READ THE SPELLING WORDS

1.	kindness	*kindness*	He always treats people with **kindness**.
2.	treatment	*treatment*	When you are ill, you need **treatment**.
3.	stillness	*stillness*	I left in the **stillness** of the night.
4.	apartment	*apartment*	She lives in a large **apartment**.
5.	fitness	*fitness*	They use **fitness** equipment at home.
6.	pavement	*pavement*	The **pavement** was wet with rain.
7.	weakness	*weakness*	Arriving late is his **weakness**.
8.	shipment	*shipment*	A **shipment** of goods arrived today.
9.	brightness	*brightness*	The sun's **brightness** made me squint.
10.	agreement	*agreement*	We will try to reach an **agreement**.
11.	placement	*placement*	Father works at a **placement** bureau.
12.	illness	*illness*	He is at home because of **illness**.
13.	enjoyment	*enjoyment*	Her **enjoyment** of the movie was clear.
14.	darkness	*darkness*	I stumbled in the **darkness**.
15.	movement	*movement*	We studied the **movement** of the stars.
16.	softness	*softness*	The blanket's **softness** was comforting.
17.	boldness	*boldness*	The **boldness** of his plan surprised us.
18.	payment	*payment*	Expect the first **payment** next week.
19.	thickness	*thickness*	She measured the **thickness** of the wall.
20.	sadness	*sadness*	He has known great **sadness** and joy.

SORT THE SPELLING WORDS

1.–11. Write the spelling words that have the **-ness** suffix.

12.–20. Write the spelling words that have the **-ment** suffix.

REMEMBER THE SPELLING STRATEGY

Remember that the suffix **-ness** means "a condition or quality": **kindness**. The suffix **-ment** means "the result of an action": **enjoyment**.

Spelling ^{and} Vocabulary

Word Meanings

Write the spelling word that goes with each definition.

1. the condition of being physically healthy
2. the result of an understanding between people
3. the condition of being sad or gloomy
4. the quality of being kind and generous
5. the act of placing something
6. the condition or feeling of being weak
7. the condition of being heavy or thick
8. the result of paying something
9. the result of covering a road with a hard, smooth surface
10. the result of changing position or location

Word Structure

Add a suffix to each of the following base words to write a spelling word.

11. treat
12. bold
13. still

14. bright
15. enjoy
16. soft

Write a spelling word for each pair of synonyms below.

17. gloom; blackout
18. flat; suite

19. cargo; freight
20. ailment; malady

◆ ◆ ◆

Thesaurus Check Be sure to check synonyms in your **Writing Thesaurus**.

Word Meanings

1. _____
2. _____
3. _____
4. _____
5. _____
6. _____
7. _____
8. _____
9. _____
10. _____

Word Structure

11. _____
12. _____
13. _____
14. _____
15. _____
16. _____

Using the Thesaurus

17. _____
18. _____
19. _____
20. _____

Spelling and Reading

kindness	treatment	stillness	apartment
fitness	pavement	weakness	shipment
brightness	agreement	placement	illness
enjoyment	darkness	movement	softness
boldness	payment	thickness	sadness

Complete the Sentences Write a spelling word by adding **-ness** or **-ment** to each underlined word.

1. The <u>ship</u> is carrying a large ____.
2. When they <u>pave</u> this road, the ____ will be easier to ride on.
3. <u>Kind</u> people bring out ____ in others.
4. This <u>thick</u> board is the same ____ as those other boards.
5. As you <u>move</u> your arms, follow the ____ of the dance director.
6. Please <u>pay</u> your bill by sending your ____ by mail.
7. We <u>agree</u> that he should sign the ____ today.
8. His <u>bold</u> words match the ____ of his personality.
9. As you <u>place</u> the pieces in the jigsaw puzzle, their ____ will help create a picture.
10. The doctors will <u>treat</u> certain injuries at a special ____ center.

Complete the Paragraph Write words from the box to complete the paragraph.

The accident left Martha weak. Each day, in the __11.__ of her small __12.__, she worked with physical __13.__ equipment to overcome her __14.__. Although it was hard work, she felt much __15.__ because she knew that one day she would be strong again.

| fitness |
| weakness |
| stillness |
| enjoyment |
| apartment |

Write the Antonyms Write the spelling word that is an antonym of each of the following words.

16. hardness
17. health
18. dimness
19. happiness
20. brightness

Complete the Sentences
1.
2.
3.
4.
5.
6.
7.
8.
9.
10.

Complete the Paragraph
11.
12.
13.
14.
15.

Write the Antonyms
16.
17.
18.
19.
20.

202

Spelling and Writing

Proofread a Note

Six words are not spelled correctly in this note. Write those words correctly.

Dear Mary,

Cindy's apartmint is beautiful. The briteness and warmth of the sun streaming through her windows are comforting. At night, the stilness of the street lulls me to sleep. I try to repay her kindniss by going with her to her fitnes class. We get a lot of enjoyment from each other's company. You were right. This is good treatmint for my sadness. I'll call you this weekend.

Love,

Sharon

Proofreading Marks

≡ Make a capital.

/ Make a small letter.

∧ Add something.

℘ Take out something.

⊙ Add a period.

⌗ New paragraph

SP Spelling error

Write a Note

Expository Writing

Write a note to your family or a friend about something of interest to you. Be sure to include

- a greeting.
- your news, with descriptive details.
- a closing, with your signature.

Use as many spelling words as you can.

Writing Process

Prewriting

Drafting

Revising

Proofread Your Writing During ▶ **Editing**

Publishing

Proofread your writing for spelling errors as part of the editing stage in the writing process. Be sure to check each word carefully. Use a dictionary to check spelling if you are not sure.

VOCABULARY CONNECTIONS

Strategy Words

Review Words

1. _____
2. _____
3. _____
4. _____
5. _____

Preview Words

6. _____
7. _____
8. _____
9. _____
10. _____

Review Words: Suffixes -ness, -ment

Write a word for each clue by adding the suffix **-ness** or **-ment** to a word in the box.

high	pave	right	round	mild

1. describes one quality of a ball
2. refers to height
3. refers to the surface of a road
4. is an antonym of **wrongness**
5. might be used to describe the weather or a spice

Preview Words: Suffixes -ness, -ment

Write the word from the box that is the correct synonym or antonym.

argument	employment	government
sickness		tardiness

6. a synonym of **illness**
7. an antonym of **agreement**
8. a synonym of **lateness**
9. an antonym of **unemployment**
10. a synonym of **administration**

Content Words

Language Arts: Punctuation

Write the words from the box that complete each sentence.

colon	sentence	comma	statement	period

1. A _____ has a noun phrase and a verb phrase.

2.–3. A declarative sentence makes a _____ and ends with a _____.

4. A _____ is often used to separate ideas in a sentence.

5. A _____ is used after a word that introduces a list.

Social Studies: Deserts

Write the word from the box that matches each definition.

arid	dune	migrate	nomad	travel

6. dry

7. wanderer; roamer

8. relocate periodically; move seasonally

9. a hill of wind-blown sand

10. take a trip; journey

Apply the Spelling Strategy

Circle the suffix in one of the Content Words you wrote.

Word Study

Idioms

An **idiom** is a saying that doesn't mean what the words in it say. For example, the idiom **travel light** means "to travel with little or no luggage." Write the Strategy Word that finishes this saying, which means "the open ocean": _____ **seas**.

Language Arts: Punctuation

1. _____
2. _____
3. _____
4. _____
5. _____

Social Studies: Deserts

6. _____
7. _____
8. _____
9. _____
10. _____

Idioms

1. _____

one-word compounds

1. _____
2. _____
3. _____
4. _____
5. _____
6. _____
7. _____
8. _____
9. _____
10. _____
11. _____
12. _____
13. _____
14. _____
15. _____

two-word compounds

16. _____
17. _____
18. _____
19. _____
20. _____

Spelling and Thinking

READ THE SPELLING WORDS

1.	tablecloth	*tablecloth*	We use a red and white **tablecloth**.
2.	everyone	*everyone*	Was **everyone** at the soccer game?
3.	nearby	*nearby*	We walk to school, which is **nearby**.
4.	outdoors	*outdoors*	We play **outdoors** when it is warm.
5.	high school	*high school*	My older brother is in **high school**.
6.	anywhere	*anywhere*	You may sit **anywhere** you wish.
7.	flashlight	*flashlight*	I need a **flashlight** to find my way.
8.	air mail	*air mail*	A plane carrying **air mail** landed.
9.	whenever	*whenever*	We can go **whenever** he is ready.
10.	driveway	*driveway*	The car is parked in the **driveway**.
11.	sometimes	*sometimes*	I walk to school **sometimes**.
12.	seat belt	*seat belt*	Use your **seat belt** when in a car.
13.	basketball	*basketball*	She is our new **basketball** coach.
14.	mailbox	*mailbox*	I dropped the letter in the **mailbox**.
15.	baby sitter	*baby sitter*	She is a **baby sitter** for the twins.
16.	upstairs	*upstairs*	My bedroom is **upstairs**.
17.	everyday	*everyday*	That is one of my **everyday** chores.
18.	alarm clock	*alarm clock*	I set the **alarm clock** for 7:30.
19.	newspaper	*newspaper*	We read a **newspaper** every day.
20.	weekend	*weekend*	The **weekend** at the lake will be fun.

SORT THE SPELLING WORDS

1.–15. Write the compound words on the spelling list that are written as one word.

16.–20. Write the spelling words that are two-word compounds.

REMEMBER THE SPELLING STRATEGY

Remember that a compound word is formed from two or more smaller words. Closed compounds are written as one word: **newspaper**. Open compounds are written as two or more words: **air mail**.

Spelling _{and} Vocabulary

Word Meanings

Write the spelling word that has the same or almost the same meaning as each of the following phrases.

1. a person who takes care of a baby
2. a paper that has news in it
3. a game in which a ball is thrown through a basket
4. a school that usually includes grades nine through twelve
5. the two days at the end of the week

Antonyms

Write a spelling word that is an antonym for each of the following words.

6. faraway
7. downstairs
8. indoors
9. no one
10. nowhere

USING THE Dictionary

Find the following words in your **Spelling Dictionary**. Write each word. Then write **n., adj., adv.,** or **conj.** after it to name the part of speech it usually has.

11. whenever
12. seat belt
13. tablecloth
14. everyday
15. mailbox
16. flashlight
17. sometimes
18. driveway
19. air mail
20. alarm clock

Word Meanings

1. _____
2. _____
3. _____
4. _____
5. _____

Antonyms

6. _____
7. _____
8. _____
9. _____
10. _____

Using the Dictionary

11. _____
12. _____
13. _____
14. _____
15. _____
16. _____
17. _____
18. _____
19. _____
20. _____

Spelling and Reading

tablecloth	everyone	nearby	outdoors
high school	anywhere	flashlight	air mail
whenever	driveway	sometimes	seat belt
basketball	mailbox	baby sitter	upstairs
everyday	alarm clock	newspaper	weekend

Replace the Words Replace the underlined part of each sentence with a spelling word.

1. <u>Every person</u> can be seated now.
2. The <u>person who takes care of children</u> arrived.
3. Our post office has a special slot for <u>mail that is sent by air</u>.
4. We subscribe to a daily <u>news printed on sheets of paper</u>.
5. I <u>now and then</u> listen to the radio.

Complete the Sentences Write the spelling word that completes each sentence.

6. I always wear a _____ when riding in a car.
7. We have old dishes that Mom calls her _____ tableware.
8. I was late yesterday because my _____ did not ring.
9. I would rather be _____ than indoors.
10. My father parks his car in our _____.
11. Was there a letter in the _____?
12. I need a bright _____ for my camping trips.
13. Please put the lace _____ on the table.
14. Our school will have a _____ game tonight.
15. I squint _____ the sun is in my eyes.

Solve the Analogies Write a spelling word to solve each analogy.

16. **Wednesday** is to **weekday** as **Saturday** is to _____.
17. **Fourth grade** is to **elementary school** as **tenth grade** is to _____.
18. **Distant** is to **faraway** as **close** is to _____.
19. **First floor** is to **downstairs** as **second floor** is to _____.
20. **No one** is to **anyone** as **nowhere** is to _____.

Replace the Words
1. _____
2. _____
3. _____
4. _____
5. _____

Complete the Sentences
6. _____
7. _____
8. _____
9. _____
10. _____
11. _____
12. _____
13. _____
14. _____
15. _____

Solve the Analogies
16. _____
17. _____
18. _____
19. _____
20. _____

Spelling and Writing

Proofread a Notice

Six words are not spelled correctly in this notice. Write those words correctly.

To: All Students and Teachers

From: J. Patrick, Principal

Friday is School Picnic Day. It is important that everyune be here on time. We will go to nearbye Fellows Field for food and fun outdores. Swings, slides, and a baskitball court will be available. Bring sunscreen because sometimes the sun gets very hot. You can return to school by bus, or your parents can pick you up whenevr they wish. This is not an everday event. Let's have fun!

Proofreading Marks

≡ Make a capital.

／ Make a small letter.

∧ Add something.

℮ Take out something.

⊙ Add a period.

⌗ New paragraph

SP Spelling error

Write a Notice — Expository Writing

Write a notice for something you would like to do. Be sure to include

- to whom the notice applies.
- who wrote the notice.
- what the readers of the notice should do.
- how they should plan their time.

Use as many spelling words as you can.

Proofread Your Writing During

Proofread your writing for spelling errors as part of the editing stage in the writing process. Be sure to check each word carefully. Use a dictionary to check spelling if you are not sure.

Writing Process

Prewriting

Drafting

Revising

Editing

Publishing

209

VOCABULARY CONNECTIONS

Strategy Words

Review Words

1. _____
2. _____
3. _____
4. _____
5. _____

Preview Words

6. _____
7. _____
8. _____
9. _____
10. _____

Review Words: Compounds

Write the word from the box that matches each of the following descriptions.

anybody	anything	everything
someone	something	

1. I am a two-syllable word ending in **one**.
2. I am a two-syllable word ending in **thing**.
3. I am a three-syllable word meaning "all things."
4. I am a three-syllable word beginning with **any**.
5. I am a four-syllable word meaning "any person."

Preview Words: Compounds

Write the word from the box that matches each clue.

downstairs	good-bye	homework
itself	peanut butter	

6. an antonym of **hello**
7. himself, herself, _____
8. an open compound naming something good to eat
9. a closed compound meaning "work that is done at home"
10. a location in a building

Content Words

Science: The Sun

Write the word from the box that fits each definition.

core	solar	eclipse	sunspot	halo

1. the center part of something
2. a dark patch on the sun
3. a temporary darkening of the sun or moon
4. a ring of light around the sun or moon
5. coming from the sun

Science: Earthquakes

Write the word from the box that matches each clue.

aftershock	terror	earthquake	totter	fault

6. a shaking of the earth's surface
7. a break or crack in the earth's crust
8. the feeling of many people during an earthquake
9. how objects and people might move during an earthquake
10. a less powerful shock that follows the shaking of the earth's surface

Apply the Spelling Strategy

Circle three of the Content Words you wrote that are closed compounds.

Word Study

Make a New Word

Spot is a word that can be used to form many other words, such as **spotless** and **spotlight**. Write the Content Word that contains **spot**.

Science: The Sun
1. _____
2. _____
3. _____
4. _____
5. _____

Science: Earthquakes
6. _____
7. _____
8. _____
9. _____
10. _____

Make a New Word
1. _____

continents

1. _____
2. _____
3. _____
4. _____
5. _____
6. _____

nationalities

7. _____
8. _____
9. _____
10. _____
11. _____
12. _____
13. _____
14. _____
15. _____
16. _____
17. _____
18. _____
19. _____
20. _____

Spelling and Thinking

READ THE SPELLING WORDS

1.	Greek	*Greek*	He is of **Greek** ancestry.
2.	Russian	*Russian*	Our dog is a **Russian** wolfhound.
3.	Africa	*Africa*	They went on a safari in **Africa**.
4.	American	*American*	That is an **American** automobile.
5.	Europe	*Europe*	She traveled in **Europe** all summer.
6.	Indian	*Indian*	The **Indian** capital is New Delhi.
7.	Japanese	*Japanese*	We saw a **Japanese** temple.
8.	Australia	*Australia*	**Australia** is a small continent.
9.	French	*French*	I studied the **French** language.
10.	Antarctica	*Antarctica*	**Antarctica** is a cold, icy continent.
11.	Canadian	*Canadian*	Ontario is a **Canadian** province.
12.	Chinese	*Chinese*	The **Chinese** have an ancient culture.
13.	Mexican	*Mexican*	Do you cook **Mexican** dishes?
14.	Spanish	*Spanish*	Are your relatives of **Spanish** descent?
15.	America	*America*	**America** consists of two continents.
16.	German	*German*	We watched the **German** folk dancers.
17.	Italian	*Italian*	I love **Italian** food.
18.	British	*British*	Which countries are **British**?
19.	Asia	*Asia*	Laos is a country in **Asia**.
20.	Irish	*Irish*	We enjoy singing **Irish** songs.

SORT THE SPELLING WORDS

1.–6. Write the spelling words that name continents.

7.–20. Write the spelling words that name nationalities.

REMEMBER THE SPELLING STRATEGY

Remember that it is important to be able to spell the names of the continents and nationalities correctly.

Spelling ᵃⁿᵈ Vocabulary

Word Meanings

Write the name of the nationality that goes with the name of each of the following countries.

1. China
2. Russia
3. Ireland
4. France
5. America
6. Mexico
7. Great Britain

Beginnings and Endings

8.–12. Write the names of the continents that begin and end with the letter **a**.

Words Within Words

Write the spelling words that contain each of the following words.

13. rope
14. man
15. span
16. can

USING THE Dictionary

17.–20. Write the following spelling words in alphabetical order.

Italian   Greek   Japanese   Indian

◆ ◆ ◆

Dictionary Check Be sure to check the alphabetical order of the words in your **Spelling Dictionary**.

Word Meanings

1. _____
2. _____
3. _____
4. _____
5. _____
6. _____
7. _____

Beginnings and Endings

8. _____
9. _____
10. _____
11. _____
12. _____

Words Within Words

13. _____
14. _____
15. _____
16. _____

Using the Dictionary

17. _____
18. _____
19. _____
20. _____

Greek	Russian	Africa	American
Europe	Indian	Japanese	Australia
French	Antarctica	Canadian	Chinese
Mexican	Spanish	America	German
Italian	British	Asia	Irish

Name the Categories   Write the spelling word that is suggested by each of the following groups of words.

1. panda bears, chopsticks, Great Wall
2. maple leaf, hockey, provinces
3. shamrocks, Blarney Stone, green fields
4. snow, ice, whales, penguins
5. kangaroos, koala bears, boomerangs
6. Paris, berets, Eiffel Tower
7. Big Ben, London, Buckingham Palace
8. Olympics, mythology, Athens

Complete the Sentences   Write the spelling word that completes each sentence.

9. The largest continent in the world is _____.
10. The United States is in North _____.
11. A sari is a dress worn by many _____ women.
12. Rome is an _____ city.
13. _____ festivals are called **fiestas**.
14. Madrid is a _____ city.
15. *Sputnik I* was a _____ spacecraft, the first to orbit the earth.
16. France and Spain are countries in _____.
17. **Origami** is the _____ art of folding paper.
18. The two _____ continents are South America and North America.
19. Berlin is a large _____ city.
20. You can go on a jungle safari in _____.

Name the Categories
1. _____
2. _____
3. _____
4. _____
5. _____
6. _____
7. _____
8. _____

Complete the Sentences
9. _____
10. _____
11. _____
12. _____
13. _____
14. _____
15. _____
16. _____
17. _____
18. _____
19. _____
20. _____

Spelling and Writing

Proofread an Ad

Six words are not spelled correctly in this travel ad. Write those words correctly.

Omniworld
Offers It All

Do you want to sweat in a jungle in Africa, shiver in Antartica, visit Europ, photograph kangaroos in Australia, or explore South Americka? We have it all: Greak food, Irish hospitality, the Chineese Great Wall! Visit or call our Canadien or American offices today.

Write an Ad

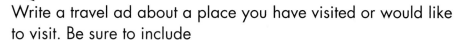

Persuasive Writing

Write a travel ad about a place you have visited or would like to visit. Be sure to include

- the name of the company placing the ad.
- what the company has to offer.
- suggested prices.
- why the reader should choose to go.
- how the reader can get more information.

Use as many spelling words as you can.

Writing Process

Prewriting

Drafting

Revising

Editing

Publishing

Proofread Your Writing During

Proofread your writing for spelling errors as part of the editing stage in the writing process. Be sure to check each word carefully. Use a dictionary to check spelling if you are not sure.

VOCABULARY CONNECTIONS

Strategy Words

Review Words: Continents and Nationalities

Write the word from the box that answers each word problem.

street	east	earth	west	south

1. best – b + w = _____
2. strong – ong + feet – f = _____
3. mouths – s – m + s = _____
4. feasting – f – ing = _____
5. dreary – dr – y + th = _____

Preview Words: Continents and Nationalities

Write the word from the box that matches each state description.

California	Colorado	New York
Texas	Washington	

6. a state bordered on the north by Oregon and on the west by the Pacific Ocean
7. a state bordered by Oregon, Idaho, and Canada
8. a state and a city in the Northeast
9. the Rocky Mountain state whose capital is Denver
10. the largest of the south-central states

Review Words

1. _____
2. _____
3. _____
4. _____
5. _____

Preview Words

6. _____
7. _____
8. _____
9. _____
10. _____

Content Words

Social Studies: Geography

Write the word from the box that matches each definition.

arctic	polar	continent	strait	iceberg

1. a narrow passage of water; a channel
2. having to do with one or both of the earth's poles
3. one of the seven main masses of land in the world
4. a body of floating ice broken off a glacier
5. extremely cold; freezing

Math: Ordinal Numbers

Write the word from the box that comes from each of the following cardinal numbers.

ninth	thirteenth	eleventh	fourteenth	twelfth

6. 12
7. 9
8. 11
9. 13
10. 14

Apply the Spelling Strategy

Circle the Content Word you wrote that means "a large land mass."

Word Study

Eponyms

An **eponym** is a word that comes from someone's name. When Spanish travelers began exploring the south-central part of what is now the United States, they met a group of Indians who called themselves the **Tejas**.

A large territory that later became a state was named after the **Tejas**. Write the Strategy Word that came from this name.

Social Studies: Geography
1. _____
2. _____
3. _____
4. _____
5. _____

Math: Ordinal Numbers
6. _____
7. _____
8. _____
9. _____
10. _____

Eponyms
1. _____

Assessment and Review

Assessment — Units 31–35

Each Assessment Word in the box fits one of the spelling strategies you have studied over the past five weeks. Read the spelling strategies. Then write each Assessment Word under the unit number it fits.

Unit 31

1.–4. Plural nouns name more than one person, place, or thing. Plurals are formed in different ways: add **-s** (**trays**), add **-es** (**lunches**), or change final **y** to **i** and add **-es** (**pennies**).

Unit 32

5.–8. Possessive nouns show ownership. Add an apostrophe and **s** (**'s**) to show possession when a noun is singular: **calf's**. Add an apostrophe (**'**) to show ownership when a plural noun ends in **-s: calves'**. When a noun is plural and does **not** end in **-s,** add an apostrophe and **s** (**'s**) to show ownership: **children's**.

Unit 33

9.–12. The suffix **-ness** means "a condition or quality": **kindness**. The suffix **-ment** means "the result of an action": **enjoyment**.

Unit 34

13.–16. A compound word is formed from two or more smaller words. Closed compounds are written as one word: **newspaper**. Open compounds are written as two or more words: **air mail**.

Unit 35

17.–20. It is important to be able to spell the names of the continents and nationalities correctly.

families
parents'
Dutch
prepayment
home run
turtleneck
cheerfulness
Korean
friend's
matches
questions
teacher's
Portuguese
peacefulness
meantime
Cuban
treaties
aunt's
swiftness
applesauce

 **Review** Unit 31: Plurals

babies	holidays	libraries	members	friends
lunches	teams	armies	patches	ladies

Write the spelling word that completes the sentence.

1. Mom sewed _____ on the holes in my shirt.
2. How many _____ are in the club?
3. Joey has two _____ of toy soldiers.
4. I have invited ten of my best _____.
5. Valentine's Day and Thanksgiving are favorite _____.
6. The men sat here, and the _____ sat there.
7. Which _____ are playing tonight?
8. I checked two _____ for that book.

9.–10. The mothers and their _____ will eat their _____ early.

 **Review** Unit 32: Possessives

brother's	children's	fathers'	mother's	watches'
fish's	sisters'	wife's	child's	sons'

Write the spelling word that completes the phrase.

11. the faces of two watches: the _____ faces
12. the eyes of one fish: the _____ eyes
13. the shoes of my sisters: my _____ shoes
14. the name of his wife: his _____ name
15. the interests of my mother: my _____ interests
16. the grades of her brother: her _____ grades
17. the toys of the children: the _____ toys
18. the tricycle of the child: the _____ tricycle
19. the lawnmowers of our fathers: our _____ lawnmowers
20. the paintings of her sons: her _____ paintings

Unit 31
1. _____
2. _____
3. _____
4. _____
5. _____
6. _____
7. _____
8. _____
9. _____
10. _____

Unit 32
11. _____
12. _____
13. _____
14. _____
15. _____
16. _____
17. _____
18. _____
19. _____
20. _____

 **Review** Unit 33: Suffixes -ness, -ment

agreement	enjoyment	kindness	thickness	stillness
movement	apartment	illness	sadness	darkness

Write the spelling word whose base word rhymes with the word below.

1. mind
2. sick
3. smart
4. spark
5. free
6. mad
7. prove
8. employ

Write the spelling word that goes with each base word.

9. ill
10. still

 **Review** Unit 34: Compounds

basketball	everyday	everyone	sometimes	newspaper
outdoors	nearby	anywhere	whenever	upstairs

Write the word that completes each sentence.

11. I looked all over but couldn't find my watch _____.
12. Nearly _____ agreed that this is best.
13. What time should we be at the gym for the _____ game?
14. Instead of staying indoors, we're going to go _____.
15. I read the article in the _____.
16. I'll be ready _____ you are.
17. These are our special dishes, and those are our _____ ones.
18. Stay here and look downstairs while I look _____.
19. Usually I eat cereal for breakfast, but _____ I have muffins.
20. Is the school far away, or is it _____?

 **Review** **Unit 35: Continents and Nationalities**

Africa	American	Chinese	Spanish	Asia
Mexican	Indian	America	Irish	French

Write the word that fits the description.

1. a child born in Ireland
2. a type of food eaten in Mexico
3. the language spoken in China
4. the music and dance of Spain
5. the continent that includes China and Vietnam
6. the continent where Ethiopia and South Africa are
7. a woman born in the United States of America
8. the language spoken in France
9. someone from India
10. South _____, the continent south of North America

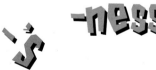

Unit 35

1. _____
2. _____
3. _____
4. _____
5. _____
6. _____
7. _____
8. _____
9. _____
10. _____

WORD SORT **Spelling Study Strategy**

Sorting by Endings

One good way to practice spelling words is to place words into groups according to some spelling pattern. Here is a way to practice some of the spelling words you have been studying in the past few weeks.

1. Make six columns across a large piece of paper.

2. Write one of these words, including the underlined parts, at the top of each column: **lunch<u>es</u>, friend<u>s</u>, brother'<u>s</u>, fathers<u>'</u>, dark<u>ness</u>, enjoy<u>ment</u>**.

3. Have a partner choose a spelling word from Units 31, 32, and 33 and say it aloud.

4. Write the spelling word in the column under the word with the same ending.

-s

-ment

s'

-es

's

-ness

Grammar, Usage, and Mechanics

Adverbs

An adverb that ends in **-ly** usually tells about a verb. It tells how something is done, or how often it is done.

The actor walked **quietly** across the stage.

The hare ran **quickly**.

Slowly but **surely,** the tortoise won the race.

A. Write the adverb in each sentence below.

1. Someone carelessly left a shoe on the floor.
2. Tawana smiled cheerfully at the audience.
3. People are sleeping, so talk softly.
4. George packed his suitcase carefully.
5. With trembling hands, I excitedly opened the huge envelope.

B. Which sentences contain adverbs? Write the adverbs you see in each sentence. Write **no** if a sentence has no adverb.

6. The audience cheered loudly for both teams.
7. I love staying in this quiet library.
8. Your brother's watch ticks noisily.
9. The door slammed suddenly and startled me.
10. The delicious aroma filled the room completely.

A.
  1.
  2.
  3.
  4.
  5.
B.
  6.
  7.
  8.
  9.
  10.

Proofreading Strategy

Box It Up!

Good writers always proofread their writing for spelling errors. Here's a strategy that you can use to proofread your work.

Cut a small hole or box in a piece of paper. Slide it over your writing so that just one or two words appear inside the box. You won't be able to see a whole sentence. Instead of reading **The rocket blasted off into space,** you might see **rocket blasted** or **off into**.

This may sound like a strange way to proofread, but boxing in a few words at a time helps you focus on the spelling of words. You pay no attention to their meanings this way. Try it!

Electronic Spelling

1. _____
2. _____
3. _____
4. _____
5. _____
6. _____

Electronic Spelling

Searching for Information

Computers and the Internet allow you to find information quickly and easily. However, you must know how to look. You can tell your search engine to look for a key word in a source. Suppose you wanted information on a state. In this case, you could type in the two-letter postal abbreviation, such as **NY** for **New York**.

Many of these abbreviations look alike. Can you tell which are which? Write the name of the state that matches each abbreviation.

1. Does AR stand for Arkansas or Arizona?
2. Does CO stand for Connecticut or Colorado?
3. Does IA stand for Indiana or Iowa?
4. Does MS stand for Missouri or Mississippi?
5. Does NE stand for Nebraska or Nevada?
6. Does MA stand for Massachusetts or Maine?

Challenge Activities

perhaps	catfish	ticket
	begun	vinegar

A. Write the challenge word that fits each group.

1. maybe, possibly, _____
2. trout, perch, _____
3. started, gone, _____
4. check, bill, _____
5. salad, oil, _____

B. Correct the misspelling in each challenge word. Write the word.

1. The performance has already beggun.
2. Do you have the tiket for the show?
3. Can you believe that there is an act with a catfesh as a magician!
4. Purhaps we can learn some tricks!
5. This viniger is very sour!

C. Write a paragraph to describe this make-believe catfish performer in the picture. Tell a little about how it is dressed, and describe one of the tricks. Use the challenge words, when you can, as well as other words of your choice.

A.
1. _____
2. _____
3. _____
4. _____
5. _____
B.
1. _____
2. _____
3. _____
4. _____
5. _____

| fuse | female | trapeze |
| antelope | otherwise |

A. Write the challenge word that rhymes with each word below. After each challenge word, write **a, e, i, o,** or **u** to tell which long vowel sound you hear in the word. One word has two different long vowel sounds in it.

1. detail

2. cantaloupe

3. green peas

4. pews

5. surprise

B. Use the letter that comes before each letter of the alphabet in the underlined words to write the challenge words.

Example: dbqf = cape

1. Can an <u>boufmpqf</u> run swiftly?

2. Does a <u>gvtf</u> have to do with electricity?

3. Is your mom a <u>gfnbmf</u>?

4. Can you find a <u>usbqfaf</u> in an oven?

5. If I think <u>puifsxjtf</u>, am I right?

Now go back and answer **Yes** or **No** to each question.

C. Make up at least ten sentences with the words "If I were . . . I might be. . . ." Use challenge words and other words you know to complete the sentences. For example, "If I were on a car, I might be a tire" or "If I were made of ice, I might be a cube." Choose one of your sentences to illustrate.

A.
1.
2.
3.
4.
5.
B.
1.
2.
3.
4.
5.

Challenge Activities

| nickname | stadium | replay |
| regain | trainer | |

A. Look at the vowel spellings for **long a** in the words below. Write the word that does not belong in each group.

1. flavor, stadium, regain, able
2. stadium, aim, rail, trainer
3. anyway, relay, nickname, holiday
4. trailer, rail, replay, brain
5. lazy, lady, paper, trainer

B. Write the challenge word that fits each "What Am I?" statement.

1. Sometimes I am Patty, and other times I am Tricia, Patsy, or "Smartie."
2. I am huge. I have a playing field, bleachers, reserved seats, and a scoreboard.
3. I am someone who teaches and helps athletes prepare for sports competitions.
4. You see me on television. Sometimes I'm in slow motion. I'm often seen as an exciting part of a game, such as a football touchdown.
5. I have a prefix that means "do again."

C. Imagine that you are a radio sports announcer. You have just witnessed a football game or some other sports event. First tell who you are and where you are broadcasting from. Write what you would say about the highlights in the exciting game. Try to use all the challenge words. You might wish to make your classmates players on the teams.

A.
1.
2.
3.
4.
5.
B.
1.
2.
3.
4.
5.

Challenge Activities

wreath	treason	keenly
breed	belief	

A. Write the challenge words that rhyme with the words below.

1. relief
2. creed
3. queenly
4. reason
5. beneath

B. Write a challenge word to complete each sentence.

1. If you betray your country by aiding the enemy, you are guilty of _____.
2. If you have faith in something, you have a _____.
3. If your eyes are sharp, you see _____.
4. A ring made of flowers, leaves, or small branches is a _____.
5. A group of animals, such as beagles, can be called a _____.

C. List several answers to each question below. Look over your lists to see whether one of your answers suggests something you could write about. Then write a short paragraph using the word or words you selected.

1. What are some names for different breeds of dogs?
2. Where might a person put a wreath?
3. What do you feel keenly, or very strongly, about?

A.
1. _____
2. _____
3. _____
4. _____
5. _____

B.
1. _____
2. _____
3. _____
4. _____
5. _____

Challenge Activities

dial	rely	hydrant
lightly	blight	

A.
1.
2.
3.
4.
5.

B.
1.
2.
3.
4.

A. Write the challenge word that matches each vowel pattern and goes with each definition. Circle the letter or letters that spell the **long i** sound.

1. control knob   __ i __ __
2. disease   __ __ i g h __
3. fireplug   __ y __ __ __ __ __
4. without force   __ i g h __ __ __ __
5. depend   __ __ __ y

B. Write the letter that tells which meaning of **lightly** is used in the sentence.

   a. with little weight or pressure
   b. a little amount of something
   c. not seriously
   d. without serious penalty

1. My uncle says that he'll buy me a pony, but I take it lightly.
2. I wasn't hungry, so I ate lightly at lunch.
3. The principal let the tardy student off lightly.
4. Please press down lightly to glue each corner.

C. Answer each question with several examples. If you wish, add details to explain your answers.

1. What things have a dial?
2. When should you rely on others?
3. Why do we have fire hydrants?
4. What might you hear that you would take lightly?

Challenge Activities

| bonus | banjo | poach |
| decode | following |

A. Write the challenge word that fits with each group.

1. gift, reward, _____
2. unscramble, solve, _____
3. guitar, ukulele, _____
4. fry, boil, _____
5. leading, passing, _____

B. Write the challenge word that completes each analogy.

1. **Tuba** is to **trumpet** as **ukulele** is to _____.
2. **Extra** is to **more** as _____ is to **reward**.
3. **Read** is to **greeting card** as _____ is to **secret message**.
4. **Fish** is to **broil** as **eggs** are to _____.
5. **Pass** is to **passing** as **follow** is to _____.

| A. |
| 1. |
| 2. |
| 3. |
| 4. |
| 5. |
| B. |
| 1. |
| 2. |
| 3. |
| 4. |
| 5. |

C. Choose a challenge word. Write it at the top of your paper. Then write **Who? What? Where? Why?** and **When?** along the left-hand edge of the paper. Write questions using the **W-**words and the challenge word. Then think about how you could answer each question. Use your questions and answers to write a paragraph.

Challenge Activities

menu	fuel	nephew
duties	blueberry	

A. Write the challenge word that completes each analogy.

1. **Sister** is to **brother** as **niece** is to _____.
2. **Telephone numbers** are to **directory** as **dinners** are to _____.
3. **Berry** is to **berries** as **duty** is to _____.
4. **Vegetable** is to **carrot** as **fruit** is to _____.
5. **Portable radio** is to **batteries** as **car** is to _____.

B. Write a challenge word to answer each question.

1. I am things you ought to do. What am I?
2. I am something you read and order from in a restaurant. What am I?
3. I am a boy who is the son of your sister or brother. What is my relationship to you?
4. I am used to produce heat in homes or power in automobiles. What am I?
5. You can pick me and put me in a dish with other fruit or into a pie. What am I?

C. Imagine that you have each job mentioned below. You think your job is very interesting and special. Write what some of your duties are. Use some of the challenge words.

1. You work at a gasoline station.
2. You are in charge of preparing menus in a famous restaurant.
3. You grow fruit and sell it.

A.
1.
2.
3.
4.
5.

B.
1.
2.
3.
4.
5.

Challenge Activities

spout	bountiful	scowl
hoist	buoyant	

A. Write the challenge word that best replaces each underlined phrase.

   1. She likes to swim with an inner tube because it is <u>able to float</u>.

   2. The <u>angry frown</u> showed how he felt when the team lost the game.

   3. The hot water came from the kettle's <u>narrow opening</u>.

   4. The heavy ropes helped them <u>lift up</u> the box off the ship and onto the dock.

   5. The pirate's chest overflowed with <u>more than enough</u> treasure.

B. Write the challenge word for each number to complete the story.

   What was that in the water? It looked heavy but it floated on the surface, so it was __1.__ . I eased our boat over to it and tried to __2.__ it in, but it weighed a ton. A __3.__ on each of our faces showed how unhappy we were. We hoped it would overflow with a __4.__ treasure! Finally, we got it out of the water and opened it. What do you think it was? A trunkful of toy, wind-up whales! We couldn't resist trying them, so we put them in the water. They began to __5.__ !

C. Write a tall tale about your own treasure hunt. Exaggerate as much as you can. Use some of the challenge words.

A.
1. _____
2. _____
3. _____
4. _____
5. _____
B.
1. _____
2. _____
3. _____
4. _____
5. _____

Challenge Activities

audio	naughty	oriole
	toward	dinosaur

A. Replace the definition in ( ) with a challenge word. Write the word. Then answer the question with **Yes** or **No**.

1.–2. Could a (prehistoric reptile) perch daintily on the head of an (orange songbird)?

3. Can (relating to sound) refer to a television set?

4. Can shoes be (behaving badly)?

5.–6. Can an (orange songbird) swim (in the direction of) land?

B. Read each group of words. Write the challenge word you associate with each group.

1. brontosaurus, stegosaurus, styracosaurus

2. overturned water dish, chewed book, muddy paws

3. Baltimore, songbird, orange and black feathers

4. AM/FM, stereo, radio

5. forward, near

C. Pretend that a dinosaur was playing a loud radio while you were trying to read. Write a paragraph describing what you would do. Use as many challenge words as possible.

A.
1.
2.
3.
4.
5.
6.
B.
1.
2.
3.
4.
5.

Challenge Activities

terse	burden	skirted
reindeer	earrings	

A. Use the clues in each equation to make a challenge word. Write the word.

1. + = _____

2. + = _____

3. + = _____

4. + = _____

5. + = _____

B. Write the challenge words for the **R** puzzle. Use the definitions as clues.

1. __ __ __ __ brief

2. __ __ __ __ __ passed around or avoided

3. __ __ __ __ __ __ jewelry worn on the ears

4. __ __ __ __ __ a load

5. __ __ __ __ __ __ __ __ animal with antlers

C. Imagine that a reindeer is a rock star. Write a story about his or her adventures. Use as many challenge words as possible.

A.	
1.	_____
2.	_____
3.	_____
4.	_____
5.	_____
B.	
1.	_____
2.	_____
3.	_____
4.	_____
5.	_____

Challenge Activities

arch   harness   tardy

glare   snare

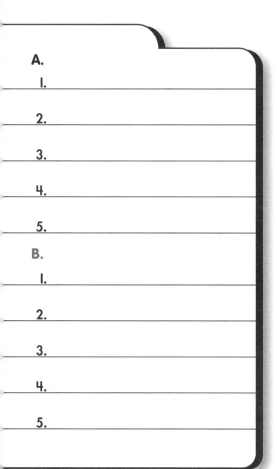

A.

1.

2.

3.

4.

5.

B.

1.

2.

3.

4.

5.

A. Write the challenge words that match the definitions below.

   1. an angry look; a bright light

   2. late or delayed

   3. leather straps and bands

   4. trap or catch

   5. a curved structure that carries weight over an opening; to form a curve

B. 1.–5. Find the misspelled challenge words or forms of them in the story. Write each one correctly.

My horse and I were walking along a road. It was hot, so I took off his harnes. Instead of walking slowly with me, he galloped off. I glaired at him, but he would not come back. I was afraid I'd be tardie for dinner, so I ran after him. I was finally able to snair him and bring him through the gate with the arrch and into the corral. I quickly washed my hands and face and went into the kitchen.

"I was just about to call you to dinner," Dad said.

C. Write a mystery story about something missing or unusual. Use some of the challenge words to tell about the mystery and to describe clues. Perhaps you can tell about a ranch and a missing saddle from the tack room where all the horses' equipment is stored.

Challenge Activities

wealth	threat	pheasant
biscuit	tortoise	

A. "Pick" or take out the flowers in these sentences. Write a challenge word to replace each one.

1. The rose would taste delicious with jam.
2. Was that a daisy I saw fly by?
3. The tulip pulled its head back into its shell.
4. The gray cloud was a dandelion to the picnic.
5. The millionaire offered to donate some of his great sunflower to build a new hospital.

B. Write a challenge word to complete each sentence.

1. A _____ is a kind of bread.
2. A _____ may be a sign of trouble.
3. A _____ is a kind of bird.
4. A _____ is a kind of turtle.
5. _____ is a large amount of riches.

C. Write a fable about a tortoise and a pheasant. Use some of the challenge words to tell what happens. Many fables end with a wise saying that sums up the fable. Use one of the sayings below or another one that you know. You may want to make up your own wise saying!

1. Nothing ventured, nothing gained.
2. He who laughs last, laughs best.
3. Don't count your chickens before they're hatched.

A.
1. _____
2. _____
3. _____
4. _____
5. _____

B.
1. _____
2. _____
3. _____
4. _____
5. _____

Challenge Activities

gnaw	gnat	cough
prompt	knuckle	

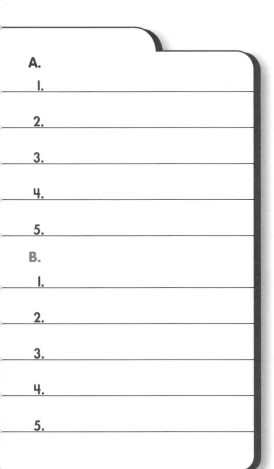

A.
1.
2.
3.
4.
5.
B.
1.
2.
3.
4.
5.

A. Write a challenge word to go with each clue.

1. a joint in your finger
2. quick
3. to bite on something, such as a bone
4. a small flying insect
5. a sound you often make when you have a cold

B. Look at the dictionary respelling in parentheses. Then write the challenge word it stands for.

1. The restaurant gave us (prŏmpt) service.
2. I scratched my (**nuk'** əl) on the bricks.
3. We gave the dog a bone to (nô).
4. The (năt) tried to bite me.
5. Does your cold make you (kôf)?

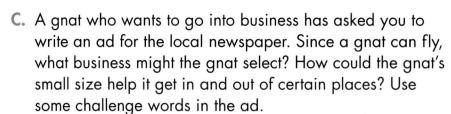

C. A gnat who wants to go into business has asked you to write an ad for the local newspaper. Since a gnat can fly, what business might the gnat select? How could the gnat's small size help it get in and out of certain places? Use some challenge words in the ad.

Challenge Activities

| quartz | quaint | quiver |
| squid | squirt |

A. Add a challenge word with the same beginning sound to each group. Be sure not to add the challenge word that is already in the list. The words are in alphabetical order.

   1. _____, quartz, quiet, quiver

   2. squad, squeal, squid, _____

   3. quaint, _____, quill, quiver

   4. squeeze, _____, squirm, squirt

   5. quaint, quartz, quiet, _____

B. What am I? Write the challenge word that answers each description.

   1. I'm an animal that looks like an octopus.

   2. I'm a hard rock.

   3. I'm what you can do with a hose.

   4. I'm what you do when you shake just a little.

   5. I'm attractive in an old-fashioned way.

C. Write two tongue twisters. Use two challenge words in each sentence and underline them. Try to make most of the words in your sentences start with the same sound.

Example: Can quartz quiver quite quickly?

A.
1.
2.
3.
4.
5.

B.
1.
2.
3.
4.
5.

Challenge Activities

gadget	gelatin	engage
beverage	rummage	

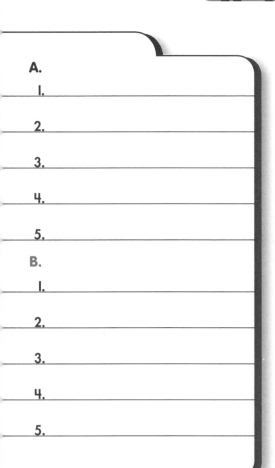

A.
1.
2.
3.
4.
5.

B.
1.
2.
3.
4.
5.

A. Write the challenge word by adding the missing consonants. Circle the **g** that stands for the **/j/** sound in each word you write.

1. __ e __ e __ a __ e
2. e __ __ a __ e
3. __ a __ __ e __
4. __ u __ __ a __ e
5. __ e __ a __ i __

B. Write the challenge word for each definition.

1. something to drink
2. a small mechanical object
3. to search for something by moving things around
4. to keep busy or to hire
5. a jellylike substance

C. You have found a mysterious-looking gadget. Write a detailed description of it, and tell what you think it is used for. If you wish, draw a picture of the strange gadget.

Challenge Activities

meddle	wriggle	sparkle
brittle	tangle

A. Write the challenge word that best completes each sentence.

1. Dried leaves and eggshells are _____.

2. To "butt in" or "intrude" is to _____.

3. A diamond or crystal will _____.

4. Hair, yarn, or string can _____.

5. A worm or a snake can _____.

s-s-s-s-s

B. Add and subtract letters to find challenge words. Write the challenge word that solves each problem.

1. wrbr – wr + i + tet – e + le = _____

2. spdl – dl + dark – d + le = _____

3. pdm – pd + edd + le = _____

4. stan – s + bgle – b = _____

5. w + rig + bg – b + le = _____

C. Imagine that your spacecraft has just landed on a planet with very strange but friendly surroundings. Write an entry for your captain's journal describing what you see. Use as many challenge words as you can.

A.
1. _____
2. _____
3. _____
4. _____
5. _____
B.
1. _____
2. _____
3. _____
4. _____
5. _____

Challenge Activities

unable	whistle	beaten
wooden	woolen	

A.
1.
2.
3.
4.
5.

B.
1.
2.
3.
4.
5.

A. Write the challenge word that answers the question.

1. What do you call an egg if the white and yolk are mixed together?
2. If a table isn't made of plastic, what kind of table might it be?
3. What means the same as **cannot**?
4. What can you do with a tune rather than sing it?
5. What type of blanket feels good on a chilly night?

B. Change one, two, or three letters in the underlined word in each sentence and write the challenge word that makes the most sense.

1. I have <u>beetle</u> the eggs.
2. I am <u>stable</u> to lift the heavy box.
3. The counselor blew a <u>whisper</u>.
4. Is this a <u>wooden</u> blanket?
5. Dad made a <u>woolen</u> train.

C. Pretend you are a carpenter. Write directions for making something out of wood. Use some of the challenge words.

Challenge Activities

halter	barber	rubber
	razor	anchor

A. Write the challenge word that goes with each spelling clue below.

    1. Which word has the **k** sound spelled **ch**?

    2. Which word rhymes with **harbor**?

    3. Which word has **long a** spelled **a**?

    4. Which word has double **b**'s?

    5. Which word begins with **h** and ends with **er**?

B. Unscramble each underlined word to find the challenge word that goes with each definition. Write the word.

    1. relhat A leather headgear for leading a horse is a _____.

    2. brerbu An article of footwear worn in the rain is a _____.

    3. brebra A person who cuts hair and trims beards is a _____.

    4. chonra A heavy object that keeps boats from drifting is an _____.

    5. zorar A tool for cutting is a _____.

C. Write about a real or an imaginary time when you had your hair cut. Did anything unusual happen? Use some challenge words if you can.

A.

1. _____

2. _____

3. _____

4. _____

5. _____

B.

1. _____

2. _____

3. _____

4. _____

5. _____

Challenge Activities

bluest	healthier	healthiest
heavier	heaviest	

A. Unscramble the challenge words and write them correctly.

1. t e s b u l

2. h e a l i t e r h

3. s e l t h a t i e h

4. v e i r e a h

5. s t e a v i e h

B. Write the missing challenge words to describe the pictures.

1. blue   bluer _____

2.–3. healthy _____ _____

4.–5. heavy _____ _____

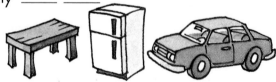

C. Describe five imaginary people. Give them names. Write a sentence about each one. Try to use challenge words in each sentence.

A.
1.
2.
3.
4.
5.

B.
1.
2.
3.
4.
5.

Challenge Activities

mist	missed	guest
	guessed	aloud

A. Write a challenge word to complete each analogy.

1. **Author** is to **write** as _____ is to **visit**.
2. **Rain** is to _____ as **cloud** is to **fog**.
3. **Pass** is to **passed** as **miss** is to _____.
4. **Guest** is to _____ as **steel** is to **steal**.
5. **Soar** is to **sore** as **allowed** is to _____.

B. Write the challenge word that makes sense in the sentence.

1. He read the story (allowed, aloud).
2. Our (guessed, guest) arrived at eight.
3. Mom (mist, missed) the bus.
4. We (guessed, guest) what was inside the box.
5. A light (missed, mist) was falling.

C. Write a paragraph about a mysterious guest who arrives unannounced and leaves unnoticed. Try to use all of the challenge words. Use other homophone pairs, too. For example, you could use **great, grate; scent, sent;** and **weigh, way**.

A.
1.
2.
3.
4.
5.
B.
1.
2.
3.
4.
5.

Unit 25

Challenge Activities

| it'll | who'll | needn't |
| wouldn't | shouldn't |

A. Write the contraction that is a short form of each word pair below.

1. who will
2. need not
3. would not
4. should not
5. it will

B. Five contractions are missing from the story. Read the story. Write the contractions.

The club is planning a party for our counselor. If I were you, I ___1.___ tell her ___2.___ be there. Then ___3.___ be a complete surprise! Also, you ___4.___ bring anything. We've already prepared the food and made decorations. The weather forecaster said it ___5.___ rain, so we'll plan to have the party outdoors.

C. Your class is having a contest for the best science invention. Write about what you will try to invent. Tell what it'll do. Use as many contractions as you can.

A.
1.
2.
3.
4.
5.
B.
1.
2.
3.
4.
5.

Challenge Activities

uncertain	unfriendly	reorder
refill	presoak	

A. The wrong prefixes are matched with base words. Think about where each prefix belongs. Write each challenge word correctly.

1. re + soak
2. un + fill
3. un + order
4. pre + certain
5. re + friendly

B. Write a challenge word to complete each sentence. More than one word might make sense.

1. A nervous animal might be _____.
2. If your pen runs out of ink, you might _____ it.
3. If your clothes are very stained, you will probably _____ them.
4. A shy child might be _____.
5. If the store runs out of an item, the manager will usually _____ it.

A.
1. _____
2. _____
3. _____
4. _____
5. _____

B.
1. _____
2. _____
3. _____
4. _____
5. _____

WASH   DRY

C. You are the manager of a coin-operated self-service laundry. Describe a bad day. What went wrong? Use as many challenge words as you can.

Challenge Activities

dancer	jogger	jeweler
forester	letter carrier	

A. Write the challenge word that describes each picture.

1.

2.

3.

4.

5.

B. Write a challenge word to answer each question.

1. Who repaired my watch?
2. Who does warm-up exercises?
3. Who cares for trees?
4. Who does ballet?
5. Who delivers mail to my house?

C. Imagine that you've chosen a career or activity named by one of the challenge words. Write a schedule showing what your day is like. Follow the example below.

9:00	Open my store.
9:00 – 10:00	Fix watches in for repair.
10:00 – 11:00	Make new sign about sale on earrings.

Before you write your schedule, you might like to interview someone who actually does these things.

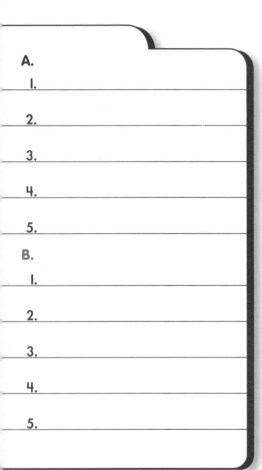

A.
1.
2.
3.
4.
5.
B.
1.
2.
3.
4.
5.

Challenge Activities

boastful	skillful	colorful
sleepless	cordless	

A. Unscramble part of each word. Then use the code to find challenge words and write them. Then write the letter of the definition that goes with each word.

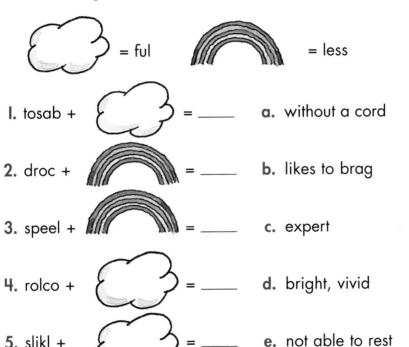

= ful   = less

1. tosab + = _____   **a.** without a cord

2. droc + = _____   **b.** likes to brag

3. speel + = _____   **c.** expert

4. rolco + = _____   **d.** bright, vivid

5. slikl + = _____   **e.** not able to rest

A.
1. _____
2. _____
3. _____
4. _____
5. _____

B.
1. _____
2. _____
3. _____
4. _____
5. _____

B. Write the challenge word that means the opposite of each definition.

1. pale, drab
2. having a cord
3. peaceful, restful
4. humble, modest
5. untrained, without ability

C. Write an advertisement for a new product. Tell why you think it is necessary for every home to have one. Use as many challenge words as you can.

Challenge Activities

Chanukah	Christmas	Easter
Passover	Thanksgiving	

A. Write the name of the holiday or holidays that fall in each season.

    1.–2. winter   **3.–4.** spring   **5.** fall

B. Write the challenge word for each dictionary respelling.

    1. On (**krĭs′** məs) we decorate a tree.
    2. On (**hä′** nə kə) we light candles.
    3. On (**ē′** stər) we paint and hide eggs.
    4. On (**păs′** ō′ vər) we eat a special dinner.
    5. On (thăngks **gĭv′** ĭng) we have a turkey dinner.

C. Pretend you're planning to celebrate one of the holidays named in the challenge words. Write a paragraph describing what you'll do on that day.

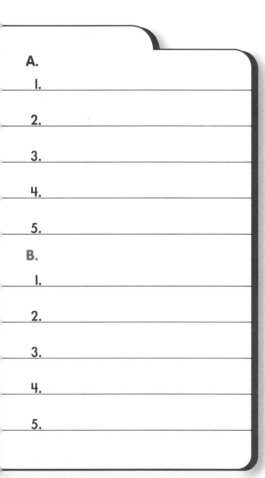

A.
1.
2.
3.
4.
5.
B.
1.
2.
3.
4.
5.

Challenge Activities

menus	sponges	arches
hobbies	strawberries	

A. Write the form of each challenge word that means one.

	one	two or more
1.	_____	arches
2.	_____	strawberries
3.	_____	sponges
4.	_____	hobbies
5.	_____	menus

B. Write the challenge word that describes the picture.

1.

3.

2.

4.

5.

A.
1.
2.
3.
4.
5.
B.
1.
2.
3.
4.
5.

C. Imagine that you own a restaurant. Write an explanation of your duties and activities during a typical day. This might include menu planning and shopping, for example. Use as many of the challenge words as you can.

Challenge Activities

infant's	nephew's	crowd's
umpires'	runners'	

A. | **1.–3.** Write the challenge words that are singular possessives.

B. | **1.–2.** Write the challenge words that are plural possessives.

C. Write the word in parentheses in the form that will correctly complete the sentence.

1. That (crowd) cheer is loud.
2. The two (umpire) gloves have been found.
3. His (nephew) hair is brown.
4. All three (runner) feet are sore.
5. The (infant) rattle is green and blue.

D. Imagine that you've found a big "lost and found" box. Your job is to get the things back to their owners. Write a list of what things are in the box and to whom they belong. Use some challenge words as well as the names of your friends as the owners. Be sure to use the apostrophe correctly to show singular or plural possession.

A.
1.
2.
3.
B.
1.
2.
C.
1.
2.
3.
4.
5.

smoothness	restfulness	happiness
emptiness	wonderment	

A. Add letters and take away letters as indicated to form challenge words.

  1. smooth + ness = _____

  2. wonder + ment = _____

  3. happy - y + i + ness = _____

  4. rest + ful + ness = _____

  5. empty - y + i + ness = _____

B. Write a challenge word to answer each question.

  1. Which word means "the condition of having nothing"?

  2. Which word means "the condition of having peace and quiet"?

  3. Which word means "the condition of surprise or amazement"?

  4. Which word means "the condition of having no rough parts"?

  5. Which word means "the condition of feeling glad"?

C. Describe a scene to illustrate one of the challenge words. Write the description, and then write the word at the bottom of the paper. Illustrate it if you wish.

A.
1. _____
2. _____
3. _____
4. _____
5. _____

B.
1. _____
2. _____
3. _____
4. _____
5. _____

Challenge Activities

yearbook	floodlight	field trip
third base	zip code	

A. Use one part of each word below to form a challenge word. Write the words you made.

1. flashlight
2. yearly
3. basement
4. zipper
5. infield

B. Write the challenge word that completes each analogy.

1. **Gas** is to **car** as **electricity** is to _____.
2. **Football** is to **yard line** as **baseball** is to _____.
3. **Words** are to **dictionary** as **pictures** are to _____.
4. **Letters** are to **name** as **numbers** are to _____.
5. **Campers** are to **hike** as **class** is to _____.

C. Make a list of words for each category below. Use the challenge words as well as other words you know. Then choose one item from your lists that you think is the most interesting or the most unusual. Write a description of it.

a. kinds of school trips
b. kinds of lighting
c. sports equipment
d. directories
e. words related to mail or post offices

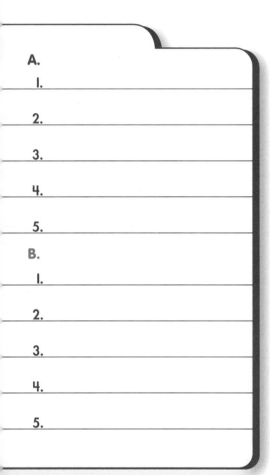

A.
1. _____
2. _____
3. _____
4. _____
5. _____

B.
1. _____
2. _____
3. _____
4. _____
5. _____

Challenge Activities

yen	lira	peso
franc	shilling	

A. Unscramble the challenge words to find out which kind of money each country uses. Write each challenge word.

1. Italy: rail
2. Japan: ney
3. Kenya: slinghli
4. Mexico: sope
5. France: crafn

B. Write the challenge word for each dictionary respelling.

1. Can you get change for a (**shĭl'** ĭng) in Nairobi, Kenya?
2. The (**pā'** sō) is used in several countries in Latin America.
3. I traded in my dollars for (yĕn) in Tokyo, Japan.
4. The (frăngk) is used in France and Belgium.
5. You'll need some (**lîr'** ə) to buy dinner in Rome, Italy.

C. Imagine you're going on a trip around the world! Make a schedule for your trip, telling where you will visit. Write a paragraph identifying and describing at least two items you might buy on your trip. Use the challenge words when you can.

A.
1. _____
2. _____
3. _____
4. _____
5. _____
B.
1. _____
2. _____
3. _____
4. _____
5. _____

WRITER'S HANDBOOK
Contents

The first step in learning your spelling words is correcting your pretest. Follow these steps with your teacher.

These tips will help you do better on your spelling tests and remember how to spell words when you are writing.

Spelling is for writing. Learning these steps in the writing process will help you become a better writer.

These ideas will help you practice the four basic types of writing: narrative, descriptive, expository, and persuasive.

Spelling Strategy
When You Take a Test

1 **Get** ready for the test. Make sure your paper and pencil are ready.

2 **Listen** carefully as your teacher says each word and uses it in a sentence. Don't write before you hear the word **and** the sentence.

3 **Write** the word carefully. Make sure your handwriting is easy to read. If you want to print your words, ask your teacher.

6 **Circle** any misspelled parts of the word.

4 **Use** a pen to correct your test. Look at the word as your teacher says it.

7 **Look** at the correctly written word. Spell the word again. Say each letter out loud.

5 **Say** the word aloud. Listen carefully as your teacher spells the word. Say each letter aloud. Check the word one letter at a time.

8 **Write** any misspelled word correctly.

Spelling Strategy
When You Write a Paper

1 **Think** of the exact word you want to use.

2 **Write** the word, if you know how to spell it.

3 **Say** the word to yourself, if you are not sure how to spell it.

4 **Picture** what the word looks like when you see it written.

5 **Write** the word.

6 **Ask** yourself whether the word looks right.

7 **Check** the word in a dictionary if you are not sure.

SPELLING AND THE Writing Process

Writing anything—a friendly letter, a paper for school—usually follows a process. The writing process has five steps. It might look like this if you tried to draw a picture of it:

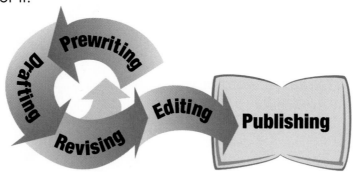

Part of that writing process forms a loop. That is because not every writing task is the same. It is also because writers often jump back and forth between the steps as they change their minds and think of new ideas.

Here is a description of each step:

Prewriting This is thinking and planning ahead to help you write.

Drafting This means writing your paper for the first time. You usually just try to get your ideas down on paper. You can fix them later.

Revising This means fixing your final draft. Here is where you rewrite, change, and add words.

Editing This is where you feel you have said all you want to say. Now you proofread your paper for spelling errors and errors in grammar and punctuation.

Publishing This is making a copy of your writing and sharing it with your readers. Put your writing in a form that your readers will enjoy.

Confident spellers are better writers. Confident writers understand better their own writing process. Know the five steps. Know how they best fit the way you write.

SPELLING AND Writing Ideas

Being a good speller can help make you a more confident writer. Writing more can make you a better writer. Here are some ideas to get you started.

Descriptive Writing Ideas for Descriptive Writing

You might…
- describe something very, very small and something very, very big.
- describe something from the point of view of an insect.
- describe your most prized possession.

Narrative Writing Ideas for Narrative Writing

You might…
- write a story about your first visit to someplace new.
- write a story about an event that helped you "grow up."
- write a story about a bad day or a best day playing your favorite sport.

Persuasive Writing Ideas for Persuasive Writing

You might…
- try to persuade your classmates to read a book you like.
- try to persuade your parents to let you have a pet.
- try to persuade your teacher to change a class rule.

Expository Writing Ideas for Expository Writing

You might…
- write how to prepare your favorite dish.
- inform your classmates how to create a craft object.
- write instructions on how to care for a lawn mower or carpentry tool.

Expository Writing More Ideas for Expository Writing

You might…
- find out how your local government works and write a report.
- interview an animal caregiver and write a report about the job.
- choose a career you might like and write a report about it.

Manuscript Handwriting Models

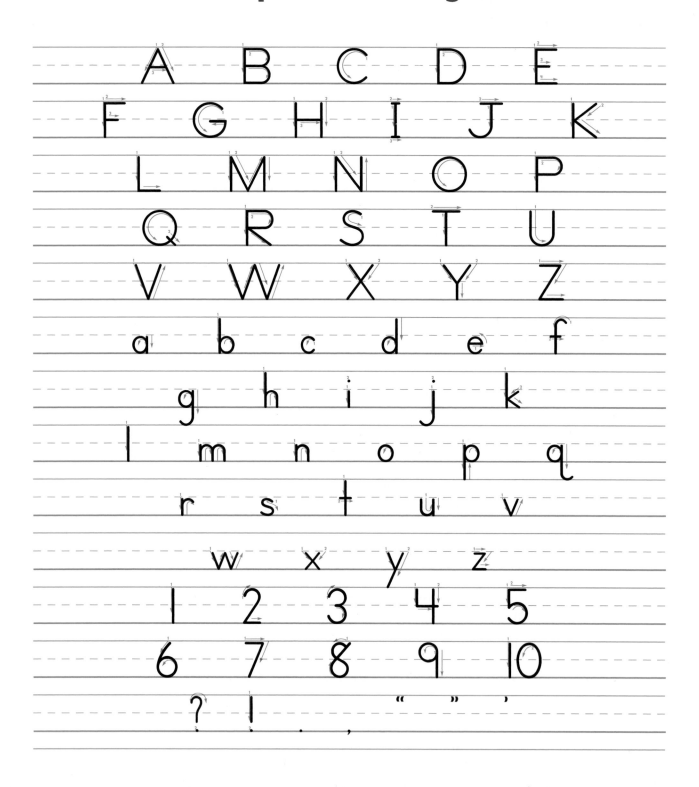

Cursive Handwriting Models

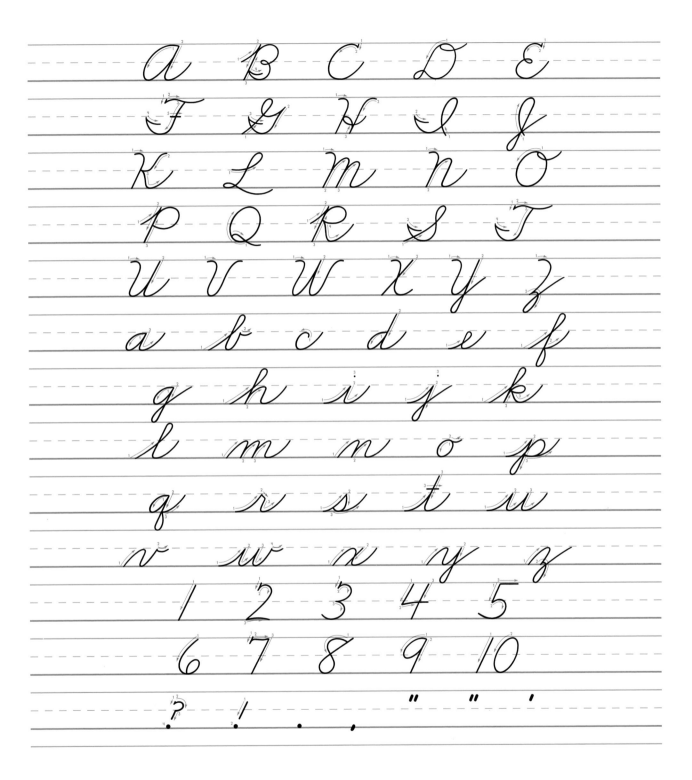

High Frequency Writing Words

A

a
about
afraid
after
again
air
all
almost
also
always
am
America
an
and
animal
animals
another
any
anything
are
around
as
ask
asked
at
ate
away

B

baby
back
bad
ball
balloons
baseball
basketball
be
bear
beautiful
because
become
bed
been
before
being
believe
best
better
big
bike
black
boat
book

books
both
boy
boys
bring
broke
brother
build
bus
but
buy
by

C

call
called
came
can
candy
can't
car
care
cars
cat
catch
caught
change

charge
children
Christmas
circus
city
class
clean
clothes
come
comes
coming
could
couldn't
country
cut

D

Dad
day
days
decided
did
didn't
died
different
dinner
do

does
doesn't
dog
dogs
doing
done
don't
door
down
dream

E

each
earth
eat
eighth
else
end
enough
even
every
everybody
everyone
everything
except
eyes

F

family
fast
father
favorite
feel
feet
fell
few
field
fight
finally
find
fire
first
fish
five
fix
food
football
for
found
four
free
Friday
friend
friends
from

front
fun
funny
future

G

game
games
gas
gave
get
gets
getting
girl
girls
give
go
God
goes
going
good
got
grade
grader
great
ground
grow

H

had
hair
half
happened
happy
hard
has
have
having
he
head
heard
help
her
here
he's
high
hill
him
his
hit
home
homework
hope
horse
horses
hot

hour	killed	lot	Mr.
house	kind	lots	Mrs.
how	knew	love	much
hurt	know	lunch	music
			must
I	**L**	**M**	my
			myself
I	lady	mad	
I'd	land	made	**N**
if	last	make	
I'm	later	making	name
important	learn	man	named
in	leave	many	need
into	left	math	never
is	let	may	new
it	let's	maybe	next
its	life	me	nice
it's	like	mean	night
	liked	men	no
J	likes	might	not
	little	miss	nothing
job	live	Mom	now
jump	lived	money	
just	lives	more	**O**
	long	morning	
K	look	most	of
	looked	mother	off
keep	looking	mouse	oh
kept	lost	move	OK
kids			old

on
once
one
only
or
other
our
out
outside
over
own

P

parents
park
party
people
person
pick
place
planet
play
played
playing
police
president
pretty
probably

problem
put

R

ran
read
ready
real
really
reason
red
responsibilities
rest
ride
riding
right
room
rules
run
running

S

said
same
saw
say
scared
school

schools
sea
second
see
seen
set
seventh
she
ship
shot
should
show
sick
since
sister
sit
sleep
small
snow
so
some
someone
something
sometimes
soon
space
sport
sports

start
started
states
stay
still
stop
stopped
store
story
street
stuff
such
sudden
suddenly
summer
sure
swimming

T

take
talk
talking
teach
teacher
teachers
team
tell
than

Thanksgiving
that
that's
the
their
them
then
there
these
they
they're
thing
things
think
this
thought
three
through
throw
time
times
to
today
together
told
too
took

top
tree
trees
tried
trip
trouble
try
trying
turn
turned
TV
two

U

united
until
up
upon
us
use
used

V

very

W

walk
walked
walking
want
wanted
war
was
wasn't
watch
water
way
we
week
weeks
well
went
were
what
when
where
which
while
white
who
whole
why

will
win
winter
wish
with
without
woke
won
won't
work
world
would
wouldn't

Y

yard
year
years
yes
you
your
you're

USING THE Dictionary

Guide Words

The **guide words** at the top of each dictionary page can help you find the word you want quickly. The first guide word tells you the first word on that page. The second guide word tells you the last word on that page. The entries on the page fall in alphabetical order between these two guide words.

Entries

Words you want to check in the dictionary are called **entries**. Entries provide a lot of information besides the correct spelling. Look at the sample entry below.

- Practice using guide words in a dictionary. Think of words to spell. Then use the guide words to find each word's entry. Do this again and again until you can use guide words easily.

- Some spellings are listed with the base word. To find **easiest,** you would look up **easy.** To find **remaining,** you would look up **remain.** To find **histories,** you would look up **history.**

- If you do not know how to spell a word, guess the spelling before looking it up. Try to find the first three letters of the word. (If you just use the first letter, you will probably take too long.)

- If you can't find a word, think of how else it might be spelled. For example, if a word starts with the **/k/ sound,** the spelling might begin with **k, c,** or even **ch**.

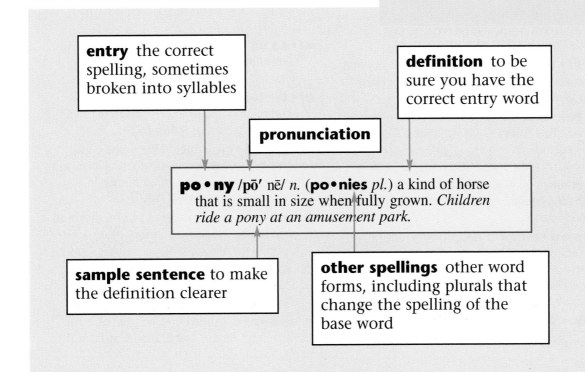

entry the correct spelling, sometimes broken into syllables

pronunciation

definition to be sure you have the correct entry word

po•ny /pō′ nē/ *n.* (**po•nies** *pl.*) a kind of horse that is small in size when fully grown. *Children ride a pony at an amusement park.*

sample sentence to make the definition clearer

other spellings other word forms, including plurals that change the spelling of the base word

a•ble /ā′ bəl/ *adj.* having power, skill, or talent. *With practice you will be able to play the piano.*

ache /āk/ *n.* a pain that continues. *The ache in the boy's tooth stopped after he saw the dentist.*

ac•id /ăs′ ĭd/ *n.* a chemical compound that can "burn" or "eat" other materials. *You learn to handle acid safely in science class.*

ad•dend /ăd′ ĕnd′/ or /ə dĕnd′/ *n.* a number to be added to another number. *In the example 50 + 25 = 75, the numbers 25 and 50 are addends.*

ad•di•tion¹ /ə dĭsh′ ən/ *n.* the adding of one number to another to get a total. *2 + 2 = 4 is an example of addition.*

ad•di•tion² /ə dĭsh′ ən/ *adj.* having to do with adding numbers: *an addition problem.*

ad•jec•tive /ăj′ ĭk′ tĭv/ *n.* a word used to describe or modify a noun. *"Sunny" is an adjective that could describe the noun "day."*

a•dult /ə dŭlt′/ or /ăd′ ŭlt/ *n.* a grown person. *You may vote when you are an adult.*

ad•verb /ăd′ vûrb′/ *n.* a word used to describe or modify a verb. *The students were asked to use the adverb "joyfully" in a sentence.*

Af•ri•ca /ăf′ rĭ kə/ *n.* a large continent that lies south of Europe. *The explorer visited jungles and deserts in Africa.*

af•ter•shock /ăf′ tər shŏk′/ *n.* a minor shock that follows an earthquake. *Because the earthquake was so slight, the aftershock was not even felt.*

a•gree /ə grē′/ *v.* to have the same opinion. *We all agree that Mr. Jansen would make a good mayor.*

a•gree•ment /ə grē′ mənt/ *n.* an arrangement or understanding between two persons or groups. *The students came to an agreement about the best day for the litter cleanup.*

a•head /ə hĕd′/ *adv.* in advance; in front. *Dad walked ahead to look for a campsite.*

aim /ām/ *v.* to point at; to direct toward. *Aim the arrow at the center of the target.*

air mail /âr′ māl′/ *n.* mail carried by airplanes. *The air mail is placed in special bags.*

air•port /âr′ pôrt′/ or /-pōrt′/ *n.* a place where airplanes take off and land. *John picked up Betty at the airport.*

air•y /âr′ ē/ *adj.* light; breezy. *The balcony of our apartment is a cool and airy place to sit.*

a•larm /ə lärm′/ *n.* a warning signal that danger is near. *The alarm went off moments after the fire started.*

a•larm clock /ə lärm′ klŏk′/ *n.* a clock that can be set to ring or buzz at a certain time. *My alarm clock wakes me up at seven every morning.*

alarm clock

a•live /ə līv′/ *adj.* living; not dead. *People sometimes forget that trees are alive.*

a•lone /ə lōn′/ *adv.* without anyone else. *The box was too heavy for one person to lift alone.*

al•pha•bet /ăl′ fə bĕt′/ *n.* the letters of a language arranged in order. *The first three letters of the English alphabet are **a**, **b**, and **c**.*

al•read•y /ôl rĕd′ ē/ *adv.* by this time; before. *We stopped to visit, but they had already left.*

al•so /ôl sō/ *adv.* too; in addition; likewise. *Geraniums grow well not only in flowerpots, but also in gardens.*

al•ti•tude /ăl′ tĭ tōōd′/ or /-tyōōd′/ *n.* height above sea level. *The altitude of the mountain pass was 9,500 feet.*

A•mer•i•ca /ə mĕr′ ĭ kə/ *n.* the continents of the western hemisphere; North and South America. *The United States of America is often called America.*

A•mer•i•can¹ /ə mĕr′ ĭ kən/ *n.* one born or living in America. *A citizen of the United States is an American.*

A•mer•i•can² /ə mĕr′ ĭ kən/ *adj.* of or from the United States. *The American flag is red, white, and blue.*

a•mount /ə mount′/ *n.* the total or sum. *We raised the amount of money needed for the books.*

an • kle /ăng′ kəl/ *n.* the joint connecting the foot with the leg. *My new sneakers are high enough to cover my ankles.*

an • swer /ăn′ sər/ *n.* **a.** a reply. *I must send my answer to her letter quickly.* **b.** a solution. *I know the answer to that math problem.*

Ant • arc • ti • ca /ănt ärk′ tĭ kə/ *n.* the continent at the South Pole. *The coldest continent on the earth is Antarctica.*

an • ten • na /ăn tĕn′ ə/ *n.* equipment for sending or receiving radio or television broadcasts. *Adjusting the TV antenna may improve the picture.*

an • y • way /ĕn′ ē wā′/ *adv.* no matter what may happen; anyhow. *It may rain tomorrow, but we are going to have the picnic anyway.*

an • y • where /ĕn′ ē hwâr′/ *adv.* at or to any place. *If you're going anywhere near a hardware store, bring me some nails.*

a • part /ə pärt′/ *adv.* to pieces; in separate pieces. *The puzzle fell apart when it slipped off the table.*

a • part • ment /ə pärt′ mənt/ *n.* a group of rooms to live in, generally in a building housing more than one family. *They live in an apartment on the second floor.*

Apr. April.

A • pril /ā′ prəl/ *n.* the fourth month of the year. *We should have some warmer weather in April.*

arc • tic[1] /ärk′ tĭk/ *n.* the region around or near the North Pole. *Scientists have been able to study the arctic in submarines.*

arc • tic[2] /ärk′ tĭk/ *adj.* extremely cold; freezing. *The winter months brought arctic temperatures.*

aren´t /ärnt/ are not.

ar • id /ăr′ ĭd/ *adj.* dry. *The desert has an arid climate.*

a • rith • me • tic /ə rĭth′ mə tĭk/ *n.* the study and use of numbers. *Arithmetic includes addition, subtraction, multiplication, and division.*

ar • my /är′ mē/ *n.* (**ar•mies** *pl.*) a large group of people who are organized and trained to serve as soldiers. *The United States Army fought in Europe during World War II.*

Pronunciation Key

ă	pat	ŏ	pot	th	**th**in
ā	pay	ō	toe	*th*	**th**is
âr	care	ô	paw, for	hw	**wh**ich
ä	father	oi	noise	zh	vi**s**ion
ĕ	pet	ou	out	ə	**a**bout,
ē	be	ŏŏ	took		it**e**m,
ĭ	pit	ōō	boot		penc**i**l,
ī	pie	ŭ	cut		gall**o**p,
îr	pier	ûr	urge		circ**u**s

ash /ăsh/ *n.* (**ash•es** *pl.*) the remains of a thing that has been burned. *We can use this pail to empty the ashes from the fireplace.*

A • sia /ā′ zhə/ *n.* the large continent that lies east of Europe. *The largest continent on the earth is Asia.*

as • pi • rin /ăs′ pə rĭn/ or /-prĭn/ *n.* a mild medicine in the form of a tablet or liquid used to relieve fever or minor pain. *The doctor told Lani to take aspirin for her cold.*

auc • tion /ôk′ shən/ *n.* a public sale at which property is sold to the highest bidder. *Mrs. Evans bought an antique vase at the auction.*

Aug. August.

Au • gust /ô′ gəst/ *n.* the eighth month of the year. *August has thirty-one days.*

Aus • tra • lia /ô strāl′ yə/ *n.* the island continent between the Pacific and Indian oceans. *At the zoo we saw a kangaroo from Australia.*

a • while /ə hwīl′/ *adv.* for a short time. *Let's rest awhile before we continue driving.*

ba • by /bā′ bē/ *n.* (**ba•bies** *pl.*) a very young child; an infant. *The baby had not learned to stand up yet.*

ba • by sit • ter /bā′ bē sĭt′ ər/ *n.* one who takes care of young children. *John's mother called a baby sitter to stay with him while she was out.*

baby

Spelling Dictionary

badge /băj/ *n.* something worn to show that a person is a member of a group or organization. *Each firefighter wore a badge.*

bag•gage /băg′ ĭj/ *n.* suitcases; luggage. *Airline passengers may pick up their baggage inside the terminal.*

bak•er /bā′ kər/ *n.* a person who makes and sells breads and pastries. *We ordered a special birthday cake from the baker.*

bank•er /băng′ kər/ *n.* a person who owns or runs a bank. *We talked to the banker about opening a savings account.*

barge /bärj/ *n.* a long, flat, unpowered boat used for transporting freight. *The tugboat pulled a barge that carried lumber.*

barn /bärn/ *n.* a farm building in which to house animals and store grain and hay. *The largest barn on the farm was filled with animals.*

barn

bar•ri•er /băr′ ē ər/ *n.* a boundary or limit. *The fence forms a barrier against intruders.*

bar•ter /bär′ tər/ *v.* to trade without the exchange of money. *She used her handmade ornaments to barter for the oriental rug.*

bas•ket•ball /băs′ kĭt bôl′/ *n.* **a.** a game in which points are scored by throwing a ball through a basket. *Basketball is usually played indoors.* **b.** the ball used in this game. *Our basketball had lost all its air.*

bass /bās/ *n.* **a.** in music, the range of notes that are lower in tone than the other notes. *A piano player plays the bass with the left hand.* **b.** a person who sings the lowest part. *A man with a deep voice is a bass.*

bas•soon /bə soon′/ *n.* a large woodwind instrument with a low tone. *The bassoon can have a mournful sound.*

bat•ter•y /băt′ ə rē/ *n.* (**bat•ter•ies** *pl.*) an electric cell used to produce a current. *My radio operates on a battery.*

bat•tle /băt′ l/ *n.* a fight between armies, navies, etc., during a war. *That battle was the turning point of the war.*

be•came /bĭ kām′/ *v.* past tense of **become**.

be•cause /bĭ kôz′/ *conj.* for the reason that. *I study because I want to learn.*

be•come /bĭ kŭm′/ *v.* (**be•comes, be•came, be•come, be•com•ing**) to come to be. *The weather will become warmer in spring.*

bee•tle /bēt′ l/ *n.* an insect that has four wings, two of which form a hard, shiny covering. *A ladybug is a small beetle that eats insects that harm garden plants.*

be•gan /bĭ găn′/ *v.* past tense of **begin**.

be•gin /bĭ gĭn′/ *v.* (**be•gins, be•gan, be•gun, be•gin•ning**) to start. *We will begin our school day with a math lesson.*

be•lieve /bĭ lēv′/ *v.* (**be•lieves, be•lieved, be•liev•ing**) to accept something as true or real. *Do you believe that cats have nine lives?*

be•side /bĭ sīd′/ *prep.* at the side of; near to. *The carton was left beside the trash can.*

be•tween /bĭ twēn′/ *prep.* in the space that separates two things. *There were four people between me and the door.*

be•ware /bĭ wâr′/ *v.* to be cautious of. *Beware of the undertow when you swim in the ocean.*

bit•ter /bĭt′ ər/ *adj.* tasting sharp and unpleasant. *Do you think black walnuts have a bitter taste?*

black•en /blăk′ ən/ *v.* to make black or dark. *Use a pencil to blacken the circle that matches the correct answer.*

blame[1] /blām/ *v.* (**blames, blamed, blam•ing**) to put the responsibility for something bad on a person or thing. *Don't blame yourself; it wasn't your fault.*

blame[2] /blām/ *n.* responsibility for a fault. *The pilot put the blame for the delay on the fog.*

blan•ket /blăng′ kĭt/ *n.* a heavy woven piece of cloth used to keep one warm. *I sleep under a wool blanket in the winter.*

blos•som[1] /blŏs′ əm/ *n.* the flower of a plant or tree. *The orange blossom smells sweet.*

blos•som[2] /blŏs′ əm/ *v.* to bloom; to produce flowers. *The trees blossom early in warm weather.*

blue jeans /blo͞o′ jēnz′/ *n.* pants made out of denim. *He likes to wear blue jeans when he goes skiing.*

boast /bōst/ *v.* to brag; to talk too much about yourself and about what you can do. *Judy likes to boast about how fast she can run.*

bold /bōld/ *adj.* not afraid to face danger; brave and daring. *The bold gymnast attempted a difficult vault.*

bold•ness /bōld′ nĭs/ *n.* the state of being bold; bravery; daring. *We were surprised by the boldness of the fawn in leaving its safe hiding place.*

bot•tle[1] /bŏt′ l/ *n.* a holder for liquids. *I think juice tastes better from a glass bottle than from a can.*

bot•tle[2] /bŏt′ l/ *v.* (**bot•tles, bot•tled, bot•tling**) to put into bottles. *Milk must be bottled under very clean conditions.*

bought /bôt/ *v.* past tense of **buy.**

brag /brăg/ *v.* (**brags, bragged, brag•ging**) to boast; to talk too much about how good you are or how much you have. *Charles often brags about his new radio.*

brain /brān/ *n.* the mass of nerve tissue in the skull that controls the body and stores knowledge. *Your brain constantly tells your heart to beat.*

brake /brāk/ *n.* a thing that slows down or stops a car, a machine, a bicycle, etc. *The driver pressed on the brake when the traffic light turned red.*

▶ **Brake** sounds like **break.**

bread /brĕd/ *n.* a food baked from dough made with flour or meal. *Sandwiches are made with bread.*

break /brāk/ *v.* (**breaks, broke, bro•ken, break•ing**) to come apart; to separate into pieces. *The dish will break if it falls on the floor.*

▶ **Break** sounds like **brake.**

break•fast /brĕk′ fəst/ *n.* the first meal of the day. *Jim ate a good breakfast of orange juice, cereal, toast, and milk.*

breeze /brēz/ *n.* a light, gentle wind. *The flag barely moved in the breeze.*

brick /brĭk/ *n.* a block of baked clay used for building or paving. *Many houses and apartment buildings are built with bricks.*

Pronunciation Key

ă	pat	ŏ	pot	th	thin
ā	pay	ō	toe	th	this
âr	care	ô	paw, for	hw	which
ä	father	oi	noise	zh	vision
ĕ	pet	ou	out	ə	about,
ē	be	o͝o	took		item,
ĭ	pit	o͞o	boot		pencil,
ī	pie	ŭ	cut		gallop,
îr	pier	ûr	urge		circus

bridge /brĭj/ *n.* a structure built over a river or a valley for people or vehicles to cross. *Thousands of cars a day cross the Mississippi River on bridges.*

bridge

brief /brēf/ *adj.* short; quick; direct. *Our meeting was brief.*

bright•en /brīt′ ən/ *v.* to lighten; to make or become bright. *The lamp will brighten the living room.*

bright•ness /brīt′ nĭs/ *n.* the state or quality of shining or giving light. *The moon's brightness made it easy to see at night.*

bring /brĭng/ *v.* (**brings, brought, bring•ing**) to take along. *Be sure to bring a gift to our party.*

Brit•ain /brĭt′ ən/ *n.* the country that includes England, Scotland, and Wales. *Britain is separated from the rest of Europe by the English Channel.*

Brit•ish[1] /brĭt′ ĭsh/ *adj.* of or from Britain. *British woolens are famous for their fine quality.*

Brit•ish[2] /brĭt′ ĭsh/ *n.* the people of Britain. *The British drive on the left side of the road.*

broth•er /brŭth′ ər/ *n.* a boy or man having the same parents as another person. *The girl had three older brothers and one younger sister.*

brought /brôt/ *v.* past tense of **bring.**

bub•ble[1] /bŭb′ əl/ *n.* a thin, round film of liquid that forms a ball around a pocket of gas or air. *The slightest touch can pop a bubble.*

bub•ble² /bŭb′ əl/ v. (bub•bles, bub•bled, bub•bling) to form bubbles. *The soup will bubble when it is hot.*

build /bĭld/ v. (builds, built, build•ing) to make; to put together. *Doug wants to build a model house out of toothpicks.*

build•er /bĭl′ dər/ n. a person whose business is putting up buildings. *My uncle is a builder working on the new school buildings.*

built /bĭlt/ v. past tense of **build**.

burst /bûrst/ v. (bursts, burst, burst•ing) to break open suddenly. *The balloon will burst if it touches the hot light.*

but•ton¹ /bŭt′ n/ n. a small, flat, hard, round piece used to fasten two parts of a garment by fitting through a slit. *The top button on my coat is loose.*

but•ton² /bŭt′ n/ v. to fasten with buttons. *I buttoned my shirt.*

buy /bī/ v. (buys, bought, buy•ing) to purchase. *Sally needs to buy a new pair of shoes before winter.*

cab•bage /kăb′ ĭj/ n. a vegetable with thick leaves growing tightly together in a solid ball. *Cabbage can be eaten raw or cooked.*

cal•en•dar /kăl′ ən dər/ n. a table or chart used to keep track of days, weeks, and months. *We must remember to change our classroom calendar on the first day of the month.*

calf /kăf/ n. (calves pl.) a young cow or bull. *A calf can walk soon after it is born.*

calm /käm/ adj. quiet; peaceful; motionless. *There wasn't even a breeze on that calm evening.*

calves /kăvz/ n. plural of **calf**.

camp•er /kăm′ pər/ n. **a.** a person who lives outdoors for a period of time, usually in a tent. *The campers pitched their tent next to a stream.* **b.** a van or trailer equipped for camping. *The family moved into the camper as the storm approached.*

Can•a•da /kăn′ ə də/ n. the country north of the United States. *Canada is larger than the United States, but it has fewer people.*

Ca•na•di•an¹ /kə nā′ dē ən/ adj. of or from Canada. *Many U.S. hockey teams have Canadian players.*

Ca•na•di•an² /kə nā′ dē ən/ n. one born or living in Canada. *Many Canadians speak French.*

ca•nal /kə năl′/ n. a waterway dug across land to connect two bodies of water. *The Panama Canal connects the Pacific Ocean and the Atlantic Ocean.*

ca•nar•y /kə nâr′ ē/ n. (ca•nar•ies pl.) a songbird with bright greenish and yellow feathers. *The canary got its name from the Canary Islands.*

card•board /kärd′ bôrd/ or /-bōrd/ n. a kind of stiff, heavy paper used in making boxes, posters, etc. *We drew posters for our school play on large pieces of cardboard.*

care•ful /kâr′ fəl/ adj. cautious; full of care. *Be careful when you cross the busy street.*

care•less /kâr′ lĭs/ adj. reckless; not cautious. *You can't afford to be careless with matches.*

car•go /kär′ gō/ n. the freight carried on a ship or other vehicle. *The barge carried a cargo of lumber to the mill.*

car•ry /kăr′ rē/ v. (car•ries, car•ried, car•ry•ing) to transport from one place to another. *She will carry the young lamb into the barn.*

cart /kärt/ n. **a.** a two-wheeled vehicle pulled by a horse or other animal. *The pony pulled a cart in the parade.* **b.** a small vehicle moved by hand. *I will push the grocery cart.*

case /kās/ n. a large box; a container. *The music teacher carries her violin in a case.*

catch /kăch/ v. (catch•es, caught, catch•ing) to seize or retrieve; to capture. *Tonight would be a good night to catch fireflies.*

catch•er /kăch′ ər/ n. one who catches, especially the player behind home plate in a baseball game. *The catcher can tell the pitcher which pitch to throw.*

cat•tle /kăt′ l/ n. cows, bulls, or oxen. *The cattle eat grass in the pasture.*

cattle

caught /kôt/ *v.* past tense of **catch**.

cause[1] /kôz/ *n.* a person or thing that makes something happen. *A snowstorm was the cause of the slow traffic.*

cause[2] /kôz/ *v.* (**caus•es, caused, caus•ing**) to make happen. *The rain caused a leak in the roof.*

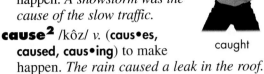

caught

cel•lar /sĕl′ ər/ *n.* an underground room, used for storage. *The family next door fixed up the cellar as a playroom for their children.*

▶ **Cellar** sounds like **seller**.

cel•lo /chĕl′ ō/ *n.* a large stringed instrument in the violin family. *The cello has a deep, rich tone.*

cen•ti•me•ter /sĕn′ tə mē′ tər/ *n.* a measure of length equal to one one-hundredth of a meter. *It takes about two centimeters to make one inch.*

cen•tu•ry /sĕn′ chə rē/ *n.* (**cen•tu•ries** *pl.*) a period of one hundred years. *The Statue of Liberty was built over a century ago.*

cer•tain /sûr′ tn/ *adj.* confident; sure; convinced. *She was certain you would win.*

charge[1] /chärj/ *v.* **a.** to ask for as payment. *That store will charge two dollars for that notebook.* **b.** to postpone payment on by recording the amount owed. *Charge the groceries to my account.*

charge[2] /chärj/ *n.* **a.** an amount asked or made as payment. *There is no charge for this service.* **b.** care; supervision: *the scientist in charge of the project.*

charm /chärm/ *v.* to delight; to please. *The child's smile charmed the audience.*

chart[1] /chärt/ *n.* information given in the form of graphs, maps, and tables. *Newspapers often print weather charts.*

chart[2] /chärt/ *v.* to make a map or diagram of. *My job is to chart our class's spelling progress.*

chase /chās/ *v.* (**chas•es, chased, chas•ing**) to run after; to try to catch. *In this game the players must chase the one with the ball.*

cheer[1] /chîr/ *n.* happiness; comfort. *A fire in the fireplace brings warmth and cheer to the room.*

Pronunciation Key

ă	pat	ŏ	pot	th	**th**in
ā	pay	ō	toe	*th*	**th**is
âr	care	ô	paw, for	hw	**wh**ich
ä	father	oi	n**oi**se	zh	vi**si**on
ě	pet	ou	**ou**t	ə	**a**bout,
ē	be	ŏŏ	t**oo**k		it**e**m,
ĭ	pit	ōō	b**oo**t		penc**i**l,
ī	pie	ŭ	c**u**t		gall**o**p,
îr	pier	ûr	**ur**ge		circ**u**s

cheer[2] /chîr/ *v.* to shout words of approval; to encourage by yelling. *We all cheered for our star player as he came on the field.*

cheer•ful /chîr′ fəl/ *adj.* happy; joyful. *Kari gave a cheerful smile.*

chick•en /chĭk′ ən/ *n.* a bird raised for its meat and its eggs; a hen or rooster. *Some chickens lay brown eggs.*

chick•en pox /chĭk′ ən pŏks/ *n.* a disease that causes a slight fever and a rash. *When Carl had chicken pox, it was hard for him to keep from scratching.*

chief /chēf/ *n.* a leader; a head of a tribe or group. *The chief leads the tribal council.*

child /chīld/ *n.* (**chil•dren** *pl.*) a young boy or girl. *Corey is the only child absent today.*

chil•dren /chĭl′ drən/ *n.* plural of **child**.

Chi•na /chī′ nə/ *n.* a country in eastern Asia. *China has more people than any other country.*

Chi•nese[1] /chī nēz′/ *adj.* of or from China. *Our city's zoo has a Chinese panda.*

Chi•nese[2] /chī nēz′/ *n.* **a.** the people of China. *Many Chinese live in rural areas.* **b.** the language of China. *Mr. Chang can speak Chinese.*

choice /chois/ *n.* a decision; a selection. *For dinner we will go to a restaurant of your choice.*

choose /chōōz/ *v.* (**choos•es, chose, cho•sen, choos•ing**) to select; to decide upon; to pick. *I will let you choose which color you would like.*

chose /chōz/ *v.* past tense of **choose**.

chuck•le /chŭk′ əl/ *n.* a small, quiet laugh. *His funny speech caused chuckles in the audience.*

cin•der /sĭn′ dər/ *n.* a piece of coal or wood that is only partly burned. *We spread cinders on the sidewalk on icy days.*

clar•i•net /klăr′ ə nĕt′/ *n.* a woodwind instrument with a bell-shaped end. *A clarinet has finger holes and keys for different notes.*

clay /klā/ *n.* soft, sticky earth that can be molded into different forms and then hardened in ovens. *Bricks, pottery, and tiles may be made of clay.*

clear /klîr/ *adj.* **a.** having no clouds; bright. *The sun shone in the clear sky.* **b.** distinct; not fuzzy. *I cannot get a clear picture on this* TV *station.*

climb /klīm/ *v.* to go up, often using both hands and feet; to move on a steep slope. *The club members climb mountains all over the state.*

climb•er /klī′ mər/ *n.* one who climbs. *Her goal was to become a mountain climber.*

clin•ic /klĭn′ ĭk/ *n.* a center like a hospital that provides care for outpatients. *Since his injuries were minor, he could be treated at the clinic.*

clos•ing /klō′ zĭng/ *n.* a phrase used to end a letter. *"Sincerely yours" is a common closing.*

clothes /klōz/ or /klōthz/ *n. pl.* garments; articles of dress; clothing. *Some people order all their clothes through a catalog.*

cloud•less /kloud′ lĭs/ *adj.* free of clouds; without clouds. *The cloudless sky was a brilliant blue.*

clue /klōō/ *n.* a piece of information that helps solve a problem or mystery. *In this game we use word clues to solve the puzzle.*

coach /kōch/ *n.* (**coach•es** *pl.*) a person who trains athletes; a person who teaches. *The basketball coach is happy when the team plays well.*

coast /kōst/ *n.* the seashore; land along the sea or ocean. *There are many beaches along the coast of the Pacific Ocean.*

coast•al /kōs′ təl/ *adj.* of or having to do with the coast or seashore. *Coastal waters are shallow.*

coil /koil/ *v.* to wind in spirals or rings; to wind around and around. *The snake coiled around the log.*

col•lar /kŏl′ ər/ *n.* the part of a shirt or coat that circles the neck. *He loosened his tie and his collar.*

co•lon /kō′ lən/ *n.* a punctuation mark (:) that introduces a list or phrase. *Use a colon before listing the names.*

col•o•ny /kŏl′ ə nē/ *n.* (**col•o•nies** *pl.*) a group of people with similar interests who live in a particular area. *The Pilgrims' colony grew as more people arrived.*

comb

comb[1] /kōm/ *n.* a tool with teeth, used to smooth or arrange the hair. *Most people carry a brush or comb.*

comb[2] /kōm/ *v.* to search carefully. *We will comb the room to find the contact lens.*

com•et /kŏm′ ĭt/ *n.* a heavenly body that looks like a star but has a tail of vapor. *A comet moves in orbit around the sun.*

com•ma /kŏm′ ə/ *n.* a punctuation mark (,) used to show a separation of words or ideas. *Commas separate items in a list.*

com•pare /kəm pâr′/ *v.* (**com•pares, com•pared, com•par•ing**) to examine things for similarities or differences. *If you compare prices, you can save money when you shop.*

con•ti•nent /kŏn′ tə nənt/ *n.* one of the seven main masses of land in the world. *We live on the continent of North America.*

core /kôr/ or /kōr/ *n.* the innermost part of something; the center; the middle. *The core of the earth contains solid metals.*

cor•ral /kə răl′/ *n.* a fenced-in place for horses, cattle, or other livestock. *Horseback riding lessons are given in the smaller corral.*

cot•tage /kŏt′ ĭj/ *n.* a small house. *We spent our vacation in a cottage on the beach.*

cou•ple /kŭp′ əl/ *n.* **a.** two of anything. *They will have to wait a couple of hours for the train.* **b.** a man and woman together. *That couple dances well together.*

craft /krăft/ *n.* **a.** skill in doing or making something. *Maria has taken up the craft of basketmaking.* **b.** a handmade item. *The crafts displayed at the fair included quilts and pottery.*

crag /krăg/ *n.* a steep mass of rock forming a cliff. *The climber reached a crag near the top of the mountain.*

cran•ber•ry /krăn′ bĕr′ ē/ *n.* (**cran•ber•ries** *pl.*) a red berry that grows on low shrubs in wet ground. *Cranberries are used in sauce and juice.*

cray•on /krā′ ŏn′/ *n.* a stick of colored wax or chalk used for drawing. *The children used crayons to add details to their paintings.*

crowd¹ /kroud/ *n.* many people gathered together. *I lost my brother in the crowd.*

crowd² /kroud/ *v.* to push or squeeze together in a small space. *The people crowded into the small room.*

crust /krŭst/ *n.* the outer surface of a loaf of bread. *Rye bread often has a dark crust.*

crys•tal /krĭs′ təl/ *n.* a clear, hard mineral with flat, regularly arranged surfaces. *Quartz is a common crystal.*

cube /kyo͞ob/ *n.* a solid figure with six square sides. *Not all ice cubes are actually in the shape of a cube.*

cure /kyo͝or/ *n.* a remedy. *Scientists have not yet found a cure for the common cold.*

cur•sive /kûr′ sĭv/ *adj.* written with the letters joined together. *Children begin to learn cursive writing when they have mastered printing.*

curve /kûrv/ *n.* a smooth bend in a line or road. *The sign warned us of a sharp curve just ahead.*

cute /kyo͞ot/ *adj.* delightfully attractive or appealing. *The child looked cute in her rabbit costume.*

cy•cle /sī′ kəl/ *n.* a series of events that occur over and over in the same order. *The seasons of the year form a cycle.*

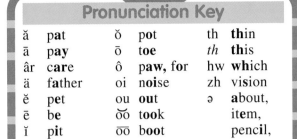

Pronunciation Key

ă	pat	ŏ	pot	th	**th**in
ā	pay	ō	toe	*th*	**th**is
âr	care	ô	paw, for	hw	**wh**ich
ä	father	oi	n**oi**se	zh	vi**s**ion
ĕ	pet	ou	**ou**t	ə	**a**bout,
ē	be	o͝o	t**oo**k		it**e**m,
ĭ	pit	o͞o	b**oo**t		penc**i**l,
ī	pie	ŭ	c**u**t		gall**o**p,
îr	pier	ûr	**ur**ge		circ**u**s

damp•en /dăm′ pən/ *v.* to make moist or wet. *Dampen the cloth before you begin cleaning.*

dan•ger /dān′ jər/ *n.* peril; chance of injury or harm. *Learning safety rules can help you avoid danger.*

dark•en /där′ kən/ *v.* to make dark. *He darkened the room by pulling down the shades.*

dark•ness /därk′ nĭs/ *n.* the state or quality of being without light or brightness. *The darkness of the sky told us a storm was coming.*

daugh•ter /dô′ tər/ *n.* a female child. *A princess is the daughter of a king or a queen.*

daughter

deal /dēl/ *v.* (**deals, dealt, deal•ing**) to handle in a certain way; to cope. *It is important to know how to deal with emergencies.*

death /dĕth/ *n.* a dying; the ending of life or existence. *The movie ended with the death of the villain.*

dec•ade /dĕk′ ād/ *n.* a period of ten years. *The royal family ruled the country for a decade.*

Dec. December.

De•cem•ber /dĭ sĕm′ bər/ *n.* the twelfth and final month of the year. *The shortest day of the year comes in December.*

Spelling Dictionary

dec•i•me•ter /děs′ ə mē′tər/ *n.* a measure of length equal to one-tenth of a meter. *There are ten decimeters in one meter.*

de•fine /dĭ fīn′/ *v.* (**de•fines, de•fined, de•fin•ing**) to describe the meaning of; to explain. *The dictionary defines words.*

de•gree /dĭ grē′/ *n.* a unit used to measure temperature. *Water freezes at thirty-two degrees Fahrenheit.*

de•nom•i•na•tor /dĭ nŏm′ ə nā′tər/ *n.* the bottom number in a fraction. *In the fraction $\frac{5}{8}$, 8 is the denominator.*

dense /děns/ *adj.* crowded together; thickly settled. *Cities are areas of dense population.*

de•pot /dē′ pō/ *n.* a station for trains or buses. *We went to the depot to meet his train.*

des•sert /dĭ zûrt′/ *n.* a food, usually sweet, served at the end of a meal. *I had an apple for dessert.*

dew /d͞oo/ or /dy͞oo/ *n.* water droplets that form at night on cool surfaces. *In the morning you may see dew on the leaves.*
▶ **Dew** sounds like **due.**

dic•tion•ar•y /dĭk′ shə něr′ē/ *n.* (**dic•tion•ar•ies** pl.) a book that explains the words used in a language. *A dictionary gives definitions, pronunciations, and word histories.*

die /dī/ *v.* (**dies, died, dy•ing**) to stop living or existing. *The tree will die if it is not watered.*
▶ **Die** sounds like **dye.**

di•et /dī′ ĭt/ *n.* a special choice of foods for improving or maintaining health. *Mr. Collins is on a special diet to control his weight.*

di•gest /dī jěst′/ or /dĭ-/ *v.* to turn food into a form the body can use. *Special juices in your stomach help your body digest food.*

dine /dīn/ *v.* (**dines, dined, din•ing**) to eat dinner. *We dine at seven o'clock.*

dis•cov•er /dĭ skŭv′ ər/ *v.* to find out. *If you read further you may discover the meaning of the word.*

dis•ease /dĭ zēz′/ *n.* a sickness; an illness. *Most common diseases, such as colds, are caused by germs.*

div•i•dend /dĭv′ ĭ děnd′/ *n.* the number to be divided. *In 60 ÷ 2 = 30, 60 is the dividend.*

di•vi•sion /dĭ vĭzh′ ən/ *n.* the act or process of dividing. *Division is the opposite of multiplication.*

di•vi•sor /dĭ vī′ zər/ *n.* a number by which another number is divided. *In 60 ÷ 2 = 30, 2 is the divisor.*

dodge /dŏj/ *v.* (**dodg•es, dodged, dodg•ing**) to try to avoid; to stay away from. *The batter stepped back from the plate to dodge the bad pitch.*

dou•ble /dŭb′ əl/ *v.* (**dou•bles, dou•bled, dou•bling**) to make or become twice as great. *The bread dough will double in size as it rises.*

doubt /dout/ *v.* to be unsure or uncertain. *I doubt that the Cortez family is home from vacation.*

drag /drăg/ *v.* (**drags, dragged, drag•ging**) to pull slowly along the ground; to haul. *They drag the sled to the top of the hill and then slide down.*

dream•er /drē′ mər/ *n.* one who dreams; one who has visions of the future. *Dreamers often have the ideas that make inventions possible.*

drive /drīv/ *v.* (**drives, drove, driv•en, driv•ing**) to operate a vehicle. *Marsha's uncle drives a school bus.*

drive•way /drīv′ wā/ *n.* a road connecting a building to the street. *We park our car in our driveway.*

driveway

drove /drōv/ *v.* past tense of **drive.**

due /d͞oo/ or /dy͞oo/ *adj.* expected; scheduled to arrive. *The bus is not due for two hours.*
▶ **Due** sounds like **dew.**

du•et /d͞oo ět′/ or /dy͞oo-/ *n.* a musical composition for two voices or instruments. *The brother and sister performed a duet in the talent show.*

dune /d͞oon/ or /dy͞oon/ *n.* a rounded hill of sand piled up by the wind. *Sand dunes are often formed in deserts.*

dye /dī/ *v.* (**dyes, dyed, dye•ing**) to give color to something or change its color. *Today we learned to dye fabric in art class.*
▶ **Dye** sounds like **die.**

ea·ger /ē′ gər/ *adj.* excitedly or impatiently wanting or expecting something. *We were eager for school to begin that day.*

ea·gle /ē′ gəl/ *n.* a large bird of prey with a hooked beak. *The bald eagle is the symbol of the United States.*

eagle

ear /îr/ *n.* the organ by which animals and humans hear. *Parts of the ear are located both inside and outside the head.*

earth·quake /ûrth′ kwāk′/ *n.* a movement of the earth's surface, sometimes caused by volcanic activity. *Earthquakes are often followed by mild aftershocks.*

ea·sy /ē′ zē/ *adj.* (eas•i•er, eas•i•est; eas•i•ly *adv.*) not hard or difficult. *The quiz was easy for me because I had studied hard.*

ech·o[1] /ĕk′ ō/ *n.* (ech•oes *pl.*) a repeated sound caused by sound waves bouncing off a surface. *We heard an echo when we shouted into the cave.*

ech·o[2] /ĕk′ ō/ *v.* to send back a sound. *Tunnels often echo.*

e·clipse /ĭ klĭps′/ *n.* the apparent covering of the sun or the moon by the other when their paths cross. *During a solar eclipse the sun is blocked from view by the moon.*

edge /ĕj/ *n.* border; side. *The cup fell from the edge of the table.*

ei·ther /ē′ thər/ or /ī′-/ *adj.* one or the other of two. *I couldn't run faster than either one of my friends.*

el·bow /ĕl′ bō/ *n.* the joint that allows the arm to bend. *I rolled my sleeves up above my elbows.*

e·lec·tion /ĭ lĕk′ shən/ *n.* a choosing or selecting by voting. *We held an election to choose a class president.*

Pronunciation Key

ă	pat	ŏ	pot	th	**th**in
ā	p**ay**	ō	t**oe**	*th*	**th**is
âr	c**are**	ô	p**aw, for**	hw	**wh**ich
ä	f**a**ther	oi	n**oi**se	zh	vi**si**on
ĕ	pet	ou	**ou**t	ə	**a**bout,
ē	be	ŏŏ	t**oo**k		item,
ĭ	pit	ōō	b**oo**t		pencil,
ī	p**ie**	ŭ	c**u**t		gallop,
îr	p**ier**	ûr	**ur**ge		circus

e·lev·enth[1] /ĭ lĕv′ ənth/ *adj.* next after the tenth. *The eleventh shopper in the new store won a prize.*

e·lev·enth[2] /ĭ lĕv′ ənth/ *n.* one of eleven equal parts. *It's hard to divide something into elevenths.*

else /ĕls/ *adj.* other; different. *Would you rather ride with someone else?*

-en a suffix that means "to cause to be," used to form verbs: *tighten.*

en·gine /ĕn′ jĭn/ *n.* a machine that changes fuel and energy into motion. *Most automobile engines use gasoline.*

Eng·land /ĭng′ glənd/ *n.* the southern part of the island of Great Britain. *London is the capital city of England.*

en·joy /ĕn joi′/ *v.* to get pleasure from. *Did you enjoy the movie last night?*

en·joy·ment /ĕn joi′ mənt/ *n.* the state of enjoying. *Her enjoyment of the play was evident from her delighted smile.*

e·nough /ĭ nŭf′/ *adj.* as much or as many as needed. *The campers had enough food and water for three days.*

en·ter /ĕn′ tər/ *v.* to come or go into. *The students enter the school through the doorway closest to their classrooms.*

en·try /ĕn′ trē/ *n.* (en•tries *pl.*) a word listed in a dictionary, along with all related information given about it. *A dictionary entry usually includes a pronunciation and one or more definitions.*

en·ve·lope /ĕn′ və lōp′/ or /ŏn′-/ *n.* a paper cover used to hold letters and other materials. *Always include the ZIP code when you address an envelope.*

Spelling Dictionary

e•qual•ly /ē′ kwə lē/ *adv.* in the same way or amount. *The two students were equally responsible for delivering the message.*

-er a suffix, used to form nouns, that means: **a.** one who: *swimmer.* **b.** thing that: *toaster.*

Eu•rope /yŏŏr′ əp/ *n.* the continent east of the Atlantic Ocean and west of Asia. *Our teacher visited France and Spain on her trip to Europe.*

ev•er•green /ĕv′ ər grēn′/ *n.* a shrub, bush, or tree that stays green all year. *The branches of evergreens are sometimes used as decorations in the winter.*

eve•ry•day /ĕv′ rē dā′/ *adj.* ordinary; all right for the usual day or event. *You should wear your everyday clothes to play outside.*

eve•ry•one /ĕv′ rē wŭn′/ *pron.* each person; everybody. *Everyone in the class received a permission slip for the field trip.*

ex•am•ple /ĭg zăm′ pəl/ *n.* a sample; a model; something that may be imitated. *If you don't understand how to do the problems, look at the example.*

ex•ert /ĭg zûrt′/ *v.* to put forth; to put into use. *If you exert pressure on the window, it will open.*

ex•plode /ĭk splōd′/ *v.* (**ex•plodes, ex•plod•ed, ex•plod•ing**) to burst violently. *Fireworks explode with a flash of color.*

eye /ī/ *n.* the part of the body with which humans and animals see. *Tears keep your eyes moist.*

fact /făkt/ *n.* something known and proved to be true. *It is a fact that gravity causes objects to fall to the earth.*

fac•tor /făk′ tər/ *n.* any of the numbers that can be multiplied together to form a given product. *The factors of 6 are 1, 2, 3, and 6.*

fac•to•ry /făk′ tə rē/ *n.* (**fac•to•ries** *pl.*) a plant where goods are manufactured. *Much of the work in a factory is done by machines.*

fail /fāl/ *v.* to be unsuccessful. *The pirates failed to find the treasure they had hidden.*

fame /fām/ *n.* the state of being well-known; respect; recognition. *George Washington was a man of great fame.*

farm /färm/ *v.* to raise crops or animals as a profession; to cultivate land. *The Ellisons farm their own land.*

farm•er /fär′ mər/ *n.* a person who owns or operates a farm. *Farmers often store chopped corn in tall towers called silos.*

fas•ten /făs′ ən/ *v.* to join; to attach. *We can fasten this lamp to the wall over my desk.*

fa•ther /fä′ thər/ *n.* the male parent. *My father helped me study my spelling.*

fault /fôlt/ *n.* **a.** a mistake; an error. *I'm sorry; it was my fault.* **b.** a break or crack in the earth's crust. *The earthquake revealed a fault that runs through the valley.*

fa•vor /fā′ vər/ *n.* **a.** a kind or thoughtful act. *We did him a favor by mowing his lawn.* **b.** a small gift. *Each child received a balloon as a party favor.*

fear¹ /fîr/ *n.* a feeling of fright or alarm. *Dogs show fear by putting their tails between their legs.*

fear² /fîr/ *v.* to be afraid of. *My little sister fears thunder and lightning.*

feast /fēst/ *n.* a large meal, often with entertainment; a banquet. *We ate so much at the feast that we all felt stuffed.*

feath•er /fĕth′ ər/ *n.* one of the light, flat parts that form the outer covering of birds. *Feathers protect birds from cold and injury.*

Feb. February.

Feb•ru•ar•y /fĕb′ rŏŏ ĕr′ ē/ *n.* the second month of the year. *February is the shortest month.*

feel /fēl/ *v.* (**feels, felt, feel•ing**) **a.** to sense by touch. *Feel how soft this cloth is!* **b.** to have a feeling or emotion. *I feel happy.*

felt /fĕlt/ *v.* past tense of **feel**.

fer•ry /fĕr′ ē/ *n.* (**fer•ries** *pl.*) a boat used to transport people or goods across a narrow body of water. *The ferry takes cars across the channel every day.*

ferry

fe•ver /fē′ vər/ *n.* a body temperature that is higher than normal. *Juanita had a cold and a slight fever.*

few /fyoo/ *adj.* not many. *Few copies of this rare book are available.*

field /fēld/ *n.* a piece of open land, usually part of a farm, often used for planting crops. *Some wheat fields are several miles wide.*

fif•ti•eth[1] /fĭf′ tē ĭth/ *adj.* next after the forty-ninth. *The couple celebrated their fiftieth year of marriage.*

fif•ti•eth[2] /fĭf′ tē ĭth/ *n.* one of fifty equal parts. *A coin worth two cents would be a fiftieth of a dollar.*

fight /fīt/ *v.* (**fights, fought, fight•ing**) to oppose strongly, especially in battle. *Our team tried to fight well, but the other team won.*

firm /fûrm/ *adj.* hard; solid. *They left the muddy road and walked on firm ground.*

fish /fĭsh/ *n.* (**fish** or **fish•es** *pl.*) an animal that lives in water, has fins, and breathes through gills. *Most fish have scales covering their bodies.*

fish

fish•er•y /fĭsh′ ə rē/ *n.* (**fish•er•ies** *pl.*) a place where fish can be caught; fishing ground. *Tuna are caught in Pacific fisheries.*

fit•ness /fĭt′ nĭs/ *n.* the state of being in good physical condition. *Many people exercise for greater fitness.*

flash•light /flăsh′ līt′/ *n.* a small light powered by batteries. *Campers carry flashlights to find their way in the dark.*

fla•vor /flā′ vər/ *n.* a particular taste. *Lemonade can have a sweet or tart flavor.*

flight /flīt/ *n.* a scheduled trip on an airplane. *The next flight to Chicago departs at 3:05.*

flood /flŭd/ *n.* water that flows over normally dry land. *The low bridge was under water for an hour after the flash flood.*

floun•der /floun′ dər/ *n.* a flat fish. *Baked flounder is a popular item on the menu.*

Pronunciation Key

ă	pat	ŏ	pot	th	**thin**
ā	pay	ō	toe	*th*	**th**is
âr	care	ô	paw, for	hw	**wh**ich
ä	father	oi	noise	zh	vision
ě	pet	ou	**out**	ə	**a**bout,
ē	be	ŏŏ	took		item,
ĭ	pit	ōō	boot		pencil,
ī	pie	ŭ	cut		gallop,
îr	pier	ûr	**ur**ge		circus

flour /flour/ *n.* a fine powder of ground grain, usually wheat. *Flour is used in making breads.*

▶ **Flour** sounds like **flower**.

flow•er /flou′ ər/ *n.* the blossom of a plant. *Many flowers bloom in the spring.*

▶ **Flower** sounds like **flour**.

flu /floo/ *n.* a very contagious disease that causes fever, aches, and tiredness; influenza. *Ann stayed in bed for a week with the flu.*

flute /floot/ *n.* a woodwind instrument with a side opening across which a player blows. *The flute makes a high, soft sound.*

foil /foil/ *n.* a sheet of metal so thin it seems like paper. *The sandwiches are wrapped in aluminum foil.*

fold /fōld/ *v.* to close or bend parts of something together in order to fit it into a smaller space. *When we take down the flag, we fold it into the shape of a triangle.*

for•est /fôr′ ĭst/ *n.* an area covered with trees; a woods. *We found pine cones in the forest.*

for•get /fôr gĕt′/ or /fər-/ *v.* (**for•gets, for•got, for•got•ten, for•get•ting**) to fail to remember. *He sometimes forgets his umbrella on rainy days.*

for•got /fôr gŏt′/ or /fər-/ *v.* past tense of **forget**.

forth /fôrth/ or /fōrth/ *adv.* forward; onward. *From that day forth the princess lived happily.*

for•ty /fôr′ tē/ *n.* one more than thirty-nine; four times ten; 40. *Her father's age is forty.*

fought /fôt/ past tense of **fight**.

four • teenth¹ /fôr tēnth'/ or /fōr-/ *adj.* next after the thirteenth. *This is the store's fourteenth year in business.*

four • teenth² /fôr tēnth'/ or /fōr-/ *n.* one of fourteen equal parts. *Two is one fourteenth of twenty-eight.*

frac • tion /frăk' shən/ *n.* one or more of the equal parts into which a thing is divided. *The fraction $\frac{3}{4}$ represents three of four equal parts.*

France /frăns/ *n.* a country in western Europe. *The Eiffel Tower is in Paris, France.*

French¹ /frĕnch/ *adj.* of or from France. *A beret is a soft French cap.*

French² /frĕnch/ *n.* **a.** the national language of France, also spoken in other parts of the world. *Can you speak French?* **b.** the people of France. *The French consider cooking an art.*

Fri. Friday.

Fri • day /frī' dē/ or /-dā/ *n.* the sixth day of the week. *Friday is the end of the school week.* [Old English *Frigedæg,* Freya's day.]

friend /frĕnd/ *n.* a person one knows and likes. *Erin and I are good friends.*

fright /frīt/ *n.* a sudden fear. *The village was filled with fright when the forest fire started.*

fruit /frōot/ *n.* (**fruit** or **fruits** *pl.*) the part of certain plants that contains seeds and is good to eat. *Oranges, grapes, and pears are types of fruit.*

fruit

-ful a suffix that means: **a.** full of or having, used to form adjectives: *meaningful.* **b.** the amount that fills, used to form nouns: *cupful.*

fun • ny /fŭn' ē/ *adj.* (**fun•ni•er, fun•ni•est**) causing laughter or amusement. *The joke was funny.*

gas /găs/ *n.* (**gas•es** *pl.*) **a.** a light substance that is neither a solid nor a liquid. *Oxygen is a gas.* **b.** a short word for gasoline. *Fill the tank with unleaded gas.*

gath • er /gă*th*' ər/ *v.* to bring or come together. *When clouds gather it often means rain.*

gem /jĕm/ *n.* a precious stone. *Diamonds and emeralds are gems.*

gen • tle /jĕn' tl/ *adj.* light; soft. *The gentle breeze rustled through the leaves.*

Ger • man¹ /jûr' mən/ *adj.* of or from Germany. *Oktoberfest is a German festival.*

Ger • man² /jûr' mən/ *n.* **a.** one born or living in Germany. *The composer Bach was a famous German.* **b.** the language spoken in Germany, Austria, and parts of Switzerland. *Many English words come from German.*

Ger • ma • ny /jûr' mə nē/ *n.* a country in north-central Europe. *Between 1949 and 1989, Germany was divided into East Germany and West Germany.*

gi • gan • tic /jī găn' tĭk/ *adj.* extremely large. *Elephants and whales are gigantic.*

gig • gle /gĭg' əl/ *v.* (**gig•gles, gig•gled, gig•gling**) to give repeated high-pitched laughs. *The children giggle when they watch cartoons.*

glow¹ /glō/ *v.* to give off light; to shine. *Fireflies glow in the dark.*

glow² /glō/ *n.* a soft light. *You can see the glow of the lamp through the window.*

glue /glōō/ *n.* a sticky liquid that hardens to hold things together. *Broken toys can be mended with glue.*

goal /gōl/ *n.* a purpose; an aim. *Mark's goal is to play the double bass in a symphony orchestra.*

gov • ern /gŭv' ərn/ *v.* to direct; to rule. *The mayor and the council govern the city.*

grab /grăb/ *v.* (**grabs, grabbed, grab•bing**) to take or grasp suddenly. *If you grab the cat's tail, he may scratch you.*

grass•hop•per /grăs' hŏp' ər/ *n.* a jumping insect with wings and powerful rear legs. *Grasshoppers feed on plants.*

Greece /grēs/ *n.* a country in southeastern Europe that borders on the Mediterranean Sea. *Corinth and Athens are cities in Greece.*

Greek¹ /grēk/ *n.* **a.** one born or living in Greece. *The ancient Greeks were the first people to stage plays.* **b.** the language of Greece. *Greek uses a different alphabet from English.*

Greek² /grēk/ *adj.* of or from Greece. *We saw Greek sculpture at the museum.*

greet•ing /grē' tĭng/ *n.* the words in a letter used to address someone. *The greeting in a friendly letter is followed by a comma.*

group /grōōp/ *n.* a gathering or arranging of people or objects. *There is a large group of people in the hotel lobby.*

grow /grō/ *v.* (**grows, grew, grown, grow•ing**) to expand or increase in size. *Trees grow slowly.*

grown /grōn/ *v.* a form of **grow**.

gym /jĭm/ *n.* a gymnasium. *The teams practice in the gym.*

gym

had•dock /hăd' ək/ *n.* (**had•dock** or **had•docks** *pl.*) a food fish of the cod family. *Haddock are found in the North Atlantic.*

had•n't /hăd' nt/ had not.

ha•lo /hā' lō/ *n.* a circle of light around the sun or moon. *A halo is caused by light reflected by ice crystals in the sky.*

hand•made /hănd' mād'/ *adj.* not made by a machine. *The handmade quilt was beautiful.*

hand•writ•ing /hănd' rī tĭng/ *n.* writing done by hand with a pen or a pencil. *Neat handwriting always makes a good impression.*

hap•py /hăp' ē/ *adj.* (**hap•pi•er, hap•pi•est; hap•pi•ly** *adv.*) feeling or showing pleasure; joyful. *The happy man whistled as he worked.*

hard•en /här' dn/ *v.* to make or become hard. *The ground hardens during cold weather.*

harp /härp/ *n.* a tall musical instrument having many strings that are plucked by hand. *A harp can make rippling patterns of notes.*

has•n't /hăz' ənt/ has not.

haul /hôl/ *v.* to pull with force; to drag. *The girls hauled their rowboat out of the water.*

have•n't /hăv' ənt/ have not.

head•ache /hĕd' āk'/ *n.* a pain in the head. *Too much noise gives some people a headache.*

head•ing /hĕd' ĭng/ *n.* the address and date at the top of a letter. *Be sure to give your complete address and ZIP code in the heading.*

heav•y /hĕv' ē/ *adj.* (**heav•i•er, heav•i•est; heav•i•ly** *adv.*) hard to move because of its weight; not light. *This heavy trunk will need two people to lift it.*

he'd /hēd/ he had, he would.

hedge /hĕj/ *n.* a thick row of bushes planted as a fence or boundary. *A hedge should be trimmed evenly.*

height /hīt/ *n.* tallness. *The height of that mountain is 15,000 feet.*

held /hĕld/ *v.* past tense of **hold**.

he·li·um /hē′ lē əm/ *n.* a chemical element that is one of the lightest gases known. *Filling balloons with helium will make them float to the ceiling.*

he'll /hēl/ he will; he shall.

hel·lo /hĕ lō′/ *interj.* something said to express greeting. *The crossing guard always says "Hello" as we go by.*

help·ful /hĕlp′ fəl/ *adj.* giving aid; useful. *It was really helpful of you to do the dishes for me.*

help·less /hĕlp′ lĭs/ *adj.* not able to help oneself or others. *We felt helpless to stop the school's litter problem until we planned a recycling program.*

herd /hûrd/ *n.* a number of animals that feed and move about together. *The herd of deer was hard to spot in the dim forest.*

he·ro /hîr′ ō/ *n.* (**he·ros** or **he·roes** *pl.*) a man or boy admired for his bravery or fine qualities. *Abraham Lincoln is a national hero.*

high /hī/ *adj.* tall; far above the ground. *Eagles build nests on high cliffs.*

high school /hī′ skool′/ *n.* a level of school that follows elementary school; secondary school. *High school usually includes grades nine through twelve.*

high·way /hī′ wā′/ *n.* a main road. *Highways are usually numbered to simplify maps and road signs.*

hike /hīk/ *v.* (**hikes, hiked, hik·ing**) to take a long walk for exercise or pleasure. *We sang marching songs as we hiked up the trail.*

hik·er /hī′ kər/ *n.* one who hikes. *Sturdy, comfortable shoes are a must for every hiker.*

hikers

hinge /hĭnj/ *n.* a joint that allows a part to move or bend. *The door swung on one hinge.*

hire /hīr/ *v.* (**hires, hired, hir·ing**) to employ; to pay a person for working. *Because of good business, the store hired three more clerks.*

hold /hōld/ *v.* (**holds, held, hold·ing**) to have or take and keep; to grasp. *Hold tightly to the dog's leash.*

hol·i·day /hŏl′ ĭ dā′/ *n.* a day on which a special event is celebrated. *Independence Day is the favorite holiday of many people.* [Middle English *holidai,* holy day]

hon·est /ŏn′ ĭst/ *adj.* tending not to lie, cheat, or steal; able to be trusted. *An honest person always tells the truth.*

hon·or[1] /ŏn′ ər/ *n.* **a.** respect or esteem. *A medal is a mark of honor.* **b.** a sense of what is good or right. *Her honor would not permit her to cheat.*

hon·or[2] /ŏn′ ər/ *v.* to show respect for. *We say the pledge of allegiance to honor our country's flag.*

hope·less /hōp′ lĭs/ *adj.* having very little chance of working out right. *After darkness fell, they decided the search for the ball was hopeless.*

hos·pi·tal /hŏs′ pĭ tl/ *n.* a place where persons who are sick or injured are cared for. *Patients who have an operation may stay in the hospital for a few days.*

ho·tel /hō tĕl′/ *n.* a place that provides guests with lodging and usually meals and other services. *Our grandparents stayed in a hotel near the beach in Florida.*

how·ev·er /hou ĕv′ ər/ *conj.* nevertheless. *I've never tasted eggplant before; however, it looks delicious.*

huge /hyooj/ *adj.* very large. *A skyscraper is a huge building.*

hu·man /hyoo′ mən/ *adj.* of or relating to persons. *It is a human weakness to put things off.*

hunt·er /hŭn′ tər/ *n.* a person or animal who hunts. *The hawk's keen eyesight makes it a good hunter.*

hur·ry /hûr′ ē/ or /hŭr′-/ *v.* (**hur·ries, hur·ried, hur·ry·ing**) to act quickly or with haste; to rush. *If we hurry, we may still catch the bus.*

ice • berg /īs′ bûrg′/ *n.* a big piece of ice that floats in the ocean. *The biggest part of an iceberg is underwater.*

i • ci • cle /ī′ sĭ kəl/ *n.* a pointed, hanging piece of ice, formed by the freezing of dripping water. *Icicles hung from the roof of the house.*

I'd /īd/ I would; I should; I had.

i • de • a /ī dē′ ə/ *n.* a thought; a plan. *Bringing plants to decorate the room was Kristin's idea.*

ill • ness /ĭl′ nĭs/ *n.* poor health; a disease. *Craig went home from school because of illness.*

im • mune /ĭ myōōn′/ *adj.* able to resist disease. *Being vaccinated against measles makes you immune to that disease.*

In • di • a /ĭn′ dē ə/ *n.* a large country in southern Asia. *Only China has more people than India.*

In • di • an¹ /ĭn′ dē ən/ *n.* one born or living in India. *He met an Indian from Bombay.*

In • di • an² /ĭn′ dē ən/ *adj.* of or from India. *She was wearing an Indian sari.*

in • fect /ĭn fĕkt′/ *v.* to make ill by the introduction of germs. *A wound can become infected if it is not kept clean.*

in • jure /ĭn′ jər/ *v.* (in•jures, in•jured, in•jur•ing) to harm. *No one was injured when the tree fell down.*

in • let /ĭn′ lĕt′/ *n.* a recess in the land along a coast; a bay or cove. *The inlet was a perfect place for sailing.*

in • sect /ĭn′ sĕkt′/ *n.* a small animal with six legs and a body that has three sections. *A beetle is an insect.*

insect

in • stead /ĭn stĕd′/ *adv.* in place of. *Since the manager wasn't in, we talked to her assistant instead.*

Pronunciation Key

ă	pat	ŏ	pot	th	**thin**
ā	pay	ō	toe	*th*	**th**is
âr	care	ô	paw, for	hw	**which**
ä	father	oi	noise	zh	vision
ĕ	pet	ou	**out**	ə	**about,**
ē	be	ŏŏ	took		**item,**
ĭ	pit	ōō	boot		**pencil,**
ī	pie	ŭ	cut		**gallop,**
îr	pier	ûr	**ur**ge		**circus**

in • vite /ĭn vīt′/ *v.* (in•vites, in•vit•ed, in•vit•ing) to ask a person to go somewhere or do something. *My mother invited my friends to lunch.*

Ire • land /īr′ lənd/ *n.* the island country west of Britain. *The shamrock is an emblem of Ireland.*

I • rish¹ /ī′ rĭsh/ *n.* the people of Ireland. *The Irish are known for their lilting accent.*

I • rish² /ī′ rĭsh/ *adj.* of or from Ireland. *The Irish countryside is green and beautiful.*

i • ron /ī′ ərn/ *v.* to press with an iron to remove wrinkles. *Most fabrics today do not need to be ironed.*

is • land /ī′ lənd/ *n.* a piece of land with water all around it. *People must take a boat or an airplane to get to an island.*

I • tal • ian¹ /ĭ tăl′ yən/ *adj.* of or from Italy. *"Pizza" is an Italian word.*

I • tal • ian² /ĭ tăl′ yən/ *n.* **a.** one born or living in Italy. *Many Italians live in Rome.* **b.** the language of Italy. *Many operas are sung in Italian.*

It • a • ly /ĭt′ ə lē/ *n.* a country in southern Europe bordering on the Mediterranean. *Italy is shaped like a boot.*

itch /ĭch/ *v.* to have or cause tickly irritation on the skin. *A poison ivy rash itches.*

I've /īv/ I have.

Jan. January.

Jan•u•ar•y /jăn′ yōō ĕr′ ē/ *n.* the first month of the year. *January has thirty-one days.*

Ja•pan /jə păn′/ *n.* a small country of islands to the east of China. *Tokyo is the capital of Japan.*

Ja•pan•ese[1] /jăp′ ə nēz′/ *adj.* of or from Japan. *Japanese writing is very different from ours.*

Ja•pan•ese[2] /jăp′ ə nēz′/ *n.* **a.** the people of Japan. *Many Japanese live in apartments.* **b.** the language of Japan. *Japanese is an interesting language to learn.*

jog /jŏg/ *v.* (**jogs, jogged, jog•ging**) to run at a slow, regular pace. *She likes to jog early in the morning.*

joint /joint/ *n.* a place where two bones are connected, allowing motion. *Your leg bends at the knee joint.*

joy /joi/ *n.* a feeling of happiness or pleasure. *Imagine my joy when I received Sandy's letter.*

joy•ful /joi′ fəl/ *adj.* full of joy. *The first and last days of school are always joyful.*

judge /jŭj/ *n.* one who presides over a court of law by hearing cases and making decisions. *A judge must be completely fair.*

juice /jōōs/ *n.* the liquid that can be squeezed out of fruits, meat, or vegetables. *He has a glass of orange juice every morning.*

Ju•ly /jōō lī′/ *n.* the seventh month of the year. *July is usually hot in Texas.*

jum•ble /jŭm′ bəl/ *v.* (**jum•bles, jum•bled, jum•bling**) to mix up. *The letters of the word were jumbled in the puzzle.*

June /jōōn/ *n.* the sixth month of the year. *June has thirty days.*

jun•gle /jŭng′ gəl/ *n.* wild land near the equator with thickly grown tropical plants. *Parrots and monkeys live in the jungle.*

ju•ror /jōōr′ ər/ *n.* one who serves on the jury of a court. *Many adult citizens take turns serving as jurors.*

ju•ry /jōōr′ ē/ *n.* (**ju•ries** *pl.*) a group of persons selected to listen to the evidence in a court case. *Robert served on a jury of twelve members.*

jus•tice /jŭs′ tĭs/ *n.* fairness. *Justice demands that you tell the truth.*

keep /kēp/ *v.* (**keeps, kept, keep•ing**) **a.** to store; to put away; to save. *I keep all my old homework.* **b.** to continue. *Let's keep looking until we find it.*

kept /kĕpt/ *v.* past tense of **keep.**

ket•tle /kĕt′ l/ *n.* a pot used for heating liquids. *Put the kettle on the stove.*

kil•o•gram /kĭl′ ə grăm/ *n.* a measure of weight equal to 1,000 grams. *A kilogram is a little over two pounds.*

kil•o•me•ter /kĭl′ ə mē′ tər/ or /kĭ lŏm′ ĭ tər/ *n.* a measure of length equal to 1,000 meters. *A kilometer is almost two-thirds of a mile.*

kind /kīnd/ *adj.* friendly; thoughtful of others. *Everyone likes kind persons.*

kind•ness /kīnd′ nĭs/ *n.* friendly or helpful behavior. *His kindness earned him the respect of the whole class.*

knee /nē/ *n.* the joint in the middle of the leg. *You bend your knees when you walk.*

knife /nīf/ *n.* (**knives** *pl.*) a flat cutting instrument with a sharp blade. *Jean sliced the carrots with a knife.*

knit /nĭt/ *v.* (**knits, knit or knit•ted, knit•ting**) to make by weaving yarn with long needles. *My father will knit a sweater for me.*

knock /nŏk/ *v.* to strike with the fist or with a hard object. *I knocked on the door but no one answered.*

knot /nŏt/ *n.* a fastening made by tying. *We joined the two ropes with a square knot.*

knot

know /nō/ *v.* (knows, knew, known, know•ing) **a.** to have the facts about; to understand. *Do you know how hail is formed?* **b.** to be acquainted with. *I know the Bakers but not where they live.*

known /nōn/ *v.* a form of **know**.

la • dy /lā′ dē/ *n.* (la•dies *pl.*) a polite term for a woman. *Ladies and gentlemen, may I have your attention?*

lamb /lăm/ *n.* a young sheep. *The lambs ran playfully in the field.*

land • scape /lănd′ skāp′/ *n.* a picture of a view of the countryside. *Some artists paint landscapes.*

laugh /lăf/ *v.* to make sounds with the voice that show amusement. *Everyone laughed at the funny movie.*

laugh • ter /lăf′ tər/ *n.* the noise of laughing. *Laughter filled the classroom during the puppet show.*

la • va /lä′ və/ *n.* the hot, melted rock that comes from a volcano. *The lava flowed down the mountain.*

la • zy /lā′ zē/ *adj.* not wanting to work. *He was too lazy to help us.*

lead¹ /lēd / *v.* (leads, led, lead•ing) to direct or show the way. *She will lead the hikers home.*

lead² /lĕd/ *n.* **a.** a soft mineral used in some pipes. *He put a weight made of lead on the fishing line.* **b.** graphite used to make the writing substance in a pencil. *My fingers had black smudges from the pencil lead.*

lead • er /lē′ dər/ *n.* one who leads. *The Scout troop needs a new leader.*

learn • er /lûr′ nər/ *n.* one who learns; a student. *A good learner listens carefully.*

least /lēst/ *adj.* smallest in size or amount. *Which game costs the least money?*

length /lĕngkth/ *n.* the distance from end to end. *The length of the boat is forty feet.*

-less a suffix that means "without," used to form adjectives: *endless.*

let's /lĕts/ let us.

Pronunciation Key

ă	pat	ŏ	pot	th	**th**in
ā	pay	ō	toe	*th*	**th**is
âr	care	ô	paw, for	hw	**wh**ich
ä	father	oi	noise	zh	vision
ĕ	pet	ou	**out**	ə	**a**bout,
ē	be	ŏŏ	took		item,
ĭ	pit	ōō	boot		penc**i**l,
ī	pie	ŭ	cut		gall**o**p,
îr	pier	ûr	**ur**ge		circus

let • ter /lĕt′ ər/ *n.* **a.** a single character in an alphabet. *The letter k was missing from the word.* **b.** a written note or message. *I got a letter in today's mail.*

lev • el /lĕv′ əl/ *adj.* flat and even. *Most floors are level.*

li • brar • y /lī′ brĕr′ ē/ *n.* a room or building containing books that may be read or borrowed. *A library is also used for research and studying.*

light • en /līt′ n/ *v.* **a.** to make brighter; to add light to. *The new paint lightens the room.* **b.** to make less heavy. *Taking out the books lightened my suitcase.*

limb /lĭm/ *n.* a branch of a tree. *We hung the swing from a strong limb.*

liq • uid /lĭk′ wĭd/ *n.* a flowing substance that is neither a solid nor a gas. *Water is a liquid.*

lis • ten /lĭs′ n/ *v.* to pay attention; to try to hear. *The audience listened closely to the speaker.*

lis • ten • er /lĭs′ ə nər/ *n.* one who listens. *A good listener remembers what is said.*

live • stock /līv′ stŏk′/ *n.* animals kept on a farm, such as horses, cattle, or sheep. *The farmer will sell some of his livestock.*

liz • ard /lĭz′ ərd/ *n.* a reptile with a long body and tail, usually having four legs and scaly skin. *Iguanas are lizards that live in a dry, desert climate.*

lizard

loan /lōn/ *n.* an amount of money lent or borrowed. *Banks charge interest on loans.*

▶ **Loan** sounds like **lone**.

lone /lōn/ *adj.* alone; single. *A lone cloud floated in the blue sky.*

▶ **Lone** sounds like **loan**.

loop /lo͞op/ *n.* the curved shape of a line that dips and crosses itself. *We hung the crepe paper in loops.*

lose /lo͞oz/ *v.* (**los•es, lost, los•ing**) **a.** to be unable to find; to misplace. *Put the key in your pocket so you won't lose it.* **b.** to fail to win. *She lost the race by less than a second.*

lunch /lŭnch/ *n.* (**lunch•es** *pl.*) a light meal usually eaten around the middle of the day. *We have lunch at noon.*

lung /lŭng/ *n.* one of the organs in the chest that are used in breathing. *The lungs take in fresh air.*

-ly a suffix, used to form adverbs, that means: **a.** like; in the manner of: *finally.* **b.** at certain intervals: *weekly.*

mag•ma /măg′ mə/ *n.* the very hot melted rock inside the earth's crust. *When magma cools, it forms igneous rock.*

mail•box /māl′ bŏks′/ *n.* **a.** a public box into which people put items to be delivered by mail. *The contents of a mailbox are taken to the post office.* **b.** a private box for a home or business to which mail is delivered. *Check the mailbox to see if you got a letter.*

ma•jor /mā′ jər/ *adj.* larger; greater; primary. *He played a major role in the project's success.*

march /märch/ *v.* (**march•es, marched, march•ing**) to walk with even, steady steps. *The band marched in the parade.*

Mar. March.

March /märch/ *n.* the third month of the year. *The weather begins to warm up in March.*

mark /märk/ *v.* to make a visible sign on or by. *Mark the wrong answers with an "x."*

mar•ket /mär′ kĭt/ *n.* a place where things can be bought and sold. *A supermarket is a large, modern market.*

mas•ter /măs′ tər/ *v.* to become skilled in. *It takes time and practice to master a foreign language.*

mat•ter /măt′ ər/ *n.* all physical or material substance; concrete objects. *Matter has weight and occupies space.*

may /mā/ *v.* (**might**) **a.** to be allowed to. *May I be excused from the table?* **b.** to be possible that. *The package may arrive today.*

May /mā/ *n.* the fifth month of the year. *Flowers bloom in May.*

mean /mēn/ *v.* (**means, meant, mean•ing**) **a.** to intend. *I didn't mean to hurt her feelings.* **b.** to signify; to carry the meaning of. *The sign "+" means "plus."*

meant /mĕnt/ past tense of **mean**.

mea•sles /mē′ zəlz/ *n.* a disease marked by red spots on the skin. *Most children have been vaccinated against measles.*

mem•ber /mĕm′ bər/ *n.* a person who belongs to a group. *Members of the club voted to have a picnic.*

-ment a suffix that means "the result of an action or process," used to form nouns: *amusement.*

met•al[1] /mĕt′ l/ *n.* any of a number of substances that shine when polished and that can conduct electricity and heat. *Most metals are found in solid form.*

met•al[2] /mĕt′ l/ *adj.* made of or containing metal. *Many foods are packed in metal cans.*

me•te•or /mē′ tē ər/ *n.* a solid fragment from space that falls into the earth's atmosphere and burns. *Meteors are sometimes called shooting stars.*

meteor

Mex•i•can[1] /mĕk′ sĭ kən/ *adj.* of or from Mexico. *A sombrero is a Mexican hat.*

Mex•i•can² /měk′ sǐ kən/ *n.* one born or living in Mexico. *Many Mexicans visit the United States each year.*

Mex•i•co /měk′ sǐ kō/ *n.* a large country located between the United States and Central America. *The capital of Mexico is Mexico City.*

mid•dle¹ /mǐd′ l/ *n.* the point or part located at the same distance from each side or end; the center. *Your nose is in the middle of your face.*

mid•dle² /mǐd′ l/ *adj.* occupying a central position. *His middle name is Michael.*

might /mīt/ past tense of **may**.

mi•grate /mī′ grāt/ *v.* (**mi•grates, mi•grat•ed, mi•grat•ing**) to travel from place to place, especially as the seasons change. *Many birds migrate south for the winter.*

mil•li•lit•er /mǐl′ ə lē′ tər/ *n.* a measure of volume equal to 1/1000 of a liter. *Chemical solutions are often measured in milliliters.*

mind¹ /mīnd/ *v.* to object to. *Would you mind holding my books for a minute?*

mind² /mīnd/ *n.* the part of a person that thinks and remembers. *Your mind directs all your conscious actions.*

mi•nor /mī′ nər/ *adj.* smaller; lesser; secondary. *Brian played a minor role, so he didn't have to learn many lines.*

mix /mǐks/ *v.* (**mix•es, mixed, mix•ing**) to form by combining unlike items. *Will you mix the salad?*

mixed /mǐkst/ *adj.* made up of different kinds. *A bowl of mixed fruit sat on the table.*

mod•el¹ /mŏd′ l/ *n.* a small, exact copy or pattern. *She built several models of old automobiles.*

mod•el² /mŏd′ l/ *v.* to make or shape something. *Let's model animals out of clay.*

moist /moist/ *adj.* somewhat wet; damp. *The grass was still moist from the rain this morning.*

mois•ten /moi′ sən/ *v.* to make or become damp; to wet. *Moisten this cloth and use it to wipe the table clean.*

mo•ment /mō′ mənt/ *n.* **a.** an instant; a very brief period. *I saw him for a moment, but I lost sight of him in the crowd.* **b.** a specific point in time. *I called the moment I heard you were sick.*

Mon. Monday.

Mon•day /mǔn′ dē/ or /-dā′/ *n.* the second day of the week, coming after Sunday and before Tuesday. *Monday is the first school day in the week.* [Old English *monandæg*, the moon's day.]

mon•key
/mǔng′ kē/ *n.* a small, furry animal with hands, thumbs, and a long tail. *Monkeys have long tails, but apes have no tails at all.*

monkey

month /mǔnth/ *n.* one of the twelve parts into which a year is divided. *We go to school for nine months of the year.*

mood /mōōd/ *n.* a state of mind; a feeling. *The sunny morning put me in a happy mood.*

mo•tel /mō tĕl′/ *n.* a hotel near a highway for people who are traveling by car. *We spent the night in a motel on our way to visit our cousins.*

moth•er /mǔ*th*′ ər/ *n.* the female parent. *My mother likes to listen to me read.*

mount /mount/ *v.* to climb onto; to get up on. *The rider mounted his horse and galloped away.*

mouth /mouth/ *n.* the opening in the head that contains the tongue and teeth and is used for taking in food and making sounds. *When you yawn, your mouth opens wide.*

move•ment /mo͞ov′ mənt/ *n.* action; a change in position or location. *The children watched the slow movement of the snail across the sidewalk.*

mul•ti•pli•ca•tion /mŭl′ tə plĭ **kā′** shən/ *n.* the adding of a number a certain number of times. *Knowing your times tables will help you solve problems in multiplication.*

mum•ble /mŭm′ bəl/ *v.* (**mum•bles, mum•bled, mum•bling**) to speak unclearly so that you are hard to understand. *If you mumble, no one will understand you.*

mu•sic /myo͞o′ zĭk/ *n.* **a.** the art of making and combining sounds using rhythm, melody, and harmony. *Music is one of the fine arts.* **b.** the sounds made and combined in this way. *We can hear many kinds of music on the radio.*

na•tion /nā′ shən/ *n.* a group of people living together under one government, who usually have many of the same customs and speak the same language. *The United States, Japan, and Sweden are nations.*

near¹ /nîr/ *adv.* not far away in time or distance. *The train drew near.*

near² /nîr/ *prep.* not far from. *The school is near my house, only a block away.*

near•by /nîr′ bī/ *adj.* not far off. *They live in a nearby town.*

nec•tar /nĕk′ tər/ *n.* a sweet liquid in the blossoms of flowers, used by bees to make honey. *Bees go from flower to flower to collect nectar.*

nei•ther¹ /nē′ thər/ or /nī′-/ *pron.* not the one and not the other. *Neither of us was invited.*

nei•ther² /nē′ thər/ or /nī′-/ *conj.* also not. *If you're not going to the park, neither am I.*

nei•ther³ /nē′ thər/ or /nī′-/ *adj.* not either. *Neither girl was tall enough for the part in the play.*

-ness a suffix that means "a state or quality," used to form nouns: *softness.*

news•pa•per /no͞oz′ pā pər/ or /nyo͞oz′-/ *n.* a printed paper that contains news, advertisements, cartoons, etc. *My grandfather likes to work the crossword puzzles in the newspaper.*

newspaper

nine•teen /nīn tēn′/ *n.* one more than eighteen; 19. *Ten plus nine is nineteen.*

nine•ty /nīn′ tē/ *n.* one more than eighty-nine; 90. *The temperature was over ninety degrees for several days this summer.*

ninth¹ /nīnth/ *adj.* next after the eighth; 9th. *Marty sat in the ninth chair.*

ninth² /nīnth/ *n.* one of nine equal parts. *We divided the cake into ninths.*

noise /noiz/ *n.* a sound, especially one that is loud and harsh. *The noise of the alarm clock startled me.*

no•mad /nō′ măd′/ *n.* a wanderer; someone without a permanent home. *In prehistoric times, tribes of nomads followed herds of animals in search of food.*

nor /nôr/ *conj.* and not; not either. *There was neither milk nor fruit juice in the refrigerator.*

noun /noun/ *n.* a word used to name a person, place, thing, or quality. *Words like* **girl, Illinois, state, tree,** *and* **honor** *are nouns.*

Nov. November.

No•vem•ber /nō vĕm′ bər/ *n.* the eleventh month of the year. *November has thirty days.*

nu•mer•al /no͞o′ mər əl/ or /nyo͞o′-/ *n.* a figure or other symbol that represents a number. *"VI" is the Roman numeral for six.*

nu•mer•a•tor /no͞o′ mə rā′ tər/ or /nyo͞o′-/ *n.* the part of a fraction written above the line. *In the fraction $\frac{3}{4}$, the numerator is 3.*

o•bey /ō bā′/ *v.* **a.** to follow the orders of. *Children obey their parents.* **b.** to act in agreement with; to carry out. *Good citizens obey the law.*

o•boe /ō′ bō/ *n.* a woodwind instrument played by blowing into a double reed. *The oboe's smooth, penetrating tone carries easily above an orchestra.*

Oct. October.

Oc•to•ber /ŏk tō′ bər/ *n.* the tenth month of the year. *Many leaves change color in October.*

of•ten /ô′ fən/ or /ŏf′ ən/ *adv.* many times; frequently. *We often see our relatives during the holidays.*

or•bit[1] /ôr′ bĭt/ *n.* the path of one body going around another. *It takes one year for the earth to travel in its orbit around the sun.*

or•bit[2] /ôr′ bĭt/ *v.* to move in an orbit around; to circle. *The moon orbits the earth.*

or•chard /ôr′ chərd/ *n.* a piece of land on which fruit trees are grown. *The apple orchard was two miles long.*

ought /ôt/ *v.* should. *You ought to wear a coat on a cold day like this.*

out•doors[1] /out dôrz′/ or /-dōrz′/ *n.* the area outside a house or building; the open air. *Campers enjoy the outdoors.*

out•doors[2] /out dôrz′/ or /-dōrz′/ *adv.* outside a building; out in the open air. *We played outdoors on the first sunny day of spring.*

out•rage /out′ rāj/ *n.* anger at an offensive act. *The community expressed outrage at the bribery scandal.*

own•er /ō′ nər/ *n.* one who owns or possesses something. *Who is the owner of this plaid jacket?*

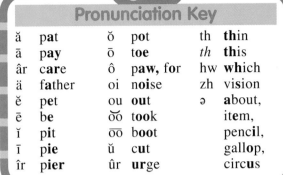

pack•age /păk′ ĭj/ *n.* a wrapped box; a parcel. *How much will it cost to mail this package?*

pain•ful /pān′ fəl/ *adj.* causing or having pain; hurting. *The blister on my heel was painful.*

paint•er /pān′ tər/ *n.* **a.** a person who paints pictures; an artist. *Some painters make abstract designs.* **b.** a person whose job is painting buildings or furniture. *The painter stood on a ladder to paint the house.*

paint•ing /pān′ tĭng/ *n.* a painted picture. *We saw many paintings in the art museum.*

pa•per /pā′ pər/ *n.* **a.** a material made in thin sheets of pulp, from wood or rags. *The pages of this book are made of paper.* **b.** a newspaper. *Have you seen the comics in today's paper?* **c.** a written article; a report. *The teacher asked us to write a paper about the moon.*

pa•per•back /pā′ pər băk′/ *n.* a book bound with a flexible paper cover and binding. *Paperbacks usually cost less than hardcover books.*

par•ent /păr′ ənt/ *n.* a father or a mother. *Either parent may write a note excusing an absence.*

par•rot /păr′ ət/ *n.* a tropical bird with a short, curved beak and brightly colored feathers. *A parrot can learn to repeat words.*

parrot

pass[1] /păs/ *v.* **a.** to go by. *They pass the fire station on the way to school.* **b.** to hand over; to give; to send. *Please pass the salad.* **c.** to succeed in. *The entire fourth grade passed the test.*

pass[2] /păs/ *n.* **a.** a written note; a permit. *Did the teacher sign your pass?* **b.** a narrow road through mountains. *We saw snow at the top of the pass.*

passed /păst/ *v.* past tense of **pass.**

▶ **Passed** sounds like **past.**

past[1] /păst/ *n.* the time that has gone by. *In the distant past, dinosaurs lived on the earth.*

▶ **Past** sounds like **passed.**

past[2] /păst/ *adj.* gone by; previous. *In the past month we had three inches of rain.*

▶ **Past** sounds like **passed.**

pas•tel /pă stĕl′/ *n.* **a.** a chalklike crayon. *Pastels smudge easily.* **b.** a light, soft color. *The pale pink roses matched the pastels of the room.*

patch[1] /păch/ *n.* (**patch•es** *pl.*) a piece of cloth sewn over a hole or a tear. *My old pants have patches on them.*

patch[2] /păch/ *v.* (**patch•es, patched, patch•ing**) to cover with a patch; to repair. *Can you patch this up?*

pave•ment /pāv′ mənt/ *n.* the surface of a road or a street made by paving. *Some pavement is made with crushed rock, clay, and tar.*

pay•ment /pā′ mənt/ *n.* an amount of money paid. *Most people who rent a house or an apartment make a monthly payment to the landlord.*

peace•ful /pēs′ fəl/ *adj.* **a.** calm; quiet. *Early morning hours are peaceful.* **b.** not liking arguments or quarrels; liking peace. *Neutral nations are peaceful.*

peach /pēch/ *n.* (**peach•es** *pl.*) a sweet, juicy fruit with a large, rough stone in the center. *When ripe, a peach has a fuzzy, pinkish-yellow skin.*

peach

peb•ble /pĕb′ əl/ *n.* a small stone. *Pebbles have been worn smooth by water running over them.*

pelt /pĕlt/ *n.* the skin of an animal with fur or hair on it. *The early settlers bartered animal pelts for food and supplies.*

pen•ny /pĕn′ ē/ *n.* (**pen•nies** *pl.*) a coin worth one cent. *Ten pennies equal one dime.*

per•fect /pûr′ fĭkt/ *adj.* **a.** having no flaws or errors; exactly right. *Charlene turned in a perfect paper in science.* **b.** excellent; unusually good. *Today is a perfect day for swimming.*

pe•ri•od /pîr′ ē əd/ *n.* **a.** a dot (.) used in printing and in writing. *Most sentences end in a period.* **b.** a length of time. *We had a period of twenty days with no rainfall.*

per•son /pûr′ sən/ *n.* a human being; a man, woman, boy, or girl. *This elevator can hold six persons.*

pet•al /pĕt′ l/ *n.* the leaflike part of a flower. *Dried rose petals have a lovely fragrance.*

pic•co•lo /pĭk′ ə lō/ *n.* a small, high-pitched flute. *Many marching bands feature a piccolo.*

piece /pēs/ *n.* a part; a segment. *Would you like a piece of my orange?*

pil•grim /pĭl′ grəm/ *n.* **a.** a person who travels to a holy place. *Pilgrims in the Middle Ages journeyed to shrines or cathedrals.* **b. Pilgrim** one of the English Puritans who founded the American colony of Plymouth in 1620. *The Pilgrims came on the Mayflower.*

pil•low /pĭl′ ō/ *n.* a support used for the head in resting or sleeping; a cushion. *Do you like to sleep on a feather pillow?*

pit•y /pĭt′ ē/ *n.* sympathy or sorrow for the suffering of another. *We felt pity for her because she looked so unhappy.*

piv•ot /pĭv′ ət/ *v.* to turn around a fixed point. *The basketball player pivoted with one foot on the floor.*

place•ment /plās′ mənt/ *n.* location; arrangement. *The placement of the flowers added the perfect touch to the dinner table.*

plan•et /plăn′ ĭt/ *n.* a large body that rotates around the sun and reflects its light. *Earth is one of nine planets in our solar system.*

play•er /plā′ ər/ *n.* **a.** a person who plays a game. *Beth is the shortest player on her soccer team.* **b.** a person who plays a musical instrument. *A guitar player is called a guitarist.*

play•ful /plā′ fəl/ *adj.* full of fun and enjoyment. *The baby was playful in his bath.*

plow¹ /plou/ *n.* a tool used in farming for turning up soil. *Plows have sharp blades and are pulled by horses, oxen, or tractors.*

plow² /plou/ *v.* to work with a plow; to till. *Fields are plowed before crops are planted.*

plum•age /plōo′ mǐj/ *n.* the feathers of a bird. *Male birds have bright plumage.*

po•em /pō′ əm/ *n.* a verbal composition arranged so that it has rhythm and appeals to the imagination. *Not all poems rhyme.*

po•et /pō′ ǐt/ *n.* a person who writes poems. *Emily Dickinson was a famous American poet.*

po•lar /pō′ lər/ *adj.* having to do with the North Pole or the South Pole. *Polar weather is cold.*

pol•len /pŏl′ ən/ *n.* the yellow powder inside a flower. *Bees carry pollen from plant to plant.*

pol•y•gon /pŏl′ ē gŏn′/ *n.* a geometric figure that has three or more angles and sides. *A pentagon is a five-sided polygon.*

po•ny /pō′ nē/ *n.* (**po•nies** *pl.*) a kind of horse that is small in size when fully grown. *Children ride a pony at an amusement park.*

pony

port /pôrt/ or /pōrt/ *n.* **a.** a town with a harbor where ships may dock. *Boston and New York are Atlantic ports.* **b.** the left-hand side of a ship, boat, or airplane as one faces forward. *Ships show a red light toward port at night.*

post•er /pō′ stər/ *n.* a sign. *The poster in the restaurant window advertised the school play.*

pow•der /pou′ dər/ *n.* a substance made of fine grains. *It's easy to grind chalk into a powder.*

Pronunciation Key

ă	pat	ŏ	pot	th	**th**in
ā	pay	ō	toe	*th*	**th**is
âr	care	ô	p**aw**, f**or**	hw	**wh**ich
ä	father	oi	n**oi**se	zh	vi**si**on
ě	pet	ou	**ou**t	ə	**a**bout,
ē	be	ŏŏ	t**oo**k		**i**tem,
ĭ	pit	ōō	b**oo**t		penc**i**l,
ī	pie	ŭ	c**u**t		gall**o**p,
îr	pier	ûr	**ur**ge		circ**u**s

pow•er¹ /pou′ ər/ *n.* great strength, force, or control. *The police have power to enforce the law.*

pow•er² /pou′ ər/ *v.* to supply with power. *The boat is powered by an engine.*

pow•er•ful /pou′ ər fəl/ *adj.* having great power; strong. *The king was a powerful ruler.*

pow•er•less /pou′ ər lǐs/ *adj.* having no strength or power; helpless. *The farmers were helpless against the drought.*

prai•rie /prâr′ ē/ *n.* a large, flat area of land with much grass but few trees. *Buffalo once grazed on the western prairies.*

pre- a prefix that means **a.** before: *preschool.* **b.** in advance: *prepay.*

pre•heat /prē hēt′/ *v.* to heat beforehand. *Please preheat the oven before you put the potatoes in to bake.*

pre•pay /prē pā′/ *v.* to pay beforehand. *The company will prepay the postage.*

pre•school /prē′ skool′/ *n.* a place of learning before elementary school. *Children aged three to five may attend preschool.*

pre•test /prē′ tĕst′/ *n.* a test given beforehand to determine readiness. *If you already know the spelling words, you'll do well on the pretest.*

pre•view /prē′ vyōō′/ *v.* to view or watch in advance. *We were invited to preview the art show.*

print /prĭnt/ *n.* **a.** letters and words made on paper. *Some books use large print.* **b.** a picture or design made by printing. *The magazine article showed a print made with a wood block.*

prob • lem /prŏb′ ləm/ *n.* a question to be worked out and answered. *Careful, step-by-step reasoning is the key to solving a math problem.*

prod • uct /prŏd′ əkt/ *n.* a number produced by multiplying two or more numbers together. *The product of 3 and 5 is 15.*

pro • noun /prō′ noun/ *n.* a word used in place of a noun. *"I," "them," and "its" are common pronouns.*

pro • vide /prə vīd′/ *v.* (**pro•vides, pro•vid•ed, pro•vid•ing**) to supply; to furnish. *The school provides hot lunches for students.*

pulse /pŭls/ *n.* the rhythm of blood in arteries, produced by regular contractions of the heart. *The nurse checked the patient's pulse.*

pump • kin /pŭmp′ kĭn/ *n.* a large yellow-orange fruit that grows on a vine. *Cooks use pumpkin in pies and breads.*

pun /pŭn/ *n.* a play on words. *A pun involves two words that sound alike.*

quake /kwāk/ *v.* (**quakes, quaked, quak•ing**) to vibrate or shake. *The ground quaked beneath us during the mild earthquake.*

quar • rel[1] /kwôr′ əl/ or /kwŏr′-/ *n.* an argument; a dispute. *The children had a quarrel about which program to watch.*

quar • rel[2] /kwôr′ əl/ or /kwŏr′-/ *v.* to fight; to disagree, using angry words. *They quarreled about whose turn it was to bat.*

quart /kwôrt/ *n.* a liquid measure equal to two pints; one-quarter of a gallon. *My mother sent me to the store for a quart of milk.*

quar • ter /kwôr′ tər/ *n.* a coin worth one fourth of a dollar, or twenty-five cents. *Two dimes and a nickel equal a quarter.*

quarter

quar • tet /kwôr tĕt′/ *n.* a group of four musicians performing together. *A string quartet consists of two violinists, one violist, and one cellist.*

queen /kwēn/ *n.* **a.** a female ruler. *The queen issued a proclamation.* **b.** the wife of a king. *When she married the king, she became his queen.*

ques • tion /kwĕs′ chən/ *n.* **a.** a sentence that asks something. *"What time is it?" is a question.* **b.** a problem. *The litter question will be discussed tonight.*

quick /kwĭk/ *adj.* fast; swift. *The rabbit made a quick leap into the bushes.*

qui • et /kwī′ ĭt/ *adj.* **a.** silent; still; having little noise. *The hum of the airplane was the only sound in the quiet night.* **b.** peaceful; calm. *Alice spent a quiet afternoon reading.*

quill /kwĭl/ *n.* a large, stiff feather or its hollow stem. *Quills were once used to make pens.*

quilt /kwĭlt/ *n.* a bed cover made of layers of cloth and padding sewn together. *Grandma told me how she made the patchwork quilt.*

quit /kwĭt/ *v.* (**quits, quit** or **quit•ted, quit•ting**) **a.** to stop. *We'll quit raking leaves when it gets dark.* **b.** to leave; to give up. *Mr. Walters quit his job to start his own business.*

quite /kwīt/ *adv.* **a.** completely; entirely. *I haven't quite finished eating.* **b.** really; truly. *His drawings are quite good.*

quiz /kwĭz/ *n.* (**quiz•zes** *pl.*) a brief test. *I missed two questions on the science quiz.*

quote[1] /kwōt/ *v.* (**quotes, quot•ed, quot•ing**) to repeat or refer to a passage from a story or poem. *Justin quoted a line from the poem in his essay.*

quote[2] /kwōt/ *n.* a quotation; a passage repeated from a story or a poem. *Quotes usually appear inside quotation marks.*

quo • tient /kwō′ shənt/ *n.* the result obtained when one number is divided by another. *If you divide 16 by 2, the quotient is 8.*

ra•di•o /rā′ dē ō/ *n.* **a.** a way of sending sounds from one place to another by electromagnetic waves. *Before radio was discovered, messages were sent over wires.* **b.** a device for receiving such sounds. *Rita heard the election results on her radio.*

radio

rail /rāl/ *n.* **a.** a bar of wood or metal. *She sat on the top rail of the fence.* **b.** railroad. *Send this package by rail.*

rail•road /rāl′ rōd′/ *n.* a track made of two parallel steel rails on which trains travel. *The railroad goes through the middle of the town.*

rail•way /rāl′ wā′/ *n.* a railroad. *Many people travel to work each day by railway.*

ranch /rănch/ *n.* (**ranch•es** *pl.*) a large farm where cattle, horses, or sheep are raised. *Some fences on their ranch are made of barbed wire.*

range /rānj/ *v.* (**rang•es, ranged, rang•ing**) **a.** to extend or vary within certain limits. *The stories in this book range from sad to funny.* **b.** to travel over; to wander through. *Giraffes range the plains of Africa.*

rare /râr/ *adj.* not often found or seen. *My uncle saves rare postage stamps.*

rate /rāt/ *n.* **a.** the amount or degree of something measured in relation to something else. *We traveled at a rate of 40 miles per hour.* **b.** a price. *The plumber's rates are high.*

rath•er /răth′ ər/ *adv.* **a.** somewhat. *The baby is rather tired after the long ride.* **b.** more readily; more gladly. *The dog would rather stay inside on cold days than go out.*

rat•tle /răt′ l/ *v.* (**rat•tles, rat•tled, rat•tling**) **a.** to make a number of short, sharp sounds. *The windows rattle when the wind blows.* **b.** to move with short, sharp sounds. *The old car rattled over the bumpy road.*

Pronunciation Key

ă	pat	ŏ	pot	th	**th**in
ā	pay	ō	toe	*th*	**th**is
âr	care	ô	paw, for	hw	**wh**ich
ä	father	oi	noise	zh	vi**s**ion
ĕ	pet	ou	**ou**t	ə	**a**bout,
ē	be	ŏŏ	took		item,
ĭ	pit	ōō	boot		penc**i**l,
ī	pie	ŭ	cut		gall**o**p,
îr	pier	ûr	**ur**ge		circ**u**s

reach /rēch/ *v.* **a.** to stretch out one's hand or arm. *Joel reached for the book on the top shelf.* **b.** to extend to. *The old road reaches the river and stops.*

read•er /rē′ dər/ *n.* a person who reads. *The teacher chose Kathy to be the reader of our lunchtime story this week.*

read•y /rĕd′ ē/ *adj.* (**read•i•er, read•i•est; read•i•ly** *adv.*) **a.** prepared. *We are ready for school.* **b.** willing. *My older brother is always ready to help me with my homework.*

reap•er /rē′ pər/ *n.* a machine that cuts and gathers grain. *The farmer used a new reaper for the harvest.*

rear[1] /rîr/ *n.* the back part. *We stood in the rear of the room.*

rear[2] /rîr/ *adj.* at or of the back. *Use the rear entrance.*

rear[3] /rîr/ *v.* to rise on the hind legs. *The horse reared suddenly and the rider fell off.*

rea•son[1] /rē′ zən/ *n.* **a.** a cause or explanation. *Your parents will write the reason for your absence.* **b.** logic; the power to think. *Use reason to solve the problem.*

rea•son[2] /rē′ zən/ *v.* to think in a sensible way; to use logic. *See if you can reason out the meaning of the word.*

re•build /rē bĭld′/ *v.* (**re•builds, re•built, re•build•ing**) to build again. *They are planning to rebuild the old school.*

re•check /rē chĕk′/ *v.* to check again. *After he finished the test, Pedro went back and rechecked his answers.*

re•cord[1] /rĭ kôrd′/ *v.* **a.** to keep an account of. *The story of our country's beginning is recorded in history.* **b.** to put sounds on a magnetic tape, phonograph record, or compact disc. *The singer recorded two new songs.*

re•cord[2] /rĕk′ ərd/ *n.* **a.** an account of facts or events. *The secretary keeps the club's records.* **b.** the best performance. *Who holds the record for the race?* **c.** a thin disc used on a phonograph to produce sound. *We listened to the singer's new record.*

re•cov•er /rĭ kŭv′ ər/ *v.* **a.** to get back. *The police recovered the stolen goods.* **b.** to regain health. *Tracy recovered quickly after her illness.*

rec•tan•gle /rĕk′ tăng′ gəl/ *n.* a parallelogram that has four right angles. *A square is a rectangle.*

reef /rēf/ *n.* an underwater ridge of rocks, sand, or coral in a shallow area. *The boat's bottom scraped against the reef.*

re- a prefix that means: **a.** again: *rebuild.* **b.** back: *recall.*

re•heat /rē hēt′/ *v.* to heat again. *Dad reheated some leftovers for dinner.*

re•lay /rē′ lā/ or /rĭ lā′/ *v.* to take and pass along to another person or place. *Will you relay a message to Joan when you see her?*

re•main /rĭ mān′/ *v.* **a.** to continue without change; to stay. *The nurse reported that the patient's condition remained good.* **b.** to be left over. *After the picnic only a few sandwiches remained.*

re•main•der /rĭ mān′ dər/ *n.* a part or amount left over. *When you divide 15 by 6, the quotient is 2 and the remainder is 3.*

re•peat /rĭ pēt′/ *v.* **a.** to say again. *Will you repeat the question, please?* **b.** to say from memory. *Tomorrow each of you will be asked to repeat this poem.*

re•ply[1] /rĭ plī′/ *n.* (**re•plies** *pl.*) an answer. *I did not hear his reply because he spoke so softly.*

re•ply[2] /rĭ plī′/ *v.* (**re•plies, re•plied, re•ply•ing**) to give an answer; to respond. *She replied to my letter immediately.*

re•port[1] /rĭ pôrt′/ or /-pōrt′/ *n.* a detailed written or spoken account. *The newspaper report of the election listed the winners.*

re•port[2] /rĭ pôrt′/ or /-pōrt′/ *v.* to give an account or statement of. *The president of the company reported that sales had increased.*

re•port•er /rĭ pôr′ tər/ or /-pōr′-/ *n.* a person who gathers news for radio, television, or newspapers. *A reporter interviewed the candidates.*

rep•tile /rĕp′ tĭl/ or /-tīl/ *n.* any of the group of cold-blooded animals whose bodies are covered with plates or scales. *Snakes, turtles, and alligators are reptiles.*

reptile

re•read /rē rēd′/ *v.* (**re•reads, re•read, re•read•ing**) to read again. *I often reread my favorite books.*

rest•ful /rĕst′ fəl/ *adj.* offering rest, peace, or quiet. *My aunt finds sewing restful after a busy day.*

rest•less /rĕst′ lĭs/ *adj.* impatient; unable to be still. *The small children grew restless after the long delay.*

re•turn /rĭ tûrn′/ *v.* **a.** to come or go back. *We will return after the game is over.* **b.** to bring, send, or give back. *Return the book when you have finished reading it.*

re•view /rĭ vyo͞o′/ *v.* to study again; to go over. *She reviewed the chapter before she took the test.*

re•write /rē rīt′/ *v.* (**re•writes, re•wrote, re•writ•ten, re•writ•ing**) to write again. *The teacher asked us to rewrite our book reports, after correcting the spelling and punctuation.*

ridge /rĭj/ *n.* **a.** a narrow, raised line or strip; a crest. *Corduroy is a type of cloth that has ridges.* **b.** a long, narrow hill or mountain. *The sun sank behind the ridge.*

rig • id /rĭj′ ĭd/ *adj.* very stiff; not able to be bent. *A cast holds a broken arm in a rigid position so it can heal.*

rise¹ /rīz/ *v.* (**ris•es, rose, ris•en, ris•ing**) **a.** to get up. *He rose from his chair to greet us.* **b.** to move upward; to ascend. *We saw the balloon rise over the heads of the crowd.*

rise² /rīz/ *n.* an increase in height or amount. *The store announced a rise in prices.*

risk¹ /rĭsk/ *n.* a chance of loss or harm. *If you don't study, you run the risk of making a low grade.*

risk² /rĭsk/ *v.* to take the risk of; to venture. *You must risk making mistakes in order to learn.*

ri • ver /rĭv′ ər/ *n.* a large natural stream of water that flows into an ocean, a lake, or a sea. *The Mississippi is a large river that flows into the Gulf of Mexico.*

role /rōl/ *n.* a part or a character in a play. *Who will play the role of Peter Pan?*

▶ **Role** sounds like **roll.**

roll /rōl/ *v.* **a.** to move by turning over and over. *The ball rolled down the hill.* **b.** to wrap something around itself. *She rolled the yarn into a ball and put it in a drawer.*

▶ **Roll** sounds like **role.**

rough /rŭf/ *adj.* **a.** not smooth or even. *The car bounced and rattled over the rough road.* **b.** harsh; violent; not gentle. *The apples were bruised by rough handling.*

roy • al /roi′ əl/ *adj.* having to do with kings and queens. *The king and queen live in the royal palace.*

rule /rōōl/ *n.* **a.** a law; a regulation. *Always obey the school safety rules.* **b.** an instruction; a direction. *The rules describe how to play the game.*

Rus • sia /rŭsh′ ə/ *n.* a large country in eastern Europe and northern Asia. *Russia was the largest republic in the former U.S.S.R.*

Rus • sian¹ /rŭsh′ ən/ *adj.* of or from Russia. *Borscht is a Russian soup.*

Rus • sian² /rŭsh′ ən/ *n.* **a.** one born or living in Russia. *Russians must dress warmly in winter.* **b.** the language of Russia. *Russian uses a different alphabet from English.*

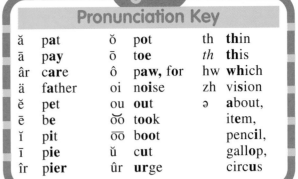

Pronunciation Key

ă	pat	ŏ	pot	th	**th**in
ā	pay	ō	toe	*th*	**th**is
âr	care	ô	paw, for	hw	**wh**ich
ä	father	oi	noise	zh	vi**s**ion
ĕ	pet	ou	**ou**t	ə	**a**bout,
ē	be	ŏŏ	t**oo**k		it**e**m,
ĭ	pit	ōō	b**oo**t		penc**i**l,
ī	pie	ŭ	c**u**t		gall**o**p,
îr	pier	ûr	**ur**ge		circ**u**s

sad • ness /săd′ nĭs/ *n.* sorrow; grief. *Tears can be an expression of sadness.*

safe /sāf/ *adj.* free from risk or harm. *The sidewalk is a safe place to walk.*

sail • boat /sāl′ bōt′/ *n.* a boat moved by sails that catch wind. *The sailboat glided across the lake.*

sam • ple¹ /săm′ pəl/ *n.* a part that shows what the rest is like. *The store gave away free samples of the new soap.*

sailboat

sam • ple² /săm′ pəl/ *v.* (**sam•ples, sam•pled, sam•pling**) to test; to try. *We sampled the cookies we had baked for the party.*

sand • wich /sănd′ wĭch/ *n.* (**sand•wich•es** *pl.*) two or more slices of bread, with a layer of meat, cheese, or other food placed between them. *I like a sandwich made of peanut butter and bananas.*

Sat. Saturday.

Sat • ur • day /săt′ ər dē/ or /-dā′/ *n.* the seventh day of the week, coming after Friday. *We have no school on Saturday.* [Old English Sæternesdæg, translated from Latin *dies Saturni,* Saturn's day.]

scale¹ /skāl/ *n.* a device or machine for weighing things. *According to the scale in the doctor's office, she weighed seventy pounds.* [Old Norse *skāl*]

scale² /skāl/ *v.* to climb up or over. *The climbers used ropes to scale the cliff.*

scare /skâr/ *v.* (**scares, scared, scar•ing**) to frighten. *The sudden loud noise scared me.*

scene /sēn/ *n.* **a.** the place where a thing happens. *Gettysburg was the scene of a famous battle.* **b.** the time and place of a story or play. *The scene of the play is a mining town in the old West.* **c.** a division of an act of a play. *I appear in the second scene of the first act of the play.*

schoon•er /skoo' nər/ *n.* a sailing ship with two or more masts. *Schooners are sometimes used as fishing vessels.*

sci•ence /sī' əns/ *n.* knowledge made up of observed facts and arranged in an ordered system. *Science helps us understand the world we live in.*

scrape¹ /skrāp/ *v.* to scratch the surface of. *The basketball player scraped his knee when he fell.*

scrape² /skrāp/ *n.* a difficulty; an unpleasant situation. *Kevin was in a scrape when he couldn't find his homework.*

scratch¹ /skrăch/ *v.* to cut or scrape a surface. *You can tell that a diamond is genuine if it scratches glass.*

scratch² /skrăch/ *n.* (**scratch•es** *pl.*) a thin cut or mark. *The top of this old desk has many scratches.*

sea•son /sē' zən/ *n.* one of the four parts into which a year is divided. *Spring is my favorite season.*

seat belt /sēt' bĕlt'/ *n.* a safety strap designed to hold a person securely in a seat. *The flight attendant asked the passengers to fasten their seat belts.*

see /sē/ *v.* (**sees, saw, seen, see•ing**) **a.** to perceive with the eyes. *She could see the light shining in the distance.* **b.** to understand; to comprehend. *She will see the meaning of the story right away.*

sell•er /sĕl' ər/ *n.* a person who sells; a vendor. *The flower seller had a stand on the street corner.*

▶ **Seller** sounds like **cellar**.

sen•tence /sĕn' təns/ *n.* a group of words that expresses a complete thought. *"Will you come to my party?" is a sentence.*

Sept. September.

Sep•tem•ber /sĕp tĕm' bər/ *n.* the ninth month of the year. *Many schools start in September.*

serve /sûrv/ *v.* **a.** to prepare and offer food. *We were served a delicious dinner.* **b.** to help others by performing a task. *Sarah will serve as club treasurer.*

set•tle /sĕt' l/ *v.* **a.** to agree; to decide. *The class settled on Saturday as the day of the picnic.* **b.** to establish residence. *Their family settled in California years ago.*

sev•en•ty /sĕv' ən tē/ *n.* the next number after sixty-nine; seven times ten; 70. *She will turn seventy next week.*

sew /sō/ *v.* (**sews, sewed, sewn** or **sewed, sew•ing**) to make by fastening with a needle and thread. *Can you sew on a sewing machine?*

share¹ /shâr/ *n.* a part; a portion. *Todd always does his share of work.*

share² /shâr/ *v.* (**shares, shared, shar•ing**) to use together. *The brothers share the same room.*

she'd /shēd/ she had; she would.

she'll /shēl/ she will; she shall.

shell /shĕl/ *n.* the hard outer covering of certain animals. *Snails, turtles, and clams have shells.*

shell

ship•ment /shĭp' mənt/ *n.* goods sent or delivered to a certain place. *The store received a shipment of clothing from the manufacturer.*

show /shō/ *v.* (**shows, showed, shown** or **showed, show•ing**) to point out; to cause to be seen. *Show me the picture you liked.*

show•er /shou' ər/ *n.* **a.** a short fall of rain. *During the afternoon there were three showers.* **b.** a bath in which water comes down in a spray. *I take a shower every morning.*

shown /shōn/ *v.* a form of **show**.

shy /shī/ *adj.* **a.** reserved; quiet. *After Josh made friends at his new school, he was no longer shy.* **b.** easily frightened. *A deer is shy.*

sig • na • ture /sĭg′ nə chər/ *n.* a person's name written by himself or herself. *In a letter, the signature goes immediately under the closing.*

sil • ly /sĭl′ ē/ *adj.* (**sil•li•er, sil•li•est**) foolish; not sensible. *It's silly to go out in the cold without a coat.*

sil • ver /sĭl′ vər/ *n.* a whitish precious metal. *Silver is used in making coins such as dimes and quarters.*

sim • ple /sĭm′ pəl/ *adj.* **a.** easy to understand. *The simple questions did not take long to answer.* **b.** plain; bare; with nothing fancy added. *She chose a simple red dress.*

sing • er /sĭng′ ər/ *n.* one who sings. *A choir is a group of singers.*

sin • gle /sĭng′ gəl/ *adj.* one alone; only one. *A single orange was left in the box.*

sis • ter /sĭs′ tər/ *n.* a girl or woman having the same parents as another person. *The two sisters were planning a surprise party for their parents' anniversary.*

skat • er /skā′ tər/ *n.* a person who skates. *The skaters checked the ice before skating on the pond.*

skiff /skĭf/ *n.* a flat-bottomed, shallow rowboat. *A skiff can be used with oars, sails, or a motor.*

skill /skĭl/ *n.* the ability to do something well as a result of practice. *His skill in playing the violin may someday make him famous.*

sky • line /skī′ līn′/ *n.* the outline of a group of buildings seen against the sky. *New York City's tall buildings give it an uneven skyline.*

skyline

slight /slīt/ *adj.* not big; small; slender. *Although it looks sunny, there's a slight chance it will rain later today.*

slip • per /slĭp′ ər/ *n.* a low, comfortable shoe that can be slipped on and off easily. *Slippers keep your feet warm on cool nights.*

Pronunciation Key

ă	pat	ŏ	pot	th	**th**in
ā	pay	ō	toe	*th*	**th**is
âr	care	ô	paw, for	hw	**wh**ich
ä	father	oi	n**oi**se	zh	vi**s**ion
ĕ	pet	ou	**ou**t	ə	**a**bout,
ē	be	ŏŏ	t**oo**k		it**e**m,
ĭ	pit	ōō	b**oo**t		penc**i**l,
ī	pie	ŭ	c**u**t		gall**o**p,
îr	p**ier**	ûr	**ur**ge		circ**u**s

smart /smärt/ *adj.* intelligent; clever; quick in mind. *A smart dog can learn many tricks.*

smell¹ /smĕl/ *v.* to get the odor or scent of through the nose. *We could smell dinner cooking as we came in.*

smell² /smĕl/ *n.* an odor; a scent. *The smell of orange blossoms filled the air.*

smog /smŏg/ *n.* fog that has become polluted with smoke. *In some cities smog makes it difficult to breathe.*

snug • gle /snŭg′ əl/ *v.* (**snug•gles, snug•gled, snug•gling**) to lie or press together; to cuddle. *The puppies snuggled close to their mother to keep warm.*

soar /sôr/ or /sōr/ *v.* to rise or fly high; to glide. *Eagles soar gracefully in the sky.*
▶ **Soar** sounds like **sore**.

sock • et /sŏk′ ĭt/ *n.* a hollow opening into which something fits. *The lamp flickered because the bulb was loose in the socket.*

soft • en /sô′ fən/ or /sŏf′ ən/ *v.* to make or become soft. *Ice cream softens in the heat.*

soft • ness /sôft′ nĭs/ or /sŏft′-/ *n.* the state or condition of being soft. *The softness of the wool blanket made it pleasant to use.*

so • lar /sō′ lər/ *adj.* of or having to do with the sun. *Solar rays can be harmful to the skin.*

sol • id /sŏl′ ĭd/ *n.* a substance with a definite shape that is neither a liquid nor a gas. *Wood, stone, and coal are solids.*

so • lo /sō′ lō/ *n.* a piece of music performed by one person. *Jim played a trumpet solo at the concert.*

some • times /sŭm′ tīmz/ *adv.* once in a while; now and then. *The sun sometimes shines when it is raining.*

Spelling Dictionary

son /sŭn/ *n.* a male child. *The mother took her son to a baseball game.*

sore /sôr/ or /sōr/ *adj.* painful; tender when touched. *His foot was sore after he stubbed his toe.*

> ▶ **Sore** sounds like **soar**.

sort /sôrt/ *v.* to separate things into like groups. *The baby can sort the blocks into two piles by color.*

sow /sō/ *v.* (**sows, sowed, sown** or **sowed, sow•ing**) to scatter seed over the ground for growing. *The farm workers were busy sowing the corn in the field.*

Spain /spān/ *n.* a country in southwestern Europe that borders on France and Portugal. *Spain and Portugal are located on the Iberian peninsula.*

Spain

Span•ish¹ /spăn′ ĭsh/ *adj.* of or from Spain. *The flamenco is a Spanish dance.*

Span•ish² /spăn′ ĭsh/ *n.* the language of Spain, Mexico, Central America, and most of South America. *Spanish is taught in many schools.*

spare /spâr/ *adj.* extra. *Every automobile should have a spare tire.*

spark /spärk/ *n.* **a.** a tiny particle of fire. *As the wood burned, it gave off bright sparks.* **b.** a brief, bright flash of light. *We saw the sparks of fireflies in the night.*

speak /spēk/ *v.* (**speaks, spoke, spo•ken, speak•ing**) to talk; to say words. *Speak clearly so that we can understand you!*

speak•er /spē′ kər/ *n.* **a.** a person who speaks or delivers public speeches. *The speaker at tonight's meeting will discuss the election.* **b.** a device that transmits sound. *These speakers will help everyone hear the music.*

speed¹ /spēd/ *n.* **a.** swiftness; quickness. *An antelope has great speed.* **b.** the rate of movement. *The airplane flies at a speed of six hundred miles an hour.*

speed² /spēd/ *v.* (**speeds, sped** or **speed•ed, speed•ing**) to go fast. *We watched the train speed past.*

spill¹ /spĭl/ *v.* to run out; to flow over. *The juice spilled on the tablecloth.*

spill² /spĭl/ *n.* an act of spilling: *an oil spill.*

spin•ach /spĭn′ ĭch/ *n.* a leafy green vegetable. *Spinach provides iron, which a healthy body needs.*

spoil /spoil/ *v.* **a.** to ruin; to damage; to destroy. *The stain will spoil your shirt if you don't wash it out quickly.* **b.** to become rotten or not fit for use. *The meat spoiled when it was left in the hot sun.*

spoke /spōk/ *v.* past tense of **speak.**

sport /spôrt/ or /spōrt/ *n.* any game involving exercise; recreation. *Swimming is a common summer sport.*

spread /sprĕd/ *v.* (**spreads, spread, spread•ing**) **a.** to open out; to unfold. *Spread out the map on the table.* **b.** to stretch out. *The bird spread its wings and flew away.*

square¹ /skwâr/ *n.* a rectangle with four equal sides. *A checkerboard is made up of squares.*

square² /skwâr/ *adj.* having four equal sides. *This room is square.*

squash /skwŏsh/ *n.* a vegetable with a hard rind and edible flesh. *Zucchini is a type of squash.* [Narragansett *askútasquash.*]

squeal¹ /skwēl/ *n.* a sharp, high-pitched cry. *The squeals of the pigs got louder as they saw the farmer bringing their food.*

squeal² /skwēl/ *v.* to make this sharp, high-pitched cry. *The baby squealed with delight.*

squeeze /skwēz/ *v.* (**squeez•es, squeezed, squeez•ing**) to press together hard; to compress. *Squeeze the sponge so that all the water comes out.*

squint /skwĭnt/ *v.* to look at with partly opened eyes. *The sun was so bright we had to squint to see.*

squirm /skwûrm/ *v.* to turn and twist the body. *We laughed to see the puppy squirm in the child's arms.*

stage /stāj/ *n.* the raised platform on which plays are presented. *When the lights came on, the actors were all on the stage.*

stake /stāk/ *n.* a stick or post with a pointed end that can be pounded into the ground. *The tent will stand straight when we tie it to these stakes.*

▶ **Stake** sounds like **steak**.

stare /stâr/ *v.* (**stares, stared, star•ing**) to look at with a steady gaze. *Mei Li stared at the painting, fascinated by the bright colors.*

state•hood /stāt′ hŏŏd′/ *n.* the condition of being a state of the United States. *Alaska and Hawaii were the last states to gain statehood.*

state•ment /stāt′ mənt/ *n.* a sentence that gives information. *Be sure your statement is accurate before you call it a fact.*

sta•tion /stā′ shən/ *n.* the place from which a service is provided or operations are directed. *The local radio station will broadcast the game.*

steak /stāk/ *n.* a slice of meat or fish for cooking. *For dinner he ordered a steak, a baked potato, a salad, and a roll with butter.*

steak

▶ **Steak** sounds like **stake**.

steal /stēl/ *v.* (**steals, stole, sto•len, steal•ing**) **a.** to take without permission. *Theft is another word for stealing.* **b.** to move quietly and secretly. *We decided to steal away before the play was over.*

▶ **Steal** sounds like **steel**.

steam /stēm/ *n.* the vapor into which water is changed by heating. *We could see steam rising from the iron.*

steel /stēl/ *n.* a strong metal made from iron by mixing it with carbon. *Steel is used for making strong tools.*

▶ **Steel** sounds like **steal**.

steer[1] /stîr/ *v.* to cause to move in the correct direction. *Use the handlebars to steer the bike.*

steer[2] /stîr/ *n.* a male of domestic cattle that is raised especially for beef. *They herded the steers into the corral.*

still•ness /stĭl′ nĭs/ *n.* quiet; silence. *After the city noise, the stillness of the country was a relief.*

Pronunciation Key

ă	pat	ŏ	pot	th	**thin**
ā	pay	ō	toe	*th*	**this**
âr	care	ô	paw, for	hw	**which**
ä	father	oi	noise	zh	vision
ĕ	pet	ou	out	ə	about,
ē	be	ŏŏ	took		item,
ĭ	pit	ōō	boot		pencil,
ī	pie	ŭ	cut		gallop,
îr	pier	ûr	urge		circus

stitch /stĭch/ *n.* (**stitch•es** *pl.*) one complete movement of a threaded needle through cloth or other material. *It took ten stitches to repair the rip in Diane's dress.*

stock /stŏk/ *n.* **a.** an amount of things to sell or to use; a supply. *For its big sale, the store ordered a large stock of clothes.* **b.** farm animals; livestock. *Some of the farmer's stock won prizes at the state fair.*

strain /strān/ *v.* **a.** to stretch; to pull tight. *The dog is straining at his rope.* **b.** to weaken; to injure; to hurt. *The pitcher strained a muscle in his arm at baseball practice.*

strait /strāt/ *n.* a narrow passage of water connecting two larger bodies of water. *Many ships sailed through the strait.*

strange /strānj/ *adj.* unusual; odd. *We were startled by the strange noise.*

strength /strĕngkth/ *n.* the quality of being strong. *He lost some of the strength in his muscles when he stopped exercising.*

stretch /strĕch/ *v.* (**stretch•es, stretched, stretch•ing**) **a.** to hold or put out; to extend. *She stretched her hand across the table.* **b.** to flex one's muscles. *Grandfather always stretches before he goes jogging.*

string /strĭng/ *n.* **a.** a thin cord or wire. *I tied a knot in the string.* **b.** **strings** the musical instruments with strings that are usually played by using a bow. *The strings form the largest section in an orchestra.*

stroke /strōk/ *n.* **a.** a complete movement that is repeated in an activity. *Swimmers practice their strokes.* **b.** a mark or movement made with a pen, pencil, or brush. *With a few strokes of the pen, the President approved the new law.*

Spelling Dictionary

stroll¹ /strōl/ *v.* to walk slowly and easily. *We strolled through the park.*

stroll² /strōl/ *n.* a slow walk for pleasure. *Our stroll in the garden was pleasant.*

stu•dent /stōōd′ nt/ or /styōōd′-/ *n.* a person who studies or goes to school. *There are three hundred students in our school.*

stum•ble /stŭm′ bəl/ *v.* to trip and almost fall. *Carlos stumbled over his sister's foot.*

sub•trac•tion /səb trăk′ shən/ *n.* the taking away of one number or part from another. *25 − 8 = 17 is an example of subtraction.*

sum•mit /sŭm′ ĭt/ *n.* **a.** the top of a mountain. *The climbers hope to reach the summit.* **b.** a high-level government conference. *The two nations discussed trade at the summit.*

Sun. Sunday.

Sun•day /sŭn′ dē/ or /-dā′/ *n.* the first day of the week. *Sunday comes before Monday.* [Old English *sunnerdæg,* translated from Latin *dies solis,* day of the sun.]

sun•spot /sŭn′ spŏt′/ *n.* any of the dark spots that appear on the surface of the sun. *Astronomers do not know exactly why sunspots appear.*

surf¹ /sûrf/ *n.* the waves of the sea as they break upon the shore. *After a rainstorm the surf is high.*

surf² /sûrf/ *v.* to ride breaking waves on a surfboard. *Mark learned to surf at the beach last summer.*

sur•prise¹ /sər prīz′/ *v.* (**sur•pris•es, sur•prised, sur•pris•ing**) to cause to feel wonder or delight; to astonish. *They surprised us by singing the song they had written.*

sur•prise² /sər prīz′/ *n.* something unexpected. *The flowers from Aunt Laura were a nice surprise.*

sweat•er /swĕt′ ər/ *n.* a knitted garment worn on the upper part of the body. *A cardigan is a sweater that opens down the front.*

sweater

swell /swĕl/ *v.* (**swells, swelled, swelled** or **swol•len, swel•ling**) to increase in size or volume; to expand. *Wood swells in damp weather.*

swol•len /swōl′ lən/ *adj.* a form of **swell**.

ta•ble /tā′ bəl/ *n.* a piece of furniture that has legs and a smooth, flat top. *We eat supper at the kitchen table.*

ta•ble•cloth /tā′ bəl klôth′/ or /-klŏth′/ *n.* a cloth used for covering a table. *Tony wiped the crumbs off the tablecloth.*

taste /tāst/ *v.* (**tastes, tast•ed, tast•ing**) to find or test the flavor of something. *Taste the sauce to see if it needs more garlic.*

taught /tôt/ *v.* past tense of **teach**.

tax¹ /tăks/ *n.* (**tax•es** *pl.*) money that citizens must pay to support the government. *Most of our city taxes are used to improve the schools.*

tax² /tăks/ *v.* to put a tax on. *The government taxes property.*

tax•i•cab /tăk′ sē kăb′/ *n.* an automobile that people hire to carry them short distances. *The meter in a taxicab keeps track of the money owed for the ride.*

teach /tēch/ *v.* (**teach•es, taught, teach•ing**) to help to learn; to instruct. *Will you teach me how to play this game?*

team /tēm/ *n.* **a.** a group of players on the same side in a game. *The gym class divided into two teams to play kickball.* **b.** a group of people working together: *a team of lawyers.*

tear¹ /târ/ *v.* (**tears, tore, torn, tear•ing**) to pull apart or into pieces. *Be careful not to tear the letter as you open the envelope.*

tear² /tîr/ *n.* a drop of liquid from the eye. *She stopped crying and wiped the tears from her face.*

tem•per /tĕm′ pər/ *n.* mood; state of mind. *Pam is always in a good temper on Fridays.*

tem•ple /tĕm′ pəl/ *n.* a building for religious worship. *The ancient Greeks built many temples.*

ten • don /tĕn′ dən/ *n.* the tough tissue that connects muscle and a bone. *Scott strained a tendon in his leg and couldn't finish the race.*

ten • or /tĕn′ ər/ *n.* **a.** the musical part for a high male voice. *My dad sings tenor.* **b.** a man who sings a high part. *Our choir has more basses than tenors.*

term /tûrm/ *n.* a period of time. *The winter school term seems long because there aren't many holidays.*

ter • ror /tĕr′ ər/ *n.* very strong fear. *The actor showed terror by trembling.*

thank • ful /thăngk′ fəl/ *adj.* feeling or showing gratitude; grateful. *She was thankful when I returned her lost purse.*

thank • less /thăngk′ lĭs/ *adj.* not showing appreciation; ungrateful. *Be sure to write Uncle Jeff a thank-you note for his gift so you won't seem like a thankless person.*

they'd /thād/ they had; they would.

they'll /thāl/ they will; they shall.

thick • en /thĭk′ ən/ *v.* to make heavier or thicker. *You can use flour to thicken gravy.*

thick • ness /thĭk′ nĭs/ *n.* the condition of being heavy or thick. *The thickness of the paint made it difficult to apply.*

thin /thĭn/ *adj.* (**thin•ner, thin•nest**) slender; not thick. *A sheet of paper is thin.*

thirst /thûrst/ *n.* a desire for something to drink caused by a dry feeling in the mouth or throat. *The horses satisfied their thirst by drinking from a stream.*

thir • teenth¹ /thûr tēnth′/ *adj.* next after the twelfth. *We rode in the thirteenth car on the train.*

thir • teenth² /thûr tēnth′/ *n.* one of thirteen equal parts. *A baker's dozen can easily be divided into thirteenths.*

though¹ /thō/ *adv.* however. *You must admit, though, that she was partly right.*

though² /thō/ *conj.* in spite of the fact that; although. *Though it was getting late, we kept playing for a while longer.*

thought¹ /thôt/ *v.* past tense of **think**.

thought² /thôt/ *n.* **a.** the act or process of thinking. *She spent many hours in thought about the problem.* **b.** an idea, opinion, or belief. *Do you have any thoughts about how to improve our school?*

Pronunciation Key

ă	pat	ŏ	pot	th	**th**in
ā	pay	ō	toe	*th*	**th**is
âr	care	ô	paw, for	hw	**wh**ich
ä	father	oi	n**oi**se	zh	vi**si**on
ĕ	pet	ou	**ou**t	ə	**a**bout,
ē	be	o͝o	t**oo**k		**i**tem,
ĭ	pit	o͞o	b**oo**t		penc**i**l,
ī	pie	ŭ	cut		gall**o**p,
îr	p**ier**	ûr	**ur**ge		circ**u**s

thought • ful /thôt′ fəl/ *adj.* **a.** engaged in thought; serious; meditative: *a thoughtful mood.* **b.** having consideration for others. *She is thoughtful of her friends and never hurts their feelings.*

thou • sand /thou′ zənd/ *n.* the next number after 999; 10 x 100; 1,000. *The figure for one thousand has four numerals.*

thun • der¹ /thŭn′ dər/ *n.* the loud noise caused by the violent expansion of air heated by lightning. *Thunder often comes before rain.*

thun • der² /thŭn′ dər/ *v.* to make this noise. *When it began to thunder, we headed for home.*

Thurs. Thursday.

Thurs • day /thûrz′ dē/ or /-dā/ *n.* the fifth day of the week, coming between Wednesday and Friday. *Our spring vacation begins on Thursday.* [Old English *dunresdæg*, Thor's day.]

tick • le /tĭk′ əl/ *v.* (**tick•les, tick•led, tick•ling**) **a.** to touch lightly to produce a shivering feeling and laughter. *She tickled me until I laughed.* **b.** to have this feeling. *His nose tickles when he has to sneeze.*

tight /tīt/ *adj.* **a.** not loose; firm. *The knot was so tight that we couldn't untie it.* **b.** fitting very closely. *My old shoes are too tight.*

tight • en /tīt′ n/ *v.* to make or become tighter. *Mother tightened her seat belt before driving away.*

tim • ber /tĭm′ bər/ *n.* trees; wooded land. *There was no timber on the mountaintop, only grasses and low shrubs.*

timber

Spelling Dictionary

times /tīmz/ *prep.* multiplied by. *Six times four is twenty-four.*

ti • ny /tī′ nē/ *adj.* (ti•ni•er, ti•ni•est) very small; wee. *An ant is a tiny animal.*

tire[1] /tīr/ *v.* to make weary or exhausted. *Exercising for a long time tires me.*

tire[2] /tīr/ *n.* an outer rim of rubber, often filled with air, that is fitted around the rim of a wheel. *I pumped air into my bicycle tire.* [Middle English, *tyre,* covering for a wheel, from *tyr,* attire.]

ti • tle /tīt′ l/ *n.* the name of a book, movie, painting, etc. *When I had finished reading the story, I couldn't remember its title.*

to • geth • er /tə gĕth′ ər/ *adv.* with each other; in one group. *We all walked to the game together.*

toot[1] /tσσt/ *n.* a short, sharp sound made by a horn or whistle. *They heard the toot of the tugboat whistle.*

toot[2] /tσσt/ *v.* to make this sound. *The engineer tooted the horn as the train entered the tunnel.*

to • tal[1] /tōt′ l/ *adj.* whole; entire. *The total price includes tax.*

to • tal[2] /tōt′ l/ *n.* an entire amount; a sum. *He added the numbers to find the total.*

tot • ter /tŏt′ ər/ *v.* to sway as if about to fall. *The child tottered as he was learning to walk.*

touch /tŭch/ *v.* to feel with the hand or other part of the body. *The builder touched the cement to see if it was still soft.*

tough /tŭf/ *adj.* strong; not easily torn or broken. *The rug is made of very tough materials.*

tour /tσσr/ *n.* **a.** a journey or trip with several visits. *The Friedmans made a driving tour of the New England states.* **b.** a brief trip of inspection. *Ms. Wright gave us a tour of her office.*

trac • tor /trăk′ tər/ *n.* a large machine on wheels, used for pulling trucks or farm equipment. *The farmer drove the tractor into the barn.*

trail • er /trā′ lər/ *n.* a large vehicle pulled or hauled by a car, truck, or tractor. *We used a trailer attached to our car to move our furniture.*

trap /trăp/ *n.* a device used to capture animals. *The tiger fell into a deep trap that the hunter had set.*

trav • el /trăv′ əl/ *v.* to go from place to place on a trip or journey. *We traveled to San Diego on our vacation.*

trawl • er /trô′ lər/ *n.* a boat used to catch fish by towing a net or line. *The trawler returned loaded with fish.*

tray /trā/ *n.* a flat, shallow holder with a low rim. *A waiter carries dishes on a tray.*

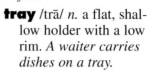

tray

treat • ment /trēt′ mənt/ *n.* **a.** a way of handling. *Baby animals receive special treatment at the zoo.* **b.** anything used to treat something. *The doctor said that ice was the best treatment for my sprain.*

trem • ble /trĕm′ bəl/ *v.* (trem•bles, trem•bled, trem•bling) to shake or quiver. *I was so nervous that my hands trembled.*

trick /trĭk/ *n.* **a.** something done to deceive. *The phone call was just a trick to get me out of the room while they planned the surprise party.* **b.** an act that requires a special skill. *Seth taught his dog the trick of rolling over.*

tri • o /trē′ ō/ *n.* a group of three performers. *Peter, Paul, and Mary were a famous singing trio.*

tri • ple /trĭp′ əl/ *v.* (tri•ples, tri•pled, tri•pling) to make three times as much or as many. *Three tripled is nine.*

trou • ble /trŭb′ əl/ *n.* **a.** something that causes worry or distress; difficulty. *The trouble with our car is that the motor won't run.* **b.** a bother; an extra effort. *It was no trouble to help her clean her room.*

true /trσσ/ *adj.* right; accurate; not false. *It is true that ostriches cannot fly.*

trust /trŭst/ *v.* **a.** to believe in; to depend or rely on. *We trust the doctor to do what is best for us.* **b.** to expect; to assume. *I trust you have finished your homework.*

truth /trσσth/ *n.* **a.** that which agrees with the facts. *The truth is that we were wrong.* **b.** honesty. *Her apology had a feeling of truth.*

tube /tσσb/ or /tyσσb/ *n.* a long, hollow cylinder used to carry or hold liquids and gases. *A drinking straw is a tube.*

Tues. Tuesday.

Tues • day /t͞ooz′ dē/ or /-dā′/ or /ty͞ooz′-/ *n.* the third day of the week, coming after Monday. *Elections are usually held on a Tuesday.* [Old English *Tiwesdæg,* Tiu's day.]

tug • boat /tŭg′ bōt′/ *n.* a powerful small boat used for towing larger vessels. *The tugboat towed the ship into the harbor.*

tu • lip /t͞oo′ lĭp/ or /ty͞oo′-/ *n.* a plant of the lily family that grows from a bulb and blooms in the spring. *Tulips have large cup-shaped flowers.*

tulip

tur • key /tûr′ kē/ *n.* a large North American bird covered with thick feathers. *Turkeys can weigh more than thirty pounds.*

twelfth¹ /twĕlfth/ *adj.* next after the eleventh. *Mary Beth celebrated her twelfth birthday.*

twelfth² /twĕlfth/ *n.* one of twelve equal parts. *Three twelfths make one fourth.*

twice /twīs/ *adv.* two times. *We liked the song so much we sang it twice.*

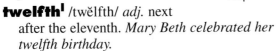

um • pire /ŭm′ pīr′/ *n.* a person who rules on the play of a game. *In baseball, the umpire calls the balls and strikes.*

un- a prefix that means "not" or "the opposite of": *unafraid.*

un • cov • er /ŭn kŭv′ ər/ *v.* **a.** to remove the cover from. *Steam rose from the hot dish as Dad uncovered it.* **b.** to reveal or expose. *The truth was uncovered during the trial.*

un • fair /ŭn fâr′/ *adj.* not fair; not honest or just. *Cheating is unfair.*

un • hap • py /ŭn hăp′ ē/ *adj.* (un•hap•pi•er, un•hap•pi•est; un•hap•pi•ly *adv.*) not happy; sad; full of sorrow. *When Maria was unhappy, we tried to cheer her up.*

un • lock /ŭn lŏk′/ *v.* to undo a lock by turning a key. *Mr. Hughes unlocked the door and let us in.*

un • luck • y /ŭn lŭk′ ē/ *adj.* (un•luck•i•er, un•luck•i•est; un•luck•i•ly *adv.*) not lucky; disappointing. *It was unlucky that we missed the bus.*

un • pack /ŭn păk′/ *v.* to remove the contents of a suitcase or a package. *After we moved, it took a week to unpack all the boxes.*

un • safe /ŭn sāf′/ *adj.* not safe; dangerous. *Running into a crowded hallway is unsafe.*

un • tie /ŭn tī′/ *v.* (un•ties, un•tied, un•ty•ing) to loosen something that has been tied. *She untied the ribbon and opened the gift.*

up • stairs¹ /ŭp′ stârz′/ *adv.* up the stairs; to a higher floor. *I went upstairs to bed.*

up • stairs² /ŭp′ stârz′/ *adj.* on a higher floor. *Did you clean the upstairs hall?*

use /y͞ooz/ *v.* (us•es, used, us•ing) to put into service. *Use the cloth to dust the shelf.*

used¹ /y͞oozd/ *v.* past tense of **use.**

used² /y͞oozd/ *adj.* not new; owned by another person in the past. *A used bike costs less than a new one.*

use • ful /y͞oos′ fəl/ *adj.* of use; helpful. *She gave me some useful advice about studying for the test.*

use • less /y͞oos′ lĭs/ *adj.* of no use; serving no purpose. *My sled is useless in the summer.*

verb /vûrb/ *n.* a word that expresses action or a state of being. *In the sentences "Go to the store" and "His dog is brown," the verbs are "go" and "is."*

view /vyōō/ *n.* **a.** what is seen; scene. *The view from the window by the beach is breathtaking.* **b.** opinion; idea. *His view was that we should change our plans.*

vil • lage /vĭl′ ĭj/ *n.* a number of houses and buildings in an area that is smaller than a town. *Everyone knows everyone else in our village.*

vi • o • la /vē ō′ lə/ *n.* a stringed instrument of the violin family. *A viola is slightly larger than a violin and has a deeper tone.*

vi • o • lin /vī ə lĭn′/ *n.* a musical instrument that has four strings and is played with a bow. *The violin is held under the chin when played.*

violin

vi • rus /vī′ rəs/ *n.* (**vi•rus•es** *pl.*) a tiny substance that causes certain diseases. *Mumps and measles are caused by viruses.*

vis • it /vĭz′ ĭt/ *v.* to go or come to see. *We visited Mrs. Gomez and her new baby after they came home from the hospital.*

vol • ca • no /vŏl kā′ nō/ *n.* (**vol•ca•noes** or **vol•ca•nos** *pl.*) a mountain formed by lava pushed out through an opening in the earth's surface. *Some islands are formed from volcanoes.*

vote /vōt/ *v.* (**votes, vot•ed, vot•ing**) to choose or decide in an election. *Our class voted to accept Joy's plan.*

vow • el /vou′ əl/ *n.* **a.** a sound made with the voice when the breath is allowed to pass out of the mouth freely. *The sound of "o" in "go" is a vowel.* **b.** any of the letters that stand for such a sound. *The most common vowels are **a, e, i, o,** and **u**.*

waist /wāst/ *n.* the narrow part of the body between the ribs and the hips. *Belts are worn around the waist.*

▶ **Waist** sounds like **waste.**

wan • der /wŏn′ dər/ *v.* to go without purpose or aim; to roam. *I wandered from room to room looking for something to do.*

was • n't /wŏz′ ənt/ or /wŭz′-/ was not.

waste /wāst/ *v.* (**wastes, wast•ed, wast•ing**) to use up carelessly or foolishly. *He wasted his money on toys he didn't need.*

▶ **Waste** sounds like **waist.**

waste • ful /wāst′ fəl/ *adj.* tending to waste; using or spending too much. *Taking more food than you can eat is wasteful.*

watch /wŏch/ *n.* (**watch•es** *pl.*) a small clock worn on the wrist or carried in a pocket. *I checked my watch to be sure I had the correct time.*

wa • ter¹ /wô′ tər/ or /wŏt′ ər/ *n.* the clear liquid that falls as rain. *Water becomes ice when it freezes.*

wa • ter² /wô′ tər/ or /wŏt′ ər/ *v.* to put water on. *Did you water the flowers today?*

wa • ter • fall /wô′ tər fôl/ or /wŏt′ ər-/ *n.* a flow of water falling from a high place. *In the spring, melting snow feeds waterfalls in the mountains.*

weak • en /wē′ kən/ *v.* to make weak; to become weak. *His legs weakened as he climbed up the mountain.*

weak • ness /wēk′ nĭs/ *n.* (**weak•ness•es** *pl.*) **a.** lack of strength or power. *An illness can cause weakness.* **b.** a weak point; a fault. *Poor fielding is the baseball team's only weakness.*

weave /wēv/ *v.* (**weaves, wove, wo•ven, weav•ing**) to make by lacing threads, yarns, or strips under and over each other. *She is weaving a basket out of straw.*

Wed. Wednesday.

Wednes•day /wěnz′ dē/ or /-dā′/ *n.* the fourth day of the week. *Wednesday is the day after Tuesday.* [Old English *Wodnesdæg,* Woden's day.]

week•end /wēk′ ěnd′/ *n.* Saturday and Sunday, as a time for rest, play, visiting, etc. *We are going bowling this weekend.*

we'll /wēl/ we will; we shall.

well-be•ing /wěl′ bē′ ĭng/ *n.* the state of being healthy and happy; welfare. *Having friends is good for your well-being.*

we've /wēv/ we have.

when•ev•er /hwěn ěv′ ər/ *conj.* at any time that. *I'm ready whenever you are.*

wheth•er /hwěth′ ər/ *conj.* if. *He didn't know whether he should laugh or cry.*

whose /hoōz/ *pron.* of whom; of which. *Whose jacket did you borrow?*

width /wĭdth/ *n.* the distance from side to side. *The width of my room is ten feet.*

wife /wīf/ *n.* (**wives** *pl.*) the woman a man is married to. *He brought flowers to his wife on her birthday.*

win•ter[1] /wĭn′ tər/ *n.* the coldest season of the year. *Winter comes between autumn and spring.*

win•ter[2] /wĭn′ tər/ *adj.* of or for the winter. *Ice skating is a winter sport.*

wire /wīr/ *n.* a thread or strand of metal. *Electricity travels through wires.*

wise /wīz/ *adj.* **a.** having good sense; showing good judgment. *She made a wise decision.* **b.** having much knowledge or information. *Scientists and professors are wise.*

wit /wĭt/ *n.* **a.** cleverness; intelligence. *It took wit to think of such a good plan.* **b.** humor. *His wit kept us all chuckling.*

wit•ty /wĭt′ ē/ *adj.* (**wit•ti•er, wit•ti•est; wit•ti•ly** *adv.*) showing wit; clever and amusing. *The witty speaker made the audience laugh.*

wives /wīvz/ *n.* plural of **wife.**

wob•ble /wŏb′ əl/ *v.* (**wob•bles, wob•bled, wob•bling**) to move in a shaky way from side to side. *The baby's legs wobbled when she tried to walk.*

Pronunciation Key

ă	pat	ŏ	pot	th	**th**in
ā	pay	ō	toe	*th*	**th**is
âr	care	ô	paw, for	hw	**wh**ich
ä	father	oi	noise	zh	vi**s**ion
ĕ	pet	ou	**ou**t	ə	**a**bout,
ē	be	ŏŏ	took		it**e**m,
ĭ	pit	ōō	boot		penc**i**l,
ī	pie	ŭ	cut		gall**o**p,
îr	pier	ûr	**ur**ge		circ**u**s

won•der /wŭn′ dər/ *v.* to be curious to know. *I wonder how the story will end.*

wring /rĭng/ *v.* (**wrings, wrung, wring•ing**) to twist and squeeze. *Wring out that wet cloth before you wipe the table.*

wrin•kle[1] /rĭng′ kəl/ *n.* a small crease or fold. *Rosa ironed the wrinkles out of her skirt.*

wrin•kle[2] /rĭng′ kəl/ *v.* to crease or crumple. *Your forehead wrinkles when you frown.*

writ•ten /rĭt′ n/ *v.* a form of **write.**

wrong /rông/ or /rŏng/ *adj.* **a.** not right; bad; wicked. *Telling lies is wrong.* **b.** not correct; not true. *Your answer was wrong.* **c.** out of order. *Do you know what's wrong with the phone?*

year /yîr/ *n.* a period of 365 days or 12 months. *The calendar year begins on January 1.*

you'd /yoōd/ you had; you would.

you'll /yoōl/ or /yŏŏl/ you will; you shall.

you're /yŏŏr/ you are.

you've /yoōv/ you have.

young /yŭng/ *adj.* not old or fully grown. *A fawn is a young deer.*

ze • ro /zîr′ ō/ or /zē′ rō/ *n.* (**ze•ros** or **ze•roes** *pl.*) the numeral 0; nothing. *If you multiply any number by zero, the product will also be zero.*

zip • per /zĭp′ ər/ *n.* a fastening device with two rows of tiny teeth that can be closed together by a sliding tab. *My boots close with a zipper.*

zipper

USING THE Thesaurus

The **Writing Thesaurus** provides synonyms—words that mean the same or nearly the same—and antonyms—words that mean the opposite—for your spelling words. Use this sample to identify the various parts of each thesaurus entry.

- **Entry words** are listed in alphabetical order and are printed in boldface type.
- The abbreviation for the **part of speech** of each entry word follows the boldface entry word.
- The **definition** of the entry word matches the definition of the word in your **Spelling Dictionary**. A **sample sentence** shows the correct use of the word in context.
- Each **synonym** for the entry word is listed under the entry word. Again, a sample sentence shows the correct use of the synonym in context.
- Where appropriate, **antonyms** for the entry word are listed at the end of the entry.

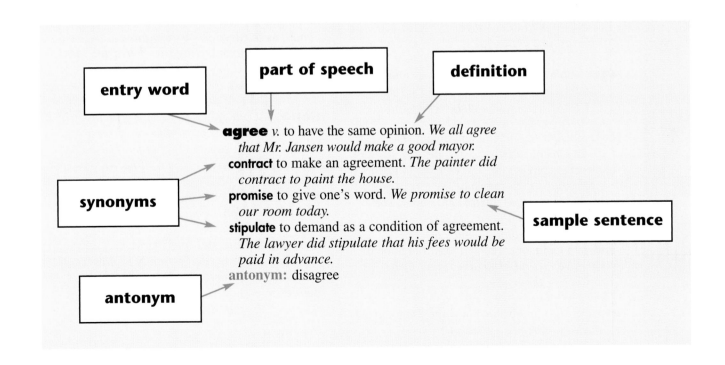

entry word

part of speech

definition

synonyms

sample sentence

antonym

agree *v.* to have the same opinion. *We all agree that Mr. Jansen would make a good mayor.*
contract to make an agreement. *The painter did contract to paint the house.*
promise to give one's word. *We promise to clean our room today.*
stipulate to demand as a condition of agreement. *The lawyer did stipulate that his fees would be paid in advance.*
antonym: disagree

able *adj.* having power, skill, or talent. *With practice you will be able to play the piano.*
competent able; qualified. *The meal was prepared by a very competent chef.*
skillful having skill. *The skillful player won the tennis game.*
talented gifted; having natural ability. *The talented musician played the piano for us.*
antonym: unable

adult *n.* a grown person. *You may vote when you are an adult.*
grown-up an adult. *The young child dressed up like a grown-up.*
human being human; person. *Every human being should exercise for good health.*
person man, woman, or child. *Each person registered to vote during the election.*

agree *v.* to have the same opinion. *We all agree that Mr. Jansen would make a good mayor.*
contract to make an agreement. *The painter did contract to paint the house.*
promise to give one's word. *We promise to clean our room today.*
stipulate to demand as a condition of agreement. *The lawyer did stipulate that his fees would be paid in advance.*
antonym: disagree

agreement *n.* an arrangement or understanding between two persons or groups. *The students came to an agreement about the best day for the litter cleanup.*
arrangement settlement; agreement. *The new arrangement satisfied everyone.*
contract an agreement. *The contract had specific terms for the car loan.*
settlement an arrangement; agreement. *The president worked for a quick settlement on wages for post office employees.*
understanding an agreement or arrangement. *We have an understanding about the terms for buying the house.*

ahead *adv.* in advance; in front. *Dad walked ahead to look for a campsite.*

before in front; ahead. *He walked before us to see that the path was clear.*
forward in front; ahead. *Once the line started to move, we all stepped forward.*
antonym: behind

aim *v.* to point at; direct toward. *Aim the arrow at the center of the target.*
beam to send out; direct. *The machine will beam the light at the sign.*
direct to point or aim. *He will direct the traffic away from the parade route.*
level to keep even. *The police officer will level his rifle at the target.*
point to aim; direct. *Ask John to point at the deer standing behind the bush.*
train to point; aim. *She will train the spotlight on the actor.*

alarm *n.* a signal warning that danger is near. *The alarm went off moments after the fire started.*
beacon light or fire used to warn. *The beacon was placed on the shoreline.*
bell anything that makes a ringing sound. *The bell rang to warn the ships in the fog.*
signal a sign of warning or notice. *A red light was the signal to indicate danger.*
siren a loud whistle. *The fire siren warned us that a fire truck was coming.*

alive *adj.* living; not dead. *People sometimes forget that trees are alive.*
existing living; having life. *The existing animals were saved from starvation.*
living being alive; having life. *The artificial plants looked like living ones.*
antonym: dead

alone *adv.* without anyone else. *The box was too heavy for one person to lift alone.*
singly by itself; separately. *Let us review each person singly to see how well his or her job is done.*
solely alone; the only one or ones. *I am solely responsible for the picnic plans.*

also *adv.* too; in addition; likewise. *Geraniums grow well not only in flowerpots but also in gardens.*
besides in addition; also. *Many people besides the parents came to the play.*

likewise also; too. *I will be there on time, and she will likewise.*

too also; besides. *The cats and dogs are hungry, too.*

amount *n.* the total or sum. *We raised the amount of money needed for the books.*

figure price; amount. *The figure for the car was less because of the rebates.*

number amount; total. *A number of people were invited to the party.*

sum amount; total. *We paid a large sum for the new house.*

total amount; sum. *A total of 100 tickets were sold for the community play.*

answer *n.* a reply. *I must send my answer to her letter quickly.*

acknowledgment something done to let one know that a service or gift was received. *An acknowledgment was sent to thank us for the gift.*

reply response; answer. *Your reply was very easy to understand.*

response an answer. *The response she gave was very prompt.*

apart *adv.* to pieces; in separate pieces. *The puzzle fell apart when it slipped off the table.*

independently on one's own. *The class members selected projects independently.*

separately individually; one at a time. *We worked separately on the project.*

antonym: together

apartment *n.* a group of rooms to live in, generally in a building housing more than one family. *They live in an apartment on the second floor.*

flat apartment or set of rooms. *We lived in a flat above the store.*

room a part of a building with walls of its own. *The hotel rented us a room for the night.*

suite set of rooms connected to each other. *The hotel suite had five rooms.*

army *n.* a large group of people who are organized and trained to serve as soldiers. *The United States Army fought in Europe during World War II.*

armed forces the army, navy, and air force of a country. *The armed forces took part in the Fourth of July parade.*

soldiers men or women in the army. *The soldiers were trained in Louisiana.*

troops soldiers. *The troops helped to rescue people after the earthquake.*

baby *n.* a very young child; an infant. *The baby had not learned to stand up yet.*

babe a baby. *The word **babe** is another word for baby.*

infant a very young child. *The new mother wrapped the infant in a soft blanket.*

young child a young boy or girl. *The young child was learning to walk.*

baby sitter *n.* one who takes care of young children. *John's mother called a baby sitter to stay with him for the afternoon.*

nanny a woman who takes care of children. *The nanny took the children to the park.*

nursemaid girl or woman who takes care of children. *The nursemaid knew how to prepare the baby's food.*

badge *n.* something worn to show that a person is a member of a group or organization. *Each firefighter wore a badge.*

emblem a badge or sign. *The police officer had an emblem on her uniform.*

name tag a badge worn that gives a name. *Everyone at the meeting wore a name tag to help people learn names.*

baggage *n.* suitcases; luggage. *Airline passengers may pick up their baggage inside the terminal.*

luggage baggage. *The passengers checked their luggage at the ticket counter.*

suitcase a flat, rectangular-shaped bag for traveling. *We packed our clothes in the suitcase.*

battle *n.* a fight between armies, navies, etc. during a war. *That battle was the turning point of the war.*
  combat a fight or struggle. *The argument was settled without any combat.*
  conflict a fight or struggle. *The conflict over wages lasted for years.*
  encounter a meeting of enemies; battle; fight. *The peaceful encounter between the two groups led to a settlement.*
  war a fight or conflict. *The war between the two groups lasted only a few days.*

because *conj.* for the reason that. *I study because I want to learn.*
  as because. *As she knew how to act better than anyone else, she became the star of the show.*
  for because. *We can't stay outside, for it is raining.*
  since because. *Since you want a new toy, you should save your money.*

begin *v.* to start. *We will begin our school day with an arithmetic lesson.*
  commence to begin; start. *The play will commence when the curtain opens.*
  open to start or set up. *They will open a new store in the shopping center.*
  start to begin. *We will start reading at the beginning of the chapter.*
  undertake to try; to attempt. *We will undertake the new assignment as soon as we get to work this morning.*
  antonyms: end, finish

believe *v.* to accept something as true or real. *Do you believe that cats have nine lives?*
  assume to suppose; to believe something to be true or real. *We could assume that the bus driver knew the correct route.*
  suppose to believe, think, or imagine. *I suppose we could try to fix the toy.*
  think to believe; to have an opinion. *I think it will rain today.*
  trust to have faith; believe. *I trust you know how to solve the math problem.*

beside *prep.* at the side of; near to. *The carton was left beside the trash cans.*
  abreast side by side. *In the parade the Boy Scouts marched four abreast.*
  alongside by the side of; side by side. *The trees were alongside the building.*

between *prep.* in the space that separates two things. *There were four people between me and the door.*
  in the midst in the middle of. *The toys were put in the midst of the children.*

bitter *adj.* tasting sharp and unpleasant. *Do you think black walnuts have a bitter taste?*
  sharp strongly affecting the senses. *The lemon drops had a very sharp taste.*
  sour having a sharp, bitter taste. *The sour lemon juice was used in the tea.*

boast *v.* to brag; to talk too much about oneself and about what one can do. *Judy likes to boast about how fast she can run.*
  bluster to talk in a noisy manner. *The man tried to complain and bluster at the clerk.*
  brag to boast; praise oneself. *Tom always seems to brag about his bicycle.*
  crow to show one's pride; boast. *We listened to the winners crow about how well they ran.*

bold *adj.* not afraid to face danger; brave and daring. *The bold gymnast attempted a difficult vault.*
  brave showing courage; without fear. *The brave firefighter saved the people in the burning house.*
  courageous brave; fearless. *The courageous child saved the animals from the cold winter storm.*
  fearless without fear. *The fearless woman raced to catch the falling child.*
  antonyms: cowardly, afraid, weak

break *v.* to come apart; separate into pieces. *The dish will break if it falls on the floor.*
  crack to break without separating into parts. *The dish might crack when it lands on the floor.*
  shatter to break into pieces. *The glass will shatter when it hits the floor.*
  snap to break suddenly. *The rope did snap when we pulled on it.*
  split to separate into pieces. *The seam split as he pulled on his jacket.*

brief *adj.* short; quick; direct. *Our meeting was brief.*
  concise short; brief. *He gave a concise report to the group.*
  little not long in time; short. *Please wait a little while before you go.*

short not long. *It took only a few minutes to read the short story.*

succinct brief; short. *The succinct comments really told the whole story.*

terse brief; to the point. *A one-word answer is a terse reply.*

brighten *v.* to lighten; make or become bright. *The lamp will brighten the living room.*

illuminate to light up; make bright. *The lights will illuminate the sky.*

lighten to make brighter; to add light to. *The new paint does lighten the room.*

antonym: darken

bubble *n.* a thin, round film of liquid that forms a ball around a pocket of gas or air. *The slightest touch can pop a bubble.*

bead any small, round object like a bubble. *A bead of water formed on the newly waxed car.*

blob a small drop. *A blob of jelly fell on the floor.*

build *v.* to make; put together. *Doug wants to build a model house out of toothpicks.*

construct to build; to fit together. *The builders will construct a new office tower.*

erect to put up; to build. *The highway crew can erect a new flag pole.*

make to build; put together. *We will make a tree house in the backyard.*

put up to build. *We followed the directions when we put up the tent.*

burst *v.* to break open suddenly. *The balloon will burst if it touches the light bulb.*

blow up to explode. *The balloon will blow up when Horace jumps on it.*

explode to burst with a loud noise. *The fireworks explode high in the sky.*

rupture to break; burst. *Where did the water main rupture?*

buy *v.* to purchase. *Sally had to buy a new pair of shoes before winter.*

purchase to buy. *He can purchase the jewelry at the shop by our house.*

shop to go to stores to look at or buy things. *We plan to shop for a new coat.*

antonyms: sell, market

calm *adj.* quiet; peaceful; motionless. *There wasn't even a breeze on that calm evening.*

composed quiet; calm. *The composed officer came forward to receive the award.*

cool calm; not excited. *The people kept cool and walked to the nearest exit.*

serene calm; peaceful. *A serene smile could be seen on her face.*

tranquil peaceful; quiet; calm. *The tranquil night air was very relaxing.*

antonyms: nervous, anxious

careful *adj.* cautious; full of care. *Be careful when you cross the busy street.*

cautious very careful. *The cautious player watched the ball at all times.*

considered carefully thought out. *His considered opinion was respected by everyone.*

diligent careful; steady. *He is a diligent worker.*

antonym: careless

careless *adj.* reckless; not cautious. *You can't afford to be careless with matches.*

negligent careless. *No one liked the negligent way Pat drove.*

thoughtless without thought. *Her thoughtless behavior made me angry.*

antonym: careful

cart *n.* a two-wheeled vehicle pulled by a horse or another animal. *The pony pulled a cart in the parade.*

buggy a small carriage pulled by a horse. *We rode in a buggy around the park.*

wagon a four-wheeled vehicle. *The wagon was pulled by a horse.*

case *n.* a large box; container. *Our music teacher carries her violin in a case.*

bin a box or container. *The grain was stored in a large bin.*

box container with four sides, a bottom, and a lid. *We packed the dishes in a box.*

carton a box made of cardboard. *The books were packed in a carton.*

container a box, can, etc. used to hold things. *She put the paper clips in a small container.*

certain *adj.* confident; sure; convinced. *She was certain you would win.*

decided definite; clear. *There is a decided difference between the two books on hamsters.*

definite clear; exact. *I want a definite answer to my question.*

sure certain; positive. *I am sure that is the right way to go.*

antonym: uncertain

charge *n.* an amount asked or made as payment. *There is no charge for this service.*

amount the total or sum. *We raised the amount of money needed to buy the books for our new library.*

cost price paid. *The cost of the shirt was more than I was willing to pay.*

price the amount charged for something. *The price of cars goes up every year.*

charm *v.* to delight; please. *The child's smile did charm the audience.*

delight to please greatly. *The pony rides will delight the children.*

enchant to delight. *The magician can enchant the audience with his tricks.*

fascinate to attract; enchant. *The music will fascinate all of us.*

chart *v.* to make a map or a diagram of. *My job is to chart our class's spelling progress.*

diagram to put a sketch on paper. *The builder will diagram the house plan for us.*

map to plan; arrange. *We will map out our work.*

outline to sketch; make a plan. *She tried to outline the entire trip for us.*

plot to plan secretly. *The pirate will plot a way to get the treasure.*

cheer *v.* to shout words of approval; to encourage by yelling. *We all cheer for our star player as he comes on the field.*

encourage to give courage. *The coach tried to encourage the players to do their best.*

shout to say loudly. *We shout encouragement to the runners.*

yell to shout loudly. *The fans yell cheers to the home team.*

cheerful *adj.* happy; joyful. *Kari gave a cheerful smile.*

good-humored cheerful; pleasant. *The good-humored clown entertained everyone.*

joyful full of joy. *The first and last days of school are always joyful.*

rosy bright; cheerful. *The good news meant there would be a rosy future.*

sunny happy, cheerful; bright. *May had a sunny personality that cheered everyone around her.*

antonyms: cheerless, sad, gloomy

chief *n.* a leader; a head of a tribe or group. *The chief leads the tribal council.*

captain head of a group; chief; leader. *John is the captain of the football team.*

head leader; chief person. *The head of the school was Mr. Smith.*

leader person who leads. *Jan was the leader of the debate team.*

officer person who holds an office in a club or organization. *The president is the top officer of the business.*

choice *n.* a decision; selection. *For dinner we will go to the restaurant of your choice.*

decision a choice. *I have made a decision about the theme for the food, costumes, and invitations for the big Fourth of July party.*

option choice; a choosing. *We have the option of taking a car, a bus, or a train to get to work.*

selection choice; act of selecting. *The store had a good selection of clothes for children.*

clear *adj.* having no clouds; bright. *The sun shone in the clear sky.*

bright very light or clear. *The bright day convinced us it would be a good day for a picnic.*

light clear; bright. *The lamp makes the room as light as day.*

sunny having much sunlight. *We wanted a sunny day for the parade.*

climb *v.* to go up, often using both hands and feet; to move on a steep slope. *The club members climb mountains all over the state.*

mount to go up. *We tried to mount the stairs as fast as we could.*

scale to climb. *We used ropes and hooks to scale the mountainside.*

clothes *n.* garments; articles of dress; clothing. *Some people order all of their clothes through a catalog.*

apparel clothing; dress. *This store sells very expensive women's apparel.*

dress clothing. *We studied about the dress of people from years ago.*
garments articles of clothing. *The queen's garments were made of velvet.*

clue *n.* a piece of information that helps solve a problem or mystery. *In this game we use a word clue to solve the puzzle.*
hint a sign; a suggestion. *The hint he gave us did not help us find the treasure.*
suggestion something suggested. *They gave us a suggestion to help us solve the problem.*

coach *n.* a person who trains athletes; person who teaches. *The basketball coach is happy when the team plays well.*
teacher a person who teaches. *We asked our teacher to help us with the report.*
trainer a person who trains others. *The trainer made the team practice throwing and catching.*
tutor a private teacher. *The tutor helped me learn how to do multiplication.*

coast *n.* the seashore; land along the sea or ocean. *There are many beaches along the coast of the Pacific Ocean.*
seacoast coast; land by the sea. *Maine has a beautiful seacoast.*
shore land along the sea, ocean, lake, etc. *We walked along the shore until we reached the path.*
shoreline place where water and shore meet. *The rising water changed the shoreline.*

compare *v.* to examine things for similarities or differences. *If you compare prices, you can save money when you shop.*
contrast to compare to show differences. *A list was made to contrast city living with country living.*
liken to compare. *The art collector did liken my painting to one hanging in the museum.*
match to fit together; be alike. *The curtains almost match the colors in the couch.*

cottage *n.* a small house. *We spent our vacation in a cottage on the beach.*
bungalow a small, one-floor house. *The family lived in a bungalow.*
cabin a small house, roughly built. *The mountain cabin was made of logs.*

crowd *v.* to push or squeeze together in a small space. *Many people tried to crowd into the small room.*

cram to put too many into a space. *Twenty people tried to cram into the small waiting room.*
jam to squeeze things or people together. *The riders tried to jam onto the train.*
swarm to crowd. *Hundreds of fans might swarm onto the field after the game.*

cute *adj.* delightfully attractive or appealing. *The child looked cute in her rabbit costume.*
attractive pretty; pleasing. *The attractive lady wore a black suit.*
charming attractive; very pleasing. *The children had charming roles in the play.*
pretty pleasing; attractive. *The pretty pictures decorated the walls.*
antonym: ugly

dampen *v.* to make moist or wet. *Dampen the cloth before you begin cleaning.*
moisten to make or become moist. *We will moisten the towel with water and clean up the mess.*
wet to make or become moist. *He can wet the soap to get lather.*

danger *n.* peril; chance of injury or harm. *Learning safety rules can help you avoid danger.*
hazard chance or harm. *The railroad crossing has been a serious safety hazard.*
peril chance of danger or harm. *The storm put the city in peril.*

darkness *n.* the state or quality of being without light or brightness. *The darkness of the sky warned of a coming storm.*
blackout a lack of light in a city or place due to loss of power. *The blackout lasted for two hours.*
dusk the time just before dark. *We got home at dusk.*
gloom darkness. *The gloom spread over the city as the sun set.*

deal *v.* to handle in a certain way; cope. *It is important to know how to deal with emergencies.*
cope to handle. *We will cope with the problem when it arises.*
handle to deal with. *The director will handle all of the problems.*

dew *n.* water droplets that form at night on cool surfaces. *In the morning you may see dew on the leaves.*

  mist fine drops of water in the air. *We can see the mist out in the yard.*

  moisture small drops of water in the air. *The moisture in the air made the car wet.*

  vapor moisture in the air. *The water vapor in the air made the windows steam up.*

dodge *v.* to try to avoid; stay away from. *The batter stepped back from the plate to dodge the wild pitch.*

  duck to move suddenly to keep from being hit. *She had to duck quickly to avoid the ball.*

  lurch to lean or stagger. *The man began to lurch forward when he lost his balance.*

  sidestep to step aside. *The pitcher had to sidestep to avoid being hit by the line drive.*

doubt *v.* to be unsure or uncertain. *I doubt that the Cortez family is home from vacation.*

  question to doubt. *I question the report of rainy weather since the sun is shining brightly.*

  suspect to doubt. *We suspect that he is not telling the whole story.*

drag *v.* to pull slowly along the ground; haul. *They drag the sled to the top of the hill and then slide down.*

  pull to move; drag. *We can pull the wagon up the hill.*

  tow to pull. *The truck will tow the car to the garage.*

  tug to pull hard. *He must tug on the rope to lead the horse to the barn.*

eager *adj.* excitedly or impatiently wanting or expecting something. *We were eager for school to begin that day.*

  avid very eager. *The avid fans cheered their team to victory.*

  enthusiastic eager; interested. *The class was very enthusiastic about the field trip.*

  zealous enthusiastic; eager. *The zealous efforts of the players made us feel we could win.*

easy *adj.* not hard or difficult. *The quiz was easy for me.*

  effortless easy; using little effort. *Because the work was so easy, it was an effortless job.*

  elementary basic; simple. *The computer instructor showed us the elementary steps for using the computer.*

  simple not hard; easy. *The simple problems were the best part of the test we had today.*

  antonyms: hard, difficult

echo *v.* to send back a sound. *Our shouts can echo throughout the canyon.*

  reverberate to echo back. *Our voices reverberate off the walls of the cave.*

  vibrate to resound; echo. *The clanging of the bells would vibrate in our ears.*

edge *n.* border; side. *The cup fell off the edge of the table.*

  border side or edge of something. *We crossed the state border at noon.*

  boundary a border or limit. *The river is the western boundary of our county.*

  brim edge or border. *The cup was filled to the brim.*

enjoy *v.* to get pleasure from. *Did you enjoy the movie last night?*

  delight to please greatly. *The clowns will delight the children.*

  like to wish for; enjoy. *The children like the new game a lot.*

enough *adj.* as much or as many as needed. *The backpackers had enough food and water for three days.*

  adequate enough; sufficient. *The food supply was adequate for a family of four.*

  ample as much as is needed; enough. *My ample allowance easily covers lunches and supplies.*

  sufficient as much as is needed. *We took sufficient food for the long trip.*

everyday *adj.* ordinary; all right for the usual day or event. *You should wear your everyday clothes to play outside.*

  common usual; ordinary. *Having a lot of rain is common in this area.*

  familiar common; well-known. *Coloring is a familiar activity for young children.*

  ordinary everyday; common. *Today is a very ordinary day.*

example *n.* a sample; model; something that may be imitated. *If you don't understand how to do the problems, look at the example.*

case a special condition; example. *The doctor treated a bad case of measles.*

model something to be copied or imitated. *Use the pattern as the model for your drawing.*

sample something to show what the rest are like. *The sample gave us a taste of various French foods.*

eye *v.* to look at or watch. *We wanted to eye the visitors to see if we knew any of them.*

observe to see; notice. *We tried to observe the workers to discover ways to improve production.*

peer at to look closely. *She likes to peer at the people in the cars on the street below.*

view to look at; see. *We can view the craters on the moon with our new telescope.*

watch to look at; observe. *The class will watch the movie about space travel.*

factory *n.* a plant where goods are manufactured. *Much of the work in a factory is done by machines.*

mill a building where goods are made or manufactured. *At the cotton mill they make very fine cotton cloth.*

plant a building and equipment for making something. *The printing plant has huge presses for printing books.*

shop a place where specific work is done. *At the shoe shop they can repair your boots.*

fame *n.* the state of being well-known; respect; recognition. *George Washington was a man of great fame.*

dignity position of honor; rank; title. *The dignity of the office of President is upheld through traditions.*

majesty nobility. *The majesty of the queen impressed all the guests.*

nobility people of noble title. *The nobility ruled the country until the revolution.*

fasten *v.* to join; attach. *We can fasten this lamp to the wall over my desk.*

attach to fasten; fix in place. *Attach the rope to the front of the sled.*

bind to hold together. *We can bind sticks together as a bundle.*

join to put together. *Let's join hands and walk in a circle.*

tie to fasten; bind. *I will tie the packages together with string.*

fear *n.* a feeling of fright or alarm. *A dog shows fear by putting its tail between its legs.*

fright fear; alarm. *The screeching brakes gave us a fright.*

panic fear in many people. *The earthquake caused a panic in our city.*

scare fright. *The loud noises sent a scare through all of us.*

terror great fear; fright. *The sound of thunder caused terror in the child.*

feel *v.* to sense by touch. *Feel how soft this cloth is!*

handle to touch, feel, or use with the hands. *We must handle the stuffed toy to learn how soft it is.*

sense to feel; understand. *She seemed to sense that the dog's bark was a warning.*

touch to put a hand on something. *We wanted to touch the soft pillow.*

few *adj.* not many. *There are few copies of this rare book available.*

scant not enough. *The scant supplies worried the captain of the ship.*

scarce hard to get. *Some coins have become very scarce.*

sparse meager; scant. *The lack of food put everyone on a very sparse diet.*

antonym: many

firm *adj.* hard; solid. *They left the muddy road and walked on firm ground.*

solid hard; firm. *The solid ground turned to mud because of the rain.*

stable firm; steady. *The steel construction made the building very stable.*

steady firm; solid. *He used a steady hand to guide the animal to safety.*

antonym: soft

flavor *n.* a particular taste. *Lemonade can have a sweet or tart flavor.*

tang a strong flavor. *The chili powder gave the stew a zesty tang.*

taste the special flavor of food. *The meat left a strange taste in my mouth.*

flood *n.* water that flows over normally dry land. *The low bridge was underwater for an hour after the flash flood.*
deluge a great flood. *The deluge washed the bridge away.*
downpour a very heavy rain. *The downpour caused flooding in the streets.*

flour *n.* a fine powder of ground grain, usually wheat. *Flour is used in breads.*
bran the covering of grains of wheat, rye, etc. *The cereal contained bran.*
meal anything ground to a powder. *The corn meal was ground to a fine powder.*

flower *n.* the blossom of a plant. *Tulips are flowers that bloom in the spring.*
bloom a blossom; flower. *There was one perfect rose bloom in the vase.*
blossom the flower of a seed plant. *The peach blossom smells beautiful.*
bud a partly opened flower. *The bud will soon open into a lovely flower.*
floret a small flower. *The floret was purple and pink.*

fold *v.* to close or bend parts of something together in order to fit it into a smaller space. *When we take down the flag, we fold it into the shape of a triangle.*
bend to curve; to be crooked. *Bend the paper around the edges of the box.*
crease to make a fold. *She will crease the paper as she wraps the package.*
crinkle to wrinkle. *The paper will crinkle when it is crushed.*

forth *adv.* forward; onward. *From that day forth they were good friends.*
ahead in the front; forward. *We will go ahead with the project.*
forward toward the front. *Come forward and get your prize.*
onward toward the front. *We will move onward to see the monument.*

friend *n.* a person one knows and likes. *Erin is my good friend.*
acquaintance a person one knows but not as a close friend. *Almost every day I made a new acquaintance.*
classmate member of the same class. *Our new classmate studied with us for the test.*
companion a comrade; friend. *Jane and her companion worked and played together.*

comrade a close friend; companion. *The police officer and her comrade directed traffic.*
mate companion; friend. *My mate and I will try to go to a movie.*
antonym: enemy

funny *adj.* causing laughter or amusement. *The joke was funny.*
amusing entertaining; funny. *The author wrote many amusing stories.*
humorous amusing; funny. *I like the humorous stories he tells.*
witty showing wit; clever and amusing. *The witty speaker made the audience laugh.*

gather *v.* to bring or come together. *When clouds gather it often means rain.*
accumulate to gather little by little. *Dust can accumulate under the sofa.*
assemble to gather or bring together. *The students will assemble outside the museum.*
collect to gather together. *The students want to collect aluminum cans for recycling.*

gentle *adj.* light; soft. *The gentle breeze rustled the leaves.*
easy smooth and pleasant. *His quiet, easy way made everyone around him feel relaxed.*
mild not harsh; not severe. *She had a very mild manner.*
soft quiet; gentle; mild. *She has a soft voice.*
antonym: harsh

gigantic *adj.* extremely large. *Elephants and whales are gigantic.*
huge very big; extremely large. *The huge truck was loaded with steel rails.*
stupendous immense; extremely large. *The stupendous mountains were a beautiful sight to see.*

glow *v.* to give off light; to shine. *Fireflies glow in the dark.*
gleam to give off light. *The little lamp will gleam in the darkness.*
glitter to shine with sparkling light. *The beads on the costumes seemed to glitter.*
shine to send out light; glow. *Please shine your flashlight over here.*

twinkle to shine and glitter. *Stars twinkle in the night sky.*

glue *n.* a sticky liquid that hardens to hold things together. *Broken toys can be mended with glue.*

cement something that hardens to hold things together. *Rubber cement is used to hold the pictures in the album.*

paste mixture used to hold things together. *We used white paste to make the paper chains.*

goal *n.* a purpose; aim. *Mark's goal is to play the double bass in a symphony orchestra.*

aim a purpose; goal. *The aim of the exercise is to build up leg muscles.*

objective a goal; aim. *We each wrote an objective for our science project.*

purpose an aim; plan. *The purpose of the game is to find all the numbers.*

target a goal; objective. *Our target was to walk a mile in eight minutes.*

group *n.* a gathering or arrangement of people or objects. *There is a large group of people in the hotel lobby.*

branch a part; division; local office. *That branch of the company is located in Sweden.*

division one part of a whole; group; section. *This division of the company handles the manufacturing of our product.*

section part of a city, region, etc. *The city offices are in this section of town.*

happy *adj.* feeling or showing pleasure; joyful. *The happy man whistled as he worked.*

cheerful happy; joyful. *Kari gave us a cheerful smile.*

contented pleased; satisfied. *The contented cat lay by the fire and purred.*

delighted very glad; very pleased. *I am delighted that you came to visit.*

ecstatic very happy; joyful. *The winner had an ecstatic look on her face.*

glad happy; pleased. *We are glad that you won the prize.*

antonym: sad

harden *v.* to make or become hard. *The ground does harden during the cold weather.*

temper to bring to a proper condition of hardness. *A special process of heating and cooling will temper the steel.*

toughen to make or become tough. *The hard work will toughen our hands and our bodies.*

haul *v.* to pull with force, drag. *We tried to haul the rowboat out of the water.*

lug to drag or pull along. *We must lug the boxes down the stairs.*

pull to move; drag. *We can pull the wagon up the hill.*

tug to pull hard. *He must tug on the rope to lead the horse to the barn.*

heavy *adj.* hard to move because of its weight; not light. *We will need two people to lift this heavy trunk.*

hefty weighty; heavy. *The hefty man easily picked up the big boxes.*

husky big and strong. *The job required a husky person to lift the crates.*

ponderous very heavy. *An elephant is a ponderous animal.*

weighty heavy. *The hasty decisions caused weighty problems for the city.*

antonym: light

hedge *n.* a thick row of bushes planted as a fence or boundary. *A hedge should be trimmed evenly.*

fence a wall put around a yard or field. *The bushes made a fence around the yard.*

wall a structure built around an area. *The plants made a wall of flowers around the patio.*

helpless *adj.* not able to help oneself or others. *We felt helpless to stop the school's litter problem.*

incapable lacking ability. *He is incapable of performing that complicated task.*

incompetent lacking power or ability. *She is incompetent when it comes to flying a helicopter.*

powerless without power; helpless. *The powerless leader was finally removed from office.*

useless of no use. *The old motor is useless.*

antonym: capable

hero *n.* a man or boy admired for his bravery or fine qualities. *Abraham Lincoln is a national hero.* [heroine (female)]

adventurer person who seeks adventure. *The adventurer set out to explore the jungle.*

star a person with exceptional qualities. *The little child was the star of the show.*

high *adj.* tall; far above the ground. *Eagles build nests on high cliffs.*

alpine like high mountains. *The alpine trees rise high into the sky.*

tall having great height. *The tall building could be seen for miles.*

towering very high. *They climbed up the towering mountain.*

antonym: low

highway *n.* a main road. *A highway is usually numbered to simplify maps and road signs.*

boulevard a broad street. *The boulevard was named after a president.*

interstate a highway that connects two or more states. *Hundreds of cars, trucks, and buses use the interstate.*

road a way for cars, trucks, etc. to travel. *The road went from town to the farm in the country.*

thoroughfare a main road; highway. *Route 66 was a main thoroughfare in years past.*

hire *v.* to employ; pay a person for working. *Because business is good, the store can hire three more clerks.*

employ to hire or give work to. *The company does employ many people.*

engage to hire. *We must engage a crew to rake the leaves and mow the lawn.*

antonym: fire

holiday *n.* a day on which a special event is celebrated. *The family went to Grandmother's house for the holiday.*

fiesta a holiday or festival. *The community planned a summer fiesta.*

vacation a time with no school, work, or other duties. *The summer vacation gave us time to swim and play.*

honest *adj.* tending not to lie, cheat, or steal; able to be trusted. *An honest person always tells the truth.*

conscientious taking care to do what is right. *The children were conscientious workers in school.*

honorable showing a sense of what is right. *The honorable man was elected to the city council.*

sincere real; honest. *His sincere efforts showed how much he cared about his work.*

trustworthy reliable; dependable. *The bank employees were trustworthy.*

truthful telling the truth. *The witness gave a truthful account of the accident.*

upstanding honorable. *The upstanding judge was respected by the townspeople.*

antonym: dishonest

hopeless *adj.* having very little chance of working out right. *After darkness fell, they decided the search for the ball was hopeless.*

desperate not caring; without hope. *After the tornado, they made a desperate search for the mailbox.*

despondent having lost hope; discouraged. *The helpers were despondent over the conditions left by the storm.*

discouraged lacking in courage. *The discouraged partners tried to sell the business.*

dismayed greatly troubled. *She was dismayed that she failed to get to school on time.*

antonym: hopeful

hotel *n.* a place that provides guests with lodging, meals, and other services. *Our grandparents stayed in a hotel near the beach.*

inn a place where travelers can get food and rooms. *The inn was built near a major highway.*

lodge a place to live in. *The ski lodge was located in Aspen, Colorado.*

resort a place people go to vacation. *The resort by the ocean had water sports and many other things to do.*

however *conj.* nevertheless. *I've never tasted eggplant before; however, it looks delicious.*

nevertheless however; nonetheless. *We knew what to do; nevertheless, we waited.*

yet nevertheless; however. *The game was well played, yet it would have been better if we had won.*

huge *adj.* very large. *A skyscraper is a huge building.*

enormous extremely large. *The enormous hippopotamus wandered down to the river.*

immense very large; huge. *The immense shopping center was the largest in the United States.*

tremendous very large; enormous. *The tremendous whale slowly swam in front of the ship.*

antonyms: tiny, little, small

idea *n.* a thought; a plan. *Bringing plants to decorate the room was Kristin's idea.*

impression idea; notion. *My impression of him changed when I saw how hard he worked.*

inspiration brilliant idea. *My inspiration for the design came from the patterns in the wallpaper.*

notion idea or understanding. *I don't think he has any notion of what I said.*

thought idea; what one thinks. *My thought on the topic was written in my report.*

view an idea; picture. *The outline will give you a general view of the story.*

illness *n.* poor health; a disease. *Craig went home from school because of illness.*

ailment sickness; illness. *The ailment caused her to be very tired.*

malady a disease or deep-seated illness. *Cancer is a very serious malady.*

sickness an illness. *The fever was caused by the sickness.*

invite *v.* to ask a person to go somewhere or do something. *My mother will invite my friend to lunch.*

ask to invite. *We must ask everyone to come to the school party.*

request to ask. *She did request that we go to hear the speech on safety.*

island *n.* a piece of land with water all around it. *People must take a boat or an airplane to get to an island.*

cay a low island; reef. *The cay was to the north of our hotel.*

isle a small island. *Only the lighthouse was left on the isle.*

joyful *adj.* full of joy. *The first and last days of school are always joyful.*

enjoyable giving joy. *We had a very enjoyable day at the zoo.*

pleasurable pleasant; enjoyable. *The trip was a pleasurable time for all of us.*

judge *n.* one who presides over a court of law by hearing cases and making decisions. *A judge must be completely fair.*

justice of the peace a local official who handles small cases and other minor duties. *The justice of the peace performed the wedding ceremony.*

magistrate a judge in a court. *The court magistrate asked the jury to give its verdict.*

jumble *v.* to mix up. *We had to jumble the letters of the word for the puzzle.*

muddle to make a mess of. *He did muddle his speech because he lost his notes.*

snarl to tangle. *As it ran around the room, the cat managed to snarl the yarn.*

tangle to twist together. *The rope might tangle around the post.*

jungle *n.* wild land near the equator with thickly grown tropical plants. *Parrots and monkeys live in a jungle.*

bush wild, unsettled land. *The explorers roamed the bush of Australia.*

chaparral an area of thick shrubs and small trees. *Animals live in the chaparral of the southwestern United States.*

keep *v.* to store; put away; save. *I keep all my old homework.*

hold to keep. *Please hold my book while I play on the slide.*

retain to keep; continue to have or hold. *I will retain the receipts for my income tax records.*

save to store up. *I will save the tickets to use next week.*

store to put away; save. *Squirrels store nuts for the winter.*

kettle *n.* a pot used for heating liquids. *Put the kettle on the stove.*
boiler large container. *The water was heated in the boiler.*
caldron a large kettle. *We made soup in the old, black caldron.*

kind *adj.* friendly; thoughtful of others. *Everyone likes kind people.*
friendly like a friend. *The friendly salesperson helped us with our problem.*
good-hearted caring; generous. *The good-hearted neighbor helped everyone.*
gracious kindly; pleasant. *The gracious hostess tried to make sure that her guests had a good time.*
hospitable kind and friendly. *The town was hospitable to newcomers.*
thoughtful considerate; kind. *The mayor was always thoughtful of our wishes.*
 antonyms: cruel, mean

knock *v.* to strike with the fist or with a hard object. *I did knock on the door but no one answered.*
hit to strike; knock. *The stick hit the ground with great force.*
punch to hit with the fist. *He continued to punch the bag until it ripped.*
slap to strike with an open hand. *She thought she had to slap the horse to make it move.*

know *v.* to have the facts about; understand. *Do you know how hail is formed?*
comprehend to understand the meaning of. *I can comprehend that scientific term.*
recognize to know again. *I did recognize that the story was similar to one I already knew.*
understand to get the meaning of. *I understand how to bake chicken pie.*

lady *n.* a polite term for a woman. *We knew by her manners that she was a real lady.*
female woman; girl. *Is the new student a female or a male?*
woman a grown female person. *Do you know the woman in the blue gown?*

laugh *v.* to make sounds with the voice that show amusement. *Everyone seemed to laugh at the funny movie.*

giggle to give high-pitched laughs. *The little children tried not to giggle at the cartoons.*
snicker to make a sly or silly laugh. *The teens liked to snicker at the old movie.*

lead *v.* to direct or show the way. *She will lead the hikers home.*
direct to tell or show the way. *Please direct me to the registration desk.*
guide to direct; lead. *The ranger did guide the tourists through the forest preserve.*
show to guide; direct. *I will show you the way to the museum.*

leader *n.* one who leads. *The Scout troop needs a new leader.*
captain head of a group; chief; leader. *John is the captain of the football team.*
chief a leader; a head of a tribe or group. *The chief of the tribe wore a headdress of feathers and beads.*
director person who manages or directs. *The director told the actors where to stand.*
guide person who leads or directs. *The guide showed us the way to the campsite.*
manager a person who manages. *Have you met the new store manager?*
master one who has power over others. *The master of the house made the rules.*

learner *n.* one who learns; student. *A good learner listens carefully.*
pupil a person who is learning. *He is the new pupil in the dance class.*
scholar a person in school; a learner. *The scholar studies her lessons every day.*
student a person who studies. *Which student is doing the spelling assignment?*
trainee a person who is being trained. *She is a trainee at the hospital.*

least *adj.* smallest in size or amount. *Which game costs the least money?*
lowest not tall; not high. *This is the lowest score on the test.*
slightest smallest of its kind. *The slightest one is four feet tall.*
smallest littler than others. *This is the smallest doll I have ever seen.*
 antonym: most

lighten *v.* to make brighter; to add light to. *The new paint does lighten the room.*
brighten to lighten; make or become brighter. *The lamp will brighten the living room.*

illuminate to light up; make bright. *The lights seem to illuminate the sky.*
antonym: darken

listen *v.* to pay attention; try to hear. *The audience did listen closely to the speaker.*
eavesdrop to listen secretly. *You can eavesdrop by putting your ear against the wall.*
hear to listen; to take in sounds. *We could hear everything that she said.*
heed to give attention to. *We must heed the advice we were given.*

lose *v.* to be unable to find; misplace. *Put the key in your pocket so you won't lose it.*
mislay to put away and forget where. *Where did you mislay your science book?*
misplace to put in the wrong place. *I always seem to misplace my gloves.*
antonym: find

major *adj.* larger; greater; primary. *We spent the major part of the day at the beach.*
greater better; larger. *The greater part of the afternoon was devoted to studying.*
larger bigger; greater. *The larger section of the office was used for the accounting division.*
superior better; greater. *This clothing is of superior quality.*

mark *v.* to make a visible sign on or by. *Mark the wrong answers with an "X."*
initial to mark or sign with initials. *Each member of the family needed to initial the document.*
inscribe to mark with letters, words, etc. *The jeweler will inscribe her initials on the bracelet.*
stamp to mark with some tool. *She needed to stamp the date on each letter.*

market *n.* a place where things can be bought and sold. *A supermarket is a large, modern market.*
emporium a large store selling many kinds of things. *At the emporium you can buy clothes, shoes, and things for the home.*
shop a place where things are sold. *The dress shop had an assortment of clothes to sell.*

store a place where things are kept for sale. *The store was located near my house.*

master *v.* to become skilled in. *It takes time and practice to master a foreign language.*
conquer to overcome; to get the better of. *If we want to conquer a difficult task, first divide it into small parts.*
learn to gain skill or knowledge. *We will learn about Africa in Social Studies.*

middle *n.* the point or part located at the same distance from each side or end; center. *Your nose is in the middle of your face.*
center the middle point. *The table is in the center of the room.*
midst the center. *The child is in the midst of the group.*

moment *n.* an instant; a very brief period. *I saw him for a moment, but lost sight of him in the crowd.*
instant a moment in time. *The horse stopped for an instant and then raced away.*
second instant; moment. *He paused for a second before turning the key.*

mount *v.* to climb onto; to get up on. *The rider wants to mount his horse and gallop away.*
ascend to go up. *The group can ascend the steps to the platform.*
climb to go up; ascend. *We tried to climb to the top of the tower.*
vault to leap or jump. *She could vault over the hedge.*

movement *n.* action; change in position or location. *The children watched the slow movement of the snail across the sidewalk.*
action movement; way of moving. *She enjoys the action of a hockey game.*
gesture movement of the body to give an idea. *Waving her hand was a gesture to say she did not want to be disturbed.*

mumble *v.* to speak unclearly so that you are hard to understand. *If you mumble, no one will understand you.*
murmur to say softly. *We told her not to murmur her thanks, so everyone can hear her.*
mutter to speak unclearly. *He always seems to mutter when he gets tired.*
whisper to speak softly. *I like to whisper secrets to my closest friend.*

near *adv.* not far away in time or distance. *The train drew near.*

  alongside by the side of. *The big car pulled up and parked alongside our car.*

  closely near; next to. *The books are stacked closely together.*

  antonym: far

nearby *adj.* not far off. *They live in a nearby town.*

  adjacent near or close. *The new store will be on the adjacent lot.*

  adjoining next to; bordering. *The adjoining lakes were connected by a stream.*

  close near; together. *The buildings are very close to each other.*

newspaper *n.* a printed paper that contains news, advertisements, cartoons, etc. *My grandfather likes to work the crossword puzzles in the newspaper.*

  daily a newspaper printed every day. *The article appeared in the daily.*

  paper a newspaper. *Have you seen the comics in today's paper?*

obey *v.* to follow the orders of. *Children are taught to obey their parents.*

  comply to follow a request. *I will comply with the captain's orders.*

  conform to follow a law or rule. *She didn't like to conform to the rules of the tennis club.*

  observe to keep; follow. *We always try to observe the rules about being quiet in the library.*

  antonym: disobey

often *adv.* many times; frequently. *We often see our relatives during the holidays.*

  frequently often; repeatedly. *We frequently shop at the grocery store in our neighborhood.*

  recurrently repeatedly. *He had to cough recurrently.*

repeatedly more than once. *She repeatedly asked for news of her lost puppy.*

owner *n.* one who owns or possesses something. *Who is the owner of this plaid jacket?*

  landlord person who owns a building. *We paid the rent to the landlord.*

  partner one of a group who owns a company. *Each partner invested a lot of money in the new business.*

  proprietor owner. *The proprietor of the store was very helpful to every customer.*

package *n.* a wrapped box; parcel. *How much will it cost to mail this package?*

  bundle things tied or wrapped together; package. *The bundle of gifts contained many games and toys.*

  parcel a package. *The driver delivered the parcel this morning.*

paper *n.* a written article; a report. *The teacher asked us to write a paper about the moon.*

  article a written report; composition. *The article contained factual information about air pollution.*

  document written information; report. *The lawyer found the document she wanted to use in court.*

  report a written account of something. *The report was prepared by a committee.*

pass *v.* to hand over; give; send. *Please pass the salad.*

  deliver to hand over; give out. *The postal carrier will deliver the mail in the morning.*

  hand to pass; give. *Please hand me the jar of jam.*

  transfer to move from one place to another; to hand over. *We had to transfer the order to the New York office.*

past *adj.* gone by; previous. *This past month we had three inches of rain.*

  earlier previous; coming before. *The earlier report said the president would arrive on Tuesday.*

  previous coming before; earlier. *The previous lesson showed us how to multiply.*

prior earlier; coming before. *The job did not require prior experience.*

payment *n.* an amount of money paid. *Most people who rent a house or apartment make a monthly payment to the landlord.*
compensation an amount paid. *We were given compensation for our work.*
installment part of a payment. *The loan was to be paid back in twelve monthly installments.*
settlement payment. *The court settlement helped her pay the legal fees.*

perfect *adj.* having no flaws or errors; exactly right. *Charlene turned in a perfect paper in science.*
flawless perfect; without flaw. *The flawless diamond was very valuable.*
ideal perfect; having no flaws. *This is an ideal day to go to the beach.*
impeccable perfect; faultless. *The group had impeccable manners.*

piece *n.* a part; a segment. *Would you like a piece of my orange?*
fragment a piece broken off. *We found a fragment of the broken dish near the sink.*
part a piece; less than the whole. *The best part of the dinner was the dessert.*
portion a part; share. *One portion of the work was already completed.*
segment piece or part of a whole. *She picked the shortest segment of the straw.*

placement *n.* location; arrangement. *The placement of the flowers added the perfect touch to the dinner table.*
arrangement items in proper order. *The arrangement of pictures told the story of the Little Red Hen.*
location place; position. *The store's location was ideal because it was on a corner of a busy street.*

playful *adj.* full of fun and enjoyment. *The baby was playful in his bath.*
frisky lively; playful. *The frisky puppy ran all around the yard.*
frivolous silly; full of fun. *Her frivolous behavior made us laugh.*
mischievous teasing; full of fun. *The mischievous kitten unraveled the yarn.*

port *n.* a town with a harbor where ships may dock. *Boston is an Atlantic port.*
dock platform built over water. *The ship unloaded at the dock.*
harbor a place to dock ships and boats. *The steamship docked at the harbor.*
wharf a dock; platform built out from shore. *The huge ship was tied at the wharf.*

powder *n.* a substance made of fine grains. *It's easy to grind chalk into a powder.*
dust fine, dry earth. *The dust settled all over the road.*
grit fine bits of sand or gravel. *The boat was covered with grit.*
sand tiny bits of stone in large amounts, found in the deserts and on shores along oceans, lakes, and rivers. *This beach has smooth sand.*

power *n.* great strength, force, or control. *The police have power to enforce the law.*
control power to direct. *The police have control over the traffic.*
force power; strength. *The force of the wind blew the door open.*
strength power; force. *He had the strength of a giant.*

powerful *adj.* having great power; strong. *The king was a powerful leader.*
able having power, skill, or talent. *He is an able warrior.*
forceful having much force or strength. *The forceful leader told everyone what to do.*
mighty showing strength. *The mighty ruler rode off to battle.*
strong having much force or power. *The strong woman lifted weights every day.*
antonym: powerless

powerless *adj.* having no strength or power; helpless. *The farmers were powerless against the drought.*
helpless not able to help oneself. *The helpless child needed his parents.*
sickly not strong. *A sickly person should not go hiking in the mountains.*
unable not able. *I would like to help you, but I am unable.*
antonym: powerful

Writing Thesaurus

preschool *n.* a place of learning before elementary school. *Children aged three to five may attend preschool.*

day-care center a place where young children are cared for while parents work. *Our community has a new day-care center.*

nursery school a place for children under the age of five. *The nursery school helps the young children learn about numbers and letters.*

quake *v.* to vibrate or shake. *The ground did quake beneath us during the mild earthquake.*

quaver tremble; shake. *The old house seemed to quaver as the strong winds blew.*

shake to move quickly. *Please shake the dirt off your boots.*

tremble to shake from fear, cold, etc. *We started to tremble when we heard the storm was near.*

vibrate to move rapidly. *The strings of the violin vibrate as he plays.*

quarrel *v.* to fight; to disagree, using angry words. *They always quarrel about whose turn it is to bat.*

argue to give reasons for and against an issue. *The students argued about the playground rules.*

bicker to quarrel. *The children started to bicker over whose turn was next.*

brawl to quarrel in a loud manner. *Two players started to brawl during the hockey game.*

wrangle to argue or quarrel. *The group seemed to wrangle over every topic that was brought up at the meeting.*

queen *n.* a female ruler. *The queen issued a proclamation.*

czarina a Russian empress. *The czarina wore beautiful clothes.*

empress a woman who rules an empire. *The empress was admired by everyone.*

question *n.* a problem. *The litter question will be discussed tonight.*

issue a problem; a point or topic. *The tax issue was always hotly debated.*

problem a difficult question. *The new economic problem troubled the country.*

topic subject that people write or talk about. *The topic of my report is health.*

antonym: answer

quick *adj.* fast; swift. *The rabbit made a quick leap into the bushes.*

fast moving with speed; quick. *The fast runner took the lead and won the race.*

rapid fast; quick. *They keep up a rapid pace on the assembly line.*

speedy fast; rapid; quick. *The speedy messenger delivered the package on time.*

swift very fast; rapid. *He gave a swift response to every test question.*

antonym: slow

quit *v.* to stop. *We'll quit raking leaves when it gets dark.*

cease to stop; put to an end. *The noise will cease when the speaker begins.*

stop to halt; to keep from doing something. *We couldn't stop them from winning.*

quiz *n.* a brief test. *I missed only two questions on the science quiz.*

checkup an examination; inspection. *I saw my doctor for a checkup yesterday.*

examination a test; set of questions. *We were given an examination by our teacher.*

test an examination, often consisting of a series of questions or problems. *There were twenty items on the test.*

quote *v.* to repeat or refer to a passage from a story or poem. *Justin wanted to quote a line from the poem in his essay.*

recite to say from memory. *We had to choose a poem to recite in class.*

repeat to say again. *Please repeat what you said about using the dictionary.*

range *v.* to extend or vary within certain limits. *The stories in this book range from sad to funny.*

encompass to include; contain. *The article will encompass a lot of information.*

span to extend. *The new bridge will span the rocky canyon.*

vary to change; be different. *The colors may vary in shades from light to dark.*

rare *adj.* not often found or seen. *My uncle saves rare postage stamps.*

scarce rare; hard to get. *Some jungle animals have become very scarce.*

uncommon rare; unusual. *Hummingbirds are uncommon in this state.*

unusual not common; rare. *This unusual flower only grows in the desert.*

rattle *v.* to make a number of short, sharp sounds. *The windows rattle when the wind blows.*

bang to make a loud noise. *The wind caused the shutters to bang against the house.*

clang to make a loud, harsh sound. *The bells began to clang as the wind blew.*

clatter to make a loud noise. *The dishes clatter as we stack them in the kitchen sink.*

reader *n.* a person who reads. *The teacher chose Kathy to be the reader of our lunchtime story this week.*

bookworm a person who loves to read. *Karl is a bookworm; he reads all the time.*

browser a person who looks through materials. *Robert is only a browser; he seldom reads a whole book.*

ready *adj.* prepared. *We are ready for school.*

available able to be used. *She is available to start work tomorrow.*

prepared ready. *The prepared lessons were put on tape.*

reason *n.* a cause or explanation. *Your parents will write the reason for your absence.*

cause reason for action. *What was the cause of the accident?*

explanation something that explains. *He didn't give an explanation for his absence.*

motive reason; thought or feeling. *My motive for the trip was to hike farther than any of my friends had.*

purpose reason for which something is done. *The major purpose of the lesson was to learn how to divide.*

rebuild *v.* to build again. *They are planning to rebuild the old school.*

reconstruct to construct again. *The townspeople wanted to reconstruct the library after the fire.*

restore to put back; establish again. *My uncle likes to restore old furniture.*

record *n.* an account of facts or events. *The secretary keeps the record of the club's activities.*

diary a personal record of daily events. *Her diary told about the events of her life.*

memo a short written statement. *The memo announced a special company picnic.*

remain *v.* to continue without change; stay. *The nurse reported that the patient's condition did remain good.*

continued to stay; remain. *The weather will continue to be sunny and nice.*

linger to stay on. *He could linger for hours in the library.*

loiter to linger. *We liked to loiter along the way and to look in the store windows.*

stay to continue; remain. *She decided to stay near the child until he fell asleep.*

report *v.* to give an account or statement. *The president of the company did report that sales had increased.*

disclose to tell; to make known. *I will never disclose my friend's secret.*

reveal to make known. *I will reveal my findings to the press next week.*

tell to say; put in words. *The travel agent will tell us about France and Italy.*

restful *adj.* offering rest, peace, or quiet. *My aunt finds sewing restful after a busy day.*

calm quiet; peaceful; motionless. *There wasn't even a breeze on that calm evening.*

cozy warm; comfortable. *The cozy cottage was difficult to leave.*

peaceful calm; quiet. *Early morning hours are peaceful.*

quiet stillness; peace. *The quiet library was a good place to study.*

snug warm; comfortable. *I felt snug in a warm coat.*

tranquil peaceful; quiet; calm. *The tranquil night air was very relaxing.*

antonym: restless

restless *adj.* impatient; unable to be still. *The small children grew restless after the long delay.*

agitated restless; impatient. *The agitated crowd began to yell at the speaker.*

impatient not patient; restless. *We became impatient while waiting in line.*

nervous upset; excited. *A nervous person tends to fidget a lot.*

uneasy restless; disturbed. *The tornado warnings gave us an uneasy feeling.*

antonym: restful

return *v.* to come or go back. *We will return after the game is over.*

reappear to appear again. *After the clouds pass, the stars will reappear in the night sky.*

recur to occur again. *The problem will recur if we don't make any changes.*

review *v.* to study again; go over. *She did review the chapter before she took the test.*

critique to review critically. *He had to critique the play and analyze the plot.*

examine to look closely at. *I will examine all of the information before I decide what to do.*

study to try to learn. *I will study my spelling words tonight.*

survey to examine; look over. *She will survey the situation before she decides what to do.*

rigid *adj.* very stiff; not able to be bent. *A cast holds a broken arm in a rigid position so it can heal.*

firm solid; hard. *The sailors were glad to set foot on firm ground.*

hard not soft; firm. *We couldn't pound the stakes into the hard ground.*

stiff rigid; not able to bend. *The stiff paper could not be bent around the package.*

tense stiff; stretched tight. *The tent was held up by the tense ropes.*

rise *n.* an increase in height or amount. *The store announced a rise in prices.*

boost an increase in price, amount, etc. *The boost in prices made food cost more this year.*

growth an increase; amount grown. *This year's growth has made the company very successful.*

raise an increase in amount. *The workers were given a yearly raise in pay.*

swell an increase in amount. *The swell of shoppers made the store owners happy.*

role *n.* a part or character in a play. *Who will play the role of Peter Pan?*

character a person or animal in a book, play, etc. *The main character was a big monster from outer space.*

impersonation a representation. *The woman gave an impersonation of a movie star.*

part a role; character in a play. *The students will try out for each part in the school play.*

roll *v.* to move by turning over and over. *The ball started to roll down the hill.*

revolve to move in a circle. *The planets revolve around the sun.*

rotate to turn about a center. *Earth does rotate on its axis.*

turn to rotate; move around. *The wheels will turn as the horse pulls the wagon.*

whirl to spin; turn round and round. *The dancers whirl around the stage.*

rough *adj.* not smooth or even. *The car bounced and rattled over the rough road.*

bumpy full of bumps. *We took a bumpy ride in an old wagon.*

rocky bumpy; full of rocks. *The car made lots of noise as it bounced over the rocky mountain road.*

uneven not level or flat. *The uneven ground made it hard to walk.*

royal *adj.* having to do with kings and queens. *The king and queen live in a royal palace.*

regal belonging to royalty. *The regal party was held in the palace of the king.*

sovereign having the power of a ruler. *The queen was the sovereign leader of the British Commonwealth.*

rule *n.* a law; regulation. *Always obey each and every school safety rule.*

fundamental a basic principle. *You can't learn a sport one fundamental at a time.*

law a rule or regulation made by a state, country, etc. *Each law was made by the state government.*

principle a basic law or assumption. *It is a scientific principle that what goes up must come down.*

regulation rule; law. *This regulation controls flights to all airports.*

sadness *n.* sorrow; grief. *Tears can be an expression of sadness.*

grief sadness; sorrow. *His grief made him a very quiet person.*

melancholy sadness; low spirits. *Her melancholy was caused by several painful events.*

sorrow grief; sadness. *Her sorrow was caused by the loss of her pet.*

unhappiness sorrow; sadness. *His illness caused his family much unhappiness.*
antonym: happiness

safe *adj.* free from risk or harm. *This sidewalk is a safe place to walk.*
armored protected with armor. *An armored car is a safe way to transport money.*
protected guarded; safe. *He led a very protected life.*
secure safe. *They built a secure fence all around the farm.*

sample *n.* a part that shows what the rest are like. *The store gave away a free sample of the new soap.*
example one thing that shows what others are like. *He used Dallas as an example of a Texas city.*
specimen one of a group used to show what others are like. *Janet collected a new rock specimen from her world travels.*

scale *v.* to climb up or over. *The climbers used ropes to scale the cliff.*
climb to go up; ascend. *We tried to climb to the top of the tower.*
mount to climb onto; to get up on. *The rider wanted to mount his horse and gallop away.*
vault to leap or jump. *She could vault over the hedge.*

scare *v.* to frighten. *The sudden loud noise did scare me.*
alarm to frighten; fill with fear. *The loud whistle and siren seemed to alarm everyone.*
frighten to scare; fill with fright. *The thunder did frighten us.*
startle to frighten suddenly. *He made a loud noise to startle the birds out of the tree.*

scratch *v.* to cut or scrape a surface. *You can tell that a diamond is genuine if it can scratch glass.*
claw to scratch or pull apart. *The cat will claw the chair until the stuffing comes out.*
scrape to scratch the surface of. *The basketball player did scrape his knee when he fell on the basketball court.*

season *v.* to improve the taste. *The chef will season the soup with herbs.*
flavor to season. *The spices flavor the pot of stew.*

salt to sprinkle with salt. *He always seems to salt his food more than anyone else does.*
spice to season; add spice. *She decided to spice the pie with nutmeg and cloves.*

seller *n.* a person who sells; a vendor. *The flower seller had a stand on the street corner.*
merchant a person who buys and sells. *The merchant in the shopping center is having a special sale.*
vendor a seller; peddler. *The vendor services the candy machines once a week.*

serve *v.* to help others by performing a task. *Sarah will serve as club treasurer.*
administer to be helpful; contribute. *Their job is to administer to the elderly.*
help to do what is needed. *I can help you fix up the old house.*
perform to do. *She did perform many duties as an officer of the company.*

settle *v.* to establish residence. *Their family did settle in California years ago.*
locate to establish in a place. *She will locate her business near San Francisco.*
place to put. *We will place the sign near the busy intersection.*
reside to occupy a home or place. *The decision to reside at this address was made years ago.*

share *n.* a part; a portion. *Todd always does his share of work.*
allotment a part; share. *The largest allotment was for food and housing.*
part a share. *We only wanted the part of the reward that belonged to us.*
portion a share; part. *A portion of time at the end of the day is set aside for storytime and cleanup.*

shipment *n.* the goods sent or delivered to a certain place. *The store received a clothing shipment from the manufacturer.*
cargo the freight carried on a ship or other vehicle. *The barge carried a cargo of lumber to the mill.*
freight goods carried by plane, truck, ship, or train. *The dockworker sent the freight by truck.*
load something that is carried. *The load was too heavy for the small car.*

shower *n.* a short fall of rain. *During the afternoon there was a thunder shower.*

cloudburst a sudden rain; violent rainstorm. *We were caught in the cloudburst and got very wet.*

downpour a very heavy rain. *The downpour started while we were at a picnic.*

rain water falling from the clouds in drops. *The rain came down all morning.*

torrent an outpouring. *A torrent of rain caused the river to flood the whole valley.*

shy *adj.* reserved; quiet. *After Josh made friends at his new school, he was no longer shy.*

bashful reserved; shy; easily embarrassed. *As a bashful child, she did not like to be with groups of people.*

quiet peaceful; calm. *Alice spent a quiet afternoon reading.*

reserved quiet; keeping to oneself. *The reserved child seldom spoke to anyone in his class at school.*

unsociable reserved; bashful. *Ann was an unsociable child and often kept away from other people.*

simple *adj.* easy to understand. *The simple questions did not take long to answer.*

easy not hard to do. *The science experiment was easy.*

effortless requiring little effort. *Typing is an effortless task for him.*

elementary simple; easy to learn first. *When learning a new sport, begin with the elementary principles.*

singer *n.* one who sings. *The singer joined a choir.*

artist one skilled in the performance of an art. *The opera singer was a talented artist.*

crooner a person who sings in a soft, sentimental style. *Crooners were popular in the forties.*

songster a singer. *The songster sang everyone's favorite songs.*

vocalist a singer. *The vocalist had an excellent soprano voice.*

single *adj.* one alone; only one. *A single orange was left in the box.*

lone alone; single. *A lone cloud floated in the blue sky.*

one a single unit. *One apple fell from the tree.*

only single; sole. *Rose was the only child to win two races.*

sole single; only one. *The pilot was the sole survivor of the plane crash.*

skill *n.* the ability to do something well as a result of practice. *His skill in playing the violin may someday make him famous.*

ability skill; power to do something. *She has unusual ability in mathematics.*

knowledge ability; what one knows. *His knowledge of World War II was outstanding.*

talent a natural ability. *John had a special talent for building birdhouses.*

slight *adj.* not big; small; slender. *Although it looks sunny, there is a slight chance of rain later today.*

delicate thin; of fine quality. *The blouse was trimmed with a delicate lace collar.*

faint weak. *The faint colors hardly showed on the dark paper.*

little not big; small. *The little problems could easily be solved.*

slim slender; small. *We had a slim chance of winning the game.*

small not large; little. *The picture had a small, decorated frame.*

tender not strong; delicate. *The tender flowers were hurt by the heavy rain.*

smart *adj.* intelligent; clever; quick in mind. *A smart dog can learn many tricks.*

bright clever; quick-witted. *The bright girl was the leader of the debate team.*

brilliant having great ability or skill. *The brilliant boy won a scholarship to an engineering school.*

clever bright; brilliant; quick-witted. *The clever student solved the math problem.*

intelligent having intelligence. *The intelligent animals knew when it was feeding time.*

resourceful quick-witted; able to think of ways to do things. *The resourceful team quickly scored the points they needed to win the football game.*

smell *n.* an odor; a scent. *The smell of orange blossoms filled the air.*

fragrance pleasant odor or smell. *The new fragrance smelled like fresh flowers.*

odor a smell; scent. *The odor from the bouquet of flowers made the whole room smell good.*

perfume a sweet smell. *The perfume of the roses filled the air.*

scent an odor; a smell. *The dogs followed the scent of the wolf.*

snuggle *v.* to lie or press together; cuddle. *The puppies need to snuggle close to their mother to keep warm.*

cuddle to lie closely. *The kittens like to cuddle next to each other in the blanket.*

curl up to roll up; draw up. *He wanted to curl up in his favorite chair with a blanket and a good book.*

nestle to snuggle cozily or comfortably. *She will nestle her head in the pillow.*

soar *v.* to rise or fly high; glide. *Eagles soar gracefully in the sky.*

fly to move through the air. *The planes fly high in the sky above the clouds.*

glide to move along smoothly. *The birds glide across the sky.*

sail to move smoothly. *The kite did sail high above the trees.*

soften *v.* to make or become soft. *Ice cream will soften in the heat.*

dissolve to change to a liquid. *Sugar will dissolve when mixed with water.*

melt to warm to turn into liquid. *We will melt the butter to use in the recipe.*

son *n.* a male child. *The mother took her son to a baseball game.*

boy a male child. *The boy was ten years old today.*

child a young boy or girl. *The child is the son of Mrs. James.*

descendant offspring; person born of a certain group. *He thought he was a descendant of King Henry VIII.*

offspring the young of a person or animal. *John is the only offspring of Mr. and Mrs. Smith.*

antonym: daughter

sore *adj.* painful; tender when touched. *His foot was sore after he stubbed his toe.*

aching dull, continuously painful. *The aching arm was put in a sling.*

painful full of pain; hurting. *The painful cut was bandaged by the nurse.*

tender painful; sensitive. *The bump on my arm was tender to the touch.*

sort *v.* to separate things into groups. *The baby can sort the blocks into two piles by color.*

arrange to put in order. *We can arrange the books by content.*

assort to arrange by kinds. *We tried to assort the magazines in alphabetical order.*

classify to arrange in groups or classes. *The team decided to classify the papers according to the student's last name.*

spare *adj.* extra. *Every automobile should have a spare tire.*

additional extra; more. *We can get additional tickets if we need them.*

extra additional; beyond what is needed. *The extra food makes another meal.*

reserve extra; kept back. *The reserve stock will be sold at the annual meeting.*

supplementary additional. *The supplementary books had more sports stories.*

spark *n.* a brief, bright flash of light. *We saw the spark of a firefly in the night.*

beam a ray of light. *The beam from the flashlight was seen across the road.*

flicker an unsteady light. *The flicker of the lamp was not enough light to cook by.*

gleam a beam of light. *The gleam of the spotlight was seen for miles.*

ray a beam of light. *The ray of light shone through the trees.*

speak *v.* to talk; to say words. *Speak clearly so that we can understand you.*

pronounce to speak; to make sounds. *I will pronounce each spelling word for you.*

state to express; to tell. *He will state the conditions of the agreement.*

talk to speak; use words to give ideas or feelings. *I often talk about safety.*

utter to speak; make known. *She meant to utter her opinion loudly so that everyone could hear.*

speaker *n.* a person who speaks or delivers public speeches. *The speaker at tonight's meeting will discuss the election.*

lecturer person who lectures. *The lecturer spoke to the group on the subjects of health and fitness.*

spokesperson person who speaks for others. *The group elected her as the spokesperson.*

speed *n.* swiftness; quickness. *An antelope has great speed.*

haste a hurry; trying to be fast. *He did everything in haste.*

hurry rushed movement or action. *She was in a hurry to get to the airport.*

rush a hurry. *The rush of the work schedule made everyone tired.*

spill *v.* to run out; to flow over. *He tried not to spill juice on the tablecloth.*

flow to pour out. *The water started to flow over the riverbanks.*

pour to flow steadily. *The water will pour out of the broken pipe.*

run to flow. *Water will run through the streets when it rains hard.*

stream to flow; pour out. *The light seemed to stream down from the sky.*

spoil *v.* to ruin; damage; destroy. *The stain will spoil your shirt if you don't wash it out quickly.*

damage to ruin; spoil. *The cold weather can damage the fruit.*

destroy to break into pieces. *The wind might destroy the old, wooden fence.*

ruin to spoil; destroy. *The spilled paint will ruin the carpet.*

smash to destroy; ruin. *The car did smash the bicycle that was left in the driveway.*

squeal *v.* to make a sharp, high-pitched cry. *The baby did squeal with delight.*

cheep to make a little, sharp sound. *We heard the baby birds cheep in the nest.*

cry to make an animal noise. *The wolf seemed to cry at the moon in the night sky.*

peep to make a sound like a chirp. *We heard the little chick peep for its mother.*

stillness *n.* quiet; silence. *After the city noise, the stillness of the country was a relief.*

hush silence; quiet. *A hush in the room made us wonder what was wrong.*

quiet state of rest. *The quiet of the night was perfect for sleeping.*

silence an absence of noise. *The teacher asked for silence while we read the directions for the activity.*

strange *adj.* unusual; odd. *We were startled by the strange noise.*

bizarre odd or queer in appearance. *The bizarre picture had very unusual colors.*

extraordinary very unusual; strange. *The extraordinary size of the elephants made us stop and stare.*

fantastic unusual; odd. *The fantastic shadows were caused by the huge lights.*

student *n.* a person who studies or goes to school. *Kia is a student at the new high school.*

pupil a person who goes to school. *Each pupil in the class is learning about the Civil War.*

scholar a very well-educated person. *Do you know that famous scholar?*

schoolchild a boy or girl attending school. *One schoolchild will receive an award for perfect attendance.*

surprise *v.* to cause to feel wonder or delight; to astonish. *They wanted to surprise us by singing the song they had written.*

amaze to surprise. *It did amaze me to see so many people at the parade.*

astonish to amaze; surprise. *The magic trick will astonish all of us.*

astound to surprise. *The news of winning the prize did astound all of us.*

shock to surprise; amaze. *It will shock us to hear we had won the contest.*

startle to surprise suddenly. *The loud noise certainly did startle us.*

taste *v.* to find or test the flavor of something. *Taste the sauce to see if it needs more garlic.*

sample to take part of. *We tried to sample the various foods to see what we liked best.*

savor to enjoy the taste or smell. *We did savor the spicy flavor of the chili.*

try to test. *Please try the soup to see if it has enough seasoning.*

team *n.* a group of people working together. *We hired a team of lawyers.*

crew a group working together. *The flight crew handled the passengers on the plane.*

gang a group of people working together. *The road gang was busy repairing the holes in the road.*

workers people who work. *The farm workers were hired to plant corn.*

tear *v.* to pull apart or into pieces. *Be careful not to tear the letter as you open the envelope.*

fray to become worn. *This cloth might fray along the edges.*

rip to tear apart. *I hurried to rip open the package to see what was inside.*

shred to tear or cut into pieces. *We shred the paper and make decorations out of it.*

term *n.* a period of time. *The winter school term seems long because there aren't many holidays.*

interval space in time. *We were busy during the interval between noon and three o'clock.*

period a portion of time. *Several battles were fought during the period of British rule.*

time a span for a certain activity. *The time was spent working on our science projects.*

thankless *adj.* not showing appreciation; ungrateful. *Be sure to write Uncle Jeff a thank-you note so you won't seem thankless for his gift.*

unappreciative not showing appreciation. *The unappreciative boy did not pretend to enjoy his gift.*

ungrateful not thankful. *The ungrateful citizens picketed the statehouse.*

antonym: thankful

thicken *v.* to make heavier or thicker. *You can use flour to thicken gravy.*

congeal to become solid by cooling. *The sauce will congeal as it cools.*

jell to thicken; congeal. *The fruit juice will jell if you put it in the refrigerator.*

thin *adj.* slender; not thick. *A sheet of paper is thin.*

slender slim; long and thin. *The diet helped him maintain a slender body.*

slight slender; not big. *His slight body made him a quick runner.*

slim thin; slender. *She had a slim figure because she exercised regularly.*

antonym: thick

thought *n.* the act or process of thinking. *She spent many hours in thought about the problem.*

consideration thinking about events to make a decision. *We gave careful consideration to the request.*

reflection thinking carefully, thoughtfully. *Our reflection on the game helped us understand why our team lost.*

study reading and thinking to learn. *My study of chemistry involved learning a lot of formulas.*

thoughtful *adj.* having consideration for others. *She is thoughtful of her friends and never hurts their feelings.*

considerate thoughtful of others. *A considerate person will often lend a hand to help others.*

diplomatic having skills in dealing with others. *His friends said he was diplomatic when faced with a conflict.*

tactful able to say and do the right thing. *Everyone likes a tactful person for a friend.*

antonym: thoughtless

thunder *v.* to make a sound like thunder. *When it began to thunder, we headed for home.*

boom to make a deep sound. *The announcer's voice can boom across the stadium.*

drum to tap again and again. *He likes to drum his fingers loudly.*

roar to make a loud noise. *The lions roar when it is time to eat.*

rumble to make a deep sound; make a continuous sound. *Thunder seemed to rumble in the distance.*

tiny *adj.* very small; wee. *An ant is a tiny animal.*

little small; not big. *The little car was a perfect toy for the young child.*

small little. *The small child seemed to be lost.*

wee tiny; very small. *The story was about a wee person who lived in the woods.*

antonym: huge

tire *v.* to make weary or exhausted. *Exercising for a long time does tire me.*

exhaust to tire. *The long hike over the hills did exhaust the campers.*

fatigue to make weary or tired. *The hard work will fatigue the road crew.*

weary to become tired. *The long walk will weary all of us.*

touch *v.* to feel with the hand or other part of the body. *The builder wanted to touch the cement to see if it was still soft.*

feel to touch. *Mike did feel the wood to see if it needed to be sanded more.*

handle to touch; hold. *She must handle the glass statues very carefully.*

stroke to move the hand gently. *She liked to stroke the pet kitten.*

tough *adj.* strong; not easily torn or broken. *The rug is made of very tough materials.*

hard not soft. *The ice on the lake was frozen as hard as a rock.*

rugged uneven; rough. *It was difficult to walk over the rugged countryside.*

strong having power and force. *The strong workers lifted many boxes on and off the trucks every day.*
antonym: weak

tremble *v.* to shake or quiver. *I was so nervous that my hands began to tremble.*

flutter to wave quickly. *The flag will flutter in the wind.*

quake to vibrate or shake. *She said that she began to quake every time she heard her name called.*

quaver to tremble or shake. *My voice would quaver when I tried to speak.*

shudder to tremble. *The cold winter wind made us shudder.*

trick *n.* something done to deceive. *The phone call was just a trick to get me out of the room while they planned the surprise party.*

joke something funny and clever. *Bob likes to play this joke on his friends.*

lark something that is fun. *Our trip to the house of mirrors was an interesting and exciting lark.*

prank a playful trick. *The phony message was only a prank.*

true *adj.* right; accurate; not false. *It is true that ostriches cannot fly.*

accurate without errors. *She kept accurate accounts of the company's business.*

actual real. *The actual events of the day were recorded in the newspaper.*

correct not wrong; free of mistakes. *He had the most correct answers on the test.*

factual consisting of facts. *We keep factual accounts of each experiment.*
antonym: false

truth *n.* that which agrees with the facts. *You can trust her because she always tells the truth.*

fact something true. *This fact of the case was presented in court.*

reality true state or existence. *The reality may be that these space creatures do not exist.*

uncover *v.* to reveal or expose. *They will uncover the truth during the trial.*

expose to uncover. *We will expose the truth to the television news reporter.*

reveal to make known. *We knew she would not reveal our secret to anyone.*

unearth to find out; discover. *The investigator finally was able to unearth the truth about the accident.*

unhappy *adj.* not happy, sad; full of sorrow. *When Maria was unhappy, we tried to cheer her up.*

sad not happy. *Losing the game made the team feel sad.*

sorrowful full of sorrow. *The death of a pet is a sorrowful occasion.*

unfortunate not lucky. *Losing your money for the show was an unfortunate event.*

unlucky not lucky. *With everything that has happened, he is a very unlucky person.*
antonyms: happy, glad

unlock *v.* to undo a lock by turning a key. *Mr. Hughes can unlock the door and let us in.*

unbolt to undo the bolts. *He will unbolt the door to let us into the house.*

unfasten to untie; undo. *We tried to unfasten the rope that was tied to the fence.*

unlatch to undo a latch. *The farmer was able to unlatch the door to the shed.*
antonym: lock

unsafe *adj.* not safe; dangerous. *Running in a crowded hallway is unsafe.*

dangerous risky; not safe. *The old road through the hills is a dangerous route.*

hazardous dangerous; full of risk. *The hazardous waste was to be buried in a cave.*

useful *adj.* of use; helpful. *She gave me some useful advice about studying for the test.*

helpful giving aid; useful. *My assistant is especially helpful when things get busy.*

serviceable useful. *The mixer has been serviceable for many years.*

worthy having worth. *The plan to restore the old buildings is a worthy cause.*
antonym: useless

view *n.* opinion; idea. *His view was that we should change our plans.*

idea plan or belief. *The class chose one idea about the scenery for the play.*

opinion what one thinks. *She asked my opinion on the color of dress to buy.*

outlook a view. *He has an interesting outlook on the future of the city government.*

village *n.* a number of houses and buildings in an area that is smaller than a town. *Everyone knows everyone else in our village.*

hamlet a small village. *The little hamlet was nestled in the Swiss mountains.*

suburb town or village near a city. *We live in a suburb of Chicago.*

township part of a county. *The township has police and fire departments.*

wasteful *adj.* tending to waste; using or spending too much. *Taking more food than you can eat is wasteful.*

extravagant wasteful; spending too much. *Extravagant persons often spend more than they need to.*

lavish giving or spending very generously. *The lavish gifts were too fancy to be used by anyone.*

wise *adj.* having much knowledge or information. *Scientists and professors are wise.*

knowing well-informed; having much knowledge. *My aunt had a knowing smile on her face when I explained the problem.*

profound showing great knowledge. *Robert says profound things about the future.*

sage wise. *You should listen to her sage advice.*

tactful having tact. *Beth is kind and tactful when she deals with difficult people.*

wonder *v.* to be curious to know. *I wonder how the song will end.*

disbelieve to refuse to believe. *Marie seemed to disbelieve the story about how the vase was broken.*

doubt to have difficulty believing. *I doubt if we will ever know the cause of the fire.*

question to doubt. *I still question the motives of the city officials.*

wring *v.* to twist and squeeze. *Wring out the wet cloth before you wipe the table.*

squeeze to press hard. *I will squeeze the grapefruit to get all the juice out.*

twist to wind or turn. *He should twist the rag to get out the water.*

wrinkle *n.* a small crease or fold. *Rosa ironed the wrinkle out of her skirt.*

crease a wrinkle. *The crease in his forehead showed us he was very worried.*

crinkle a wrinkle or crease. *The crinkle in the wrapping paper spoiled the package.*

rumple a wrinkle. *They pressed every rumple from the tablecloths.*

wrong *adj.* not correct; not true. *Your answer was wrong.*

false not correct; not true. *We were given false information about the crime.*

inaccurate not accurate. *Our cost estimates were wrong because we were given inaccurate information.*

incorrect not correct; wrong. *The incorrect directions caused us to get lost.*

antonym: right

young *adj.* not old or fully grown. *A fawn is a young deer.*

juvenile young; youthful. *I enjoy reading juvenile books.*

youngish rather young. *The youngish group was the first to the top of the mountain.*

youthful young; looking or acting young. *The group had very youthful spirits.*